D1070290

RELIGION, RACE, AND ETHNICITY SERIES

General Editor: Peter J. Paris

Public Religion and Urban Transformation: Faith in the City
Edited by Lowell W. Livezey

Down by the Riverside: Readings in African American Religion
Edited by Larry G. Murphy

New York Glory: Religions in the City
Edited by Tony Carnes and Anna Karpathakis

Religion and the Creation of Race and Ethnicity: An Introduction
Edited by Craig R. Prentiss

God in Chinatown:
Religion and Survival in New York's Evolving Immigrant Community
Kenneth J. Guest

Creole Religions of the Caribbean:
An Introduction from Vodou and Santería to Obeah and Espiritismo
Margarite Fernández Olmos and Lizabeth Paravisini-Gebert

The History of the Riverside Church in the City of New York
Peter J. Paris, John Wesley Cook, James Hadnut-Beumler,
Lawrence H. Mamiya, Leonora Tubbs Tisdale, and Judith Weisenfeld
Foreword by Martin E. Marty

Righteous Content: Black Women's Perspectives of Church and Faith
Daphne C. Wiggins

Beyond Christianity: African Americans in a New Thought Church
Darnise C. Martin

Deeper Shades of Purple: Womanism in Religion and Society
Edited by Stacey M. Floyd-Thomas

Afro-Pentecostalism

*Black Pentecostal and Charismatic
Christianity in History and Culture*

EDITED BY

Amos Yong and Estrelda Y. Alexander

NEW YORK UNIVERSITY PRESS
New York and London

NEW YORK UNIVERSITY PRESS
New York and London
www.nyupress.org

References to Internet Web sites (URLs) were accurate at the time of writing.
Neither the author nor New York University Press is responsible for URLs
that may have expired or changed since the manuscript was prepared.

Library of Congress Cataloging-in-Publication Data

Afro-pentecostalism : Black pentecostal and charismatic Christianity in
history and culture / edited by Amos Yong and Estrelda Y. Alexander.
p. cm. — (Religion, race, and ethnicity)
Includes bibliographical references and index.
ISBN 978-0-8147-9730-3 (cl : alk. paper) — ISBN 978-0-8147-9731-0
(pb : alk. paper) — ISBN 978-0-8147-9732-7 (ebook : alk. paper)
1. African American Pentecostal churches. I. Yong, Amos. II. Alexander,
Estrelda, 1949– III. Title. IV. Series.
BX8762.5.A67   2011
277.3'08208996073—dc22   2010047484

New York University Press books are printed on acid-free paper,
and their binding materials are chosen for strength and durability.
We strive to use environmentally responsible suppliers and materials
to the greatest extent possible in publishing our books.

Manufactured in the United States of America
c   10 9 8 7 6 5 4 3 2 1
p   10 9 8 7 6 5 4 3 2 1

In memory of Ogbu U. Kalu (1942–2009)

Contents

Acknowledgments

Most of the chapters in this book were originally shared and discussed among the contributors and other scholars in the fall of 2007 and spring of 2008. We would like to acknowledge the following for their helping to make possible this initial research and sharing of ideas:

- our former and present deans at Regent University School of Divinity—Donald Tucker, Michael Palmer, Joy Brathwaite, and Randall Pannell—each of whom supported this project variously in its different phases;
- Dr. David Bearinger and his staff at the Virginia Council for the Humanities, for a grant that underwrote some of the expenses behind this work;
- the contributors to this volume, each of whom graciously accepted our invitation to participate in this project, and who have worked diligently with us to prepare their chapters for publication;
- Louis B. Gallien Jr., who as an engaging interlocutor served as respondent to the initial chapter drafts, and who then crafted his own chapter for inclusion in this volume;
- our School of Divinity and wider university staff—Misty Martin, Pidge Bannin, Lelia Fry, Charles Eichmann, Brian McLean, and Mark Stevenson—for their behind-the-scenes work;
- graduate assistants, Bradford McCall and Bashiri Durham, for yeomen's labor, and Timothy Lim Teck Ngern, for his help with the manuscript and with the index;
- Jennifer Hammer, our expeditious and indefatigable editor at New York University Press; Peter J. Paris, series editor; and the anonymous reviewers for the Press—all of whose comments have combined to improve the volume;
- Despina P. Gimbel, for her expert copyediting, and Gabrielle Begue and others at the Press for their patient professionalism in moving the manuscript through to its various phases of publication.

Professor Ogbu Kalu passed away suddenly and without warning in early January 2009, just as we were putting together the final touches on the manuscript for this book. At the time of his death, he was one of the leading interpreters of African Christianity, the African Christian diaspora, and Afro-Pentecostalism. We are additionally grateful to Drs. Wilhelmina J. Kalu and Stella Kalu-Egwim, and Professors David D. Daniels III and Jacob Olupona, for their help with revising Professor Kalu's chapter for inclusion in this volume. The editors dedicate this book to our good friend and colleague Ogbu U. Kalu, with gratitude to God for his life and work, and with fond affection of his memory.

Estrelda Y. Alexander and Amos Yong

Introduction

Black Tongues of Fire: Afro-Pentecostalism's
Shifting Strategies and Changing Discourses

ESTRELDA Y. ALEXANDER AND AMOS YONG

African American Pentecostalism: Entering the Field

In 2006, the contemporary American Pentecostal movement passed a milestone, celebrating its one hundredth birthday. Over that time, its African American sector has been markedly influential, not only vis-à-vis other branches of Pentecostalism but also throughout the Christian church. Still, this segment of Pentecostalism has not received the kind of critical attention it has deserved. As a central contributor to historic Pentecostalism and as one of the fastest growing segments of the Black Church, the African American Pentecostal movement increasingly clamors for scholarly assessment.

Perhaps part of the reason for the neglect derives from overlooking African American agency at the origins of the movement. Even today, debates remain over who was at the forefront of the nascent modern Pentecostal movement—the white Charles Fox Parham, who is credited with laying its foundations by formulating its central doctrine of the baptism of the Holy Spirit being accompanied with the initial evidence of speaking in tongues; the black William Seymour, the leader of the 1906 Azusa Street Revival to which many, if not most, American Pentecostal denominations trace their roots; or simply the Holy Spirit, who used a variety of personalities, events, and locations to bring about the advent of the movement.[1] As Seymour's founding role has been increasingly recognized, so has the role of many other African Americans in the ongoing development of modern Pentecostalism. After a century of expansion, from a movement once considered by many as a marginalized cult to one that has come to have far-reaching global influence throughout the church and society, we are now at the point at which the important contribution of African Americans cannot be overlooked. Throughout this relatively short period within Christian history, African

Americans have been involved in every aspect of the Pentecostal movement's development: forging its worship and music styles, framing and carrying out strategies to mold its public presence, shaping its theological discourse, and contributing to the variety of deliberations, schisms, and controversies that have shaped its structure.[2]

This recovery of and emphasis on the African American contribution must acknowledge the role of black Christians in laying the groundwork for the Pentecostal revival. The nineteenth-century Holiness movement, which focused on calling the church back to personal piety through the experience of sanctification, produced such black leaders as the evangelists Jarena Lee and Amanda Berry Smith, and pastors like Charles Price Jones and William Christian, and saw the founding of several black denominations including the Church of Christ Holiness and the Church of the Living God (Christian Workers for Fellowship). Members of this movement laid the foundations for twentieth-century Pentecostalism by reincorporating John Wesley's concept of entire sanctification into a personal spirituality and piety, which they sensed was missing in their churches. These Holiness folk, who were already employing camp-meeting style revivalism and language of Holy Spirit "fire" baptism as endowment with power for service and piety, eventually made their way into the Pentecostal movement. For their part, the Pentecostals incorporated the initial sign of speaking in tongues as an indication that one had truly received the Spirit, and by so doing, made a significant shift in Holiness beliefs about practices regarding the Holy Spirit. A number of denominations that had roots in the black Holiness movement, including the United Holy Church of America and the Fire Baptized Holiness Church of America, would ultimately become Pentecostal.

From out of these late nineteenth-century Holiness movements, it is now widely accepted that blacks made up a substantial portion of William Seymour's Azusa Street congregation, which fueled the spread of the Pentecostal movement across the country beginning in 1906.[3] Once their tongues were touched by the fires of Azusa Street, blacks left Los Angeles, serving with others of every race and culture as missionaries at home and abroad, to take the message of the Spirit being poured out on them in a new way. The movement was decidedly multiracial, and black Pentecostals founded churches and denominations—some of them interracially constituted—which at first dotted the West and the South, where they were largely confined. Then they moved with the Great Migration to major urban centers in the North and East and to every town and hamlet in between, establishing predominantly black congregations. Within twenty years, no part of the American landscape and very little of the world remained untouched by the revival that emerged from Azusa Street.

This book is one of the first scholarly volumes to cover the spectrum of this African American Pentecostal—Afro-Pentecostal, for short—world. We should note that just as there is no one black Baptist denomination, or one exclusively black Methodist denomination, there is also no one black Pentecostal movement—no one type of black Pentecostal discourse, and no one form of black Pentecostal life. Instead, Afro-Pentecostals can be found in more than one hundred large and small bodies, which extend from regional groups with a handful of congregations and a few hundred members to those with international constituencies. For purposes of classification, we can identify at least four types of Afro-Pentecostal groups: classical Wesleyan-Holiness Trinitarian Pentecostals, classical Apostolic (Jesus' name or "Oneness"), charismatic independent congregations or networks, and recent neo-Pentecostal currents within the wider black church tradition.

In brief, classical Afro-Pentecostal groups involve denominations that have links to the first generation of the modern Pentecostal movement, in some way tracing their roots back to the Azusa Street revival. Included among these are denominations such as the Church of God in Christ (COGIC), with several thousand congregations and several million members in North America and around the world; the Mount Sinai Holy Church of America; the Fire Baptized Holiness Church of God of America; and the United Holy Church of America. Many of these are connected to black Holiness churches and traditions.

Apostolic or oneness churches are those who hold to the necessity of baptism by immersion "in the name of Jesus" and who, more importantly, reject the Trinitarian conception of the Godhead in lieu of a concept of God as one person who is expressed in three modes. These include the Pentecostal Assemblies of the World, the Church of Our Lord Jesus Christ of the Apostolic Faith, the Church of the Lord Jesus Christ of the Apostolic Faith, and Bible Way Church World Wide. We will mention more about these churches later.

Since the 1960s the development of the charismatic tradition has seen the rapid spread of Pentecostal theology, which incorporates a expanded pneumatology and a distinctive appreciation for the operation of spiritual gifts in the life of the individual and in corporate worship—without the strict personal piety or rigid insistence on speaking in tongues as a necessary evidence of Holy Spirit baptism—into mainline congregations and independent networks. Black charismatic churches include the Full Gospel Baptist Church Fellowship International and a number of Word-of-Faith congregations and denominations that focus on teaching that those who are favored by God and who tap into the potential of the Holy Spirit will be materially successful. Representative of these are such churches, congregations, and networks as Creflo Dollar's World Changers Church International in Atlanta, and Frederick Price's Crenshaw Christian Center in Los Angeles.

More recently, neo-Pentecostal spirituality has impacted many classically black denominations including large segments of the African Methodist Episcopal (AME) Church. Black neo-Pentecostals have generally thus remained in their classical denominational churches and may not even go by that label, but they have incorporated Pentecostal style worship practices without making major changes in theology.

This typology provides a convenient, albeit rough and provisional, framework for understanding the broad scope of Afro-Pentecostalism, at least as the term is used in the remainder of this book. In reality, however, Pentecostal spirituality has so influenced the Black Church that in many instances—perhaps with the exception of the emphasis on speaking in tongues—there is little noticeable difference in the worship styles of contemporary African American congregations, regardless of which denominations are involved.

These various churches, organizations, and networks are all bound together in part by their distinctive Pentecostal belief that the "baptism" or "outpouring" of the Holy Spirit on the believer is a distinct work of grace, subsequent to the indwelling of the Holy Spirit given at initial conversion, and is an essential aspect of the Christian experience. This experience of Spirit baptism is understood as a direct fulfillment of the prophecy of the Old Testament book of Joel, in which the Spirit would be poured out on all flesh (Joel 2:28) and, among other signs, individuals would speak with other tongues as the Spirit makes its presence known. (Acts 2:4). Pentecostal believers thus have always been marked by a sense of personal communion with God established through ecstatic religious experience, including glossolalia or "speaking in tongues" as initial objective evidence of the Holy Spirit's presence in an individual. For them, the corporate experience of this manifestation has been thought to signal the arrival of the reign of Christ. These palpable religious manifestations are also perceived as divine urgings to earnestly redouble evangelistic efforts to reach every soul with the salvation message in view of the impending end of the age. To Pentecostals, this "in-filling" of the Holy Spirit is a supernatural enablement to live a holy life and to accomplish works of righteousness on behalf of the kingdom of God.

But Holy Spirit empowerment alone was not enough to ensure that black Pentecostals would be able to overcome the social realities of American race politics in the first half of the twentieth century, within which they suffered the double indignity of racial discrimination and religious persecution. Despite Seymour's early leadership and the uncontestable contribution of other blacks such as Charles Harrison Mason, founder of the Church of God in Christ, and Garfield T. Haywood, early leader and first General Secretary of the Pentecostal Assemblies of the World,[4] blacks were denied access to positions of influence or leadership by white Pentecostals, who quickly forsook the Azusa Street ideal of interracial fellowship to embrace the existing racial status quo of the broader society. Black Pentecostals were also scorned as ignorant and uncouth by their mainline black brother and sisters, who wrote them off as members of a mysterious cult under the leadership of unscrupulous charlatans.[5] Black Pentecostals were thus forced to frame and live out a distinct self-understanding. They had to forge a particular set of strategies and peculiar set of discourses for being the "sanctified church" in an unsanctified world.[6]

Shifting Strategies and Changing Discourses

While they share a common openness to the immanent work of the Spirit within their lives and congregations, the African Americans who make up otherwise very diverse black Pentecostal groups have had to deal with the same variety of modern issues—economic and political realities, spirituality, ethics, and the like—that are of concern to other members of society. Further, black Pentecostal church leaders have historically had to wrestle with the same concerns—mission strategies, gender roles, and theological relevance—as leaders within other contexts and have employed a variety of strategies to do both. Notwithstanding common depictions of Pentecostals—black and white—as almost entirely otherworldly, what is noteworthy about Afro-Pentecostalism is the variety of modes of expressions found within it—the various ways in which its adherents were able to shift the discourse about race and social ethics and incorporate tactics to enable adequate engagement with the realities of this world. Far from being simply the monolithic, otherworldly, "tongues movement" (this terminology was used by detractors to call attention to what they saw as an overemphasis on the practice of speaking tongues in Pentecostal personal devotions and public worship) that many have depicted, Afro-Pentecostalism exhibits a wide range of responses that has informed the movement's coping with modern issues and realities.

The diversity within Afro-Pentecostalism reflects at least in part the changing dynamics of the North American socio-political, cultural, and religious context. During the Jim Crow era of the first half of the twentieth century, blacks were marginalized from engaging with the dominant structures of the nation. In this context Afro-Pentecostals were forced to form their own cultural institutions, to create their own social spaces and niches, and to articulate their own version of Pentecostal and Christian beliefs. While it is reductionistic to think that the earliest Afro-Pentecostals derived homogeneously from the lower classes, it is also undeniable that Pentecostalism made its most substantive inroads among this social stratum of the black community.[7] But the phenomenon of the emerging black middle class since the civil rights movement has transformed the shape of the Afro-Pentecostal church over the last forty years. Whereas storefront Pentecostal and Holiness black churches have not disappeared, there are now established, solidly middle-class Afro-Pentecostal congregations as well as megachurches like those of T. D. Jakes's The Potter's House in Dallas, Charles Blake's West Angeles Church of God in Christ, and John Cherry's From the Heart Ministries in suburban Washington, D.C., among many others. Afro-Pentecostalism is now televised across the continent—and around the world—in mainstream and cable TV channels, with the result that few are uninformed about African American forms of Pentecostal life.

This shift from the margins of North American society to the more-or-less mainstream has brought with it changes in Afro-Pentecostals beliefs and practices. While among the generation of Seymour the emphasis was on ecstatic worship, the current generation has tempered this with professional worship teams. While the earlier Afro-Pentecostals were more sectarian in nature in terms of their avowed apolitical or antipolitical stances and countercultural practices, the recent Pentecostals have become bolder in the public square, more willing to engage both the *polis* and the world, even while wrestling with what that means for their Pentecostal identity. These changes can be understood in terms of the social dynamics of twentieth-century American life viewed through the lens of race and ethnicity, but doing so without recognizing the agency of Afro-Pentecostal people would be to tell only one side of the story.

The shifting strategies of Afro-Pentecostal agency, for example, can be observed in the dynamics of the movement's interface with the wider society. Because of the earlier sectarian posture, interaction with the "world" outside the church was never overtly sanctioned. Afro-Pentecostal congregations, however, have always found ways to deal with the challenges besetting their parishioners and communities: poverty, homelessness, substance abuse, domestic and community violence, and, more recently, teen pregnancy and HIV/AIDS.[8] With the advent of the civil rights movement more and more

Afro-Pentecostal pastors and leaders have been motivated to enter directly into the social and political limelight, adding their voices to the prophetic activity long characteristic of the Black Church tradition. Simultaneously, African American Pentecostal congregations have cultivated virtues of honesty, ethical character, industry, and modest living that have assisted many of their members to gain middle-class status. Many larger, more successful Afro-Pentecostal congregations—especially megachurch congregations—have combined spiritual formation/discipleship, life-skills training and education, community service, social activism, and political engagement—all under the rubric of a much more sophisticated theological understanding of holistic ministry.[9]

Herein we can also observe the changing theological and doctrinal discourses of Afro-Pentecostalism. Ecclesially, whereas early Afro-Pentecostals were predominantly shaped by the Holiness movement, contemporary Afro-Pentecostalism is much more diverse, and much less denominationally linked or constrained. Theologically, the traditional doctrinal emphasis on sanctification, understood as separation from the world, has given way to an implicit theology of cultural affirmation, framed in terms of contextualization or the cultural relevance of the gospel. Such an overall theological adjustment has more often than not been implicit, rather than explicit. These theological revisions exist at the oral and lived levels of African American Pentecostal pastoral and congregational life, rather than in the formally crafted manuals, handbooks, or theological texts. Indeed, there has only been slight revision of long-held doctrines that have been handed down from generation to generation, particularly in churches that are and remain denominationally affiliated.

This trend—of a fairly conservative official theological platform—is not peculiar to African American Pentecostalism. The wider Pentecostal movement, both in North America and elsewhere, remains theologically conservative. But if other Pentecostals can attend their denominationally sponsored (and accredited) colleges, universities, and seminaries, Afro-Pentecostals do not usually have such options. There are a handful of Afro-Pentecostal institutions of higher education such as the All Saints Bible College and Charles H. Mason Theological Seminary under the auspices of the Church of God in Christ, Aenon Bible College of the Pentecostal Assemblies of the World, and the Church of Our Lord Jesus Christ's Bonner Bible College. The majority of theologically trained African American Pentecostals receive their formative academic education in non-Pentecostal settings either in historically black colleges and universities such as Howard University, Morehouse College, or Spellman College, or in institutions friendly to the Black Church and with programs that address the concerns of black Christians such as Candler School of Theology, Duke, Vanderbilt, or Crozer Divinity Schools, or Princeton Theological Seminary.

The result of increasing matriculation of African American Pentecostals in such programs has been the gradual emergence of the Afro-Pentecostal academy. Whereas a strong anti-intellectual strain existed in earlier generations who often rejected the "higher learning" of liberal institutions that might undercut Pentecostal faith and piety, more recent sentiments have sustained the healthy tension of receiving and engaging the specificity of Afro-Pentecostal commitments amid the less parochial forms of black theology and the more "universal" evangelical and ecumenical Christian discourses. Thus Afro-Pentecostal scholars have from their beginnings been firmly rooted in the wider Black Church tradition, drawing simultaneously on slave traditions as well as the black liberation and political theologies that began to appear at the end of the 1960s. More recently, some scholars are also exploring the possibility of a convergence between African American Pentecostal theology and certain strands of Liberationist and even Womanist theology.[10] The Afro-Pentecostal academy, in other words, has always walked a fine line between the much more theological conservative orientations of the pastors and congregations they serve and the more progressive and even radical trajectories of the black theological academy under whom many were tutored and within which many continue to be engaged in dialogue.

The ongoing maturation of the Afro-Pentecostal theological academy should be understood, however, as part of wider globalization processes. While black Pentecostal scholarship had begun in North America with the work of James F. Tinney, Bennie Goodwin, James Forbes, Leonard Lovett, and others in the 1970s, the present generation has built on their work to rethink black Pentecostal identity in global context. In this wider context, the discourses of the African Christian diaspora are increasingly considered. The voices of African Pentecostal scholars as well as those of Caribbean Pentecostals are slowly emerging. At the vanguard of this stream of global Pentecostalism is the work of black Pentecostal theologians in the UK like Robert Beckford and Joseph Aldred, among others.[11] While there are distinct differences between black Pentecostalism in the UK and in the United States, many Afro-Pentecostals are seeing links that can be forged around common histories, concerns, and issues. Globalization trends related to migration, transnationalism, and market capitalism are being registered more regularly and forcefully in Afro-Pentecostal thinking.[12]

It is notable that black Pentecostal Apostolics have, like their white counterparts in North America and elsewhere, attempted to hold out longer against the dominant social, cultural, and religious forces that have impinged upon them. One of the distinctive ways black Apostolics persisted counterculturally was by remaining the most racially integrated segment of the movement over the longest period of time. In addition, and here in substantial contrast to the experience of white Oneness Pentecostals, black Apostolics have tended to be less divided from their Trinitarian counterparts in the Pentecostal movement and even in the wider Black Church tradition. Perhaps because of common cause in resisting racism, political marginalization, and economic injustice, the Black Church has been generally more inclusive when engaging these issues, so that black Apostolics have stood in solidarity with Trinitarians when the opportunities have arisen. Yet these same Apostolics have firmly held their theological ground concerning the Oneness of the Godhead, salvation understood in terms that include the necessity of both baptism by immersion in the name of Jesus and the reception of the Holy Spirit with the evidence of speaking in tongues, and rigid holiness standards in personal piety. In these matters, black Apostolics have been as staunchly resistant to ecumenical "accommodation" as any white Oneness organization or denomination.

Clearly, African American Pentecostalism has evolved as a complex reality: it has always been "home" to a dynamic population, and has constantly served the needs of a wide range of people representing different socio-economic, geographical, cultural, and even theological backgrounds. It is precisely this diversity of beliefs and practices that is at the heart of this book.

Overview

Afro-Pentecostalism explores the ways in which adherents of African American Pentecostalism, the antecedent black Holiness movement that spawned it, and the descendent charismatic movement, which inserted Pentecostal spirituality into black mainline and nondenominational congregations, have adapted strategies to faithfully engage the broader social, political, and economic culture while formulating discursive practices of worship and spirituality consistent with their self-identities and ethical and ideological commitments. The scholars in this volume, representing diverse traditions from within and outside of the Pentecostal movement, examine four major aspects of the Afro-Pentecostal movement: (1) its historical trajectories, (2) issues of gender and culture, (3) the nature and central features of Afro-Pentecostal ethics, and

(4) its changing theological discourses. Through their extensive experience with Pentecostal culture or scholarship, these authors embody the breadth of its expression within the African American community. Their work demonstrates the range of strategies African American Pentecostals have employed—sometimes successfully, sometimes unsuccessfully—to deal with the issues of spirituality, culture race, gender, sexuality, economics, and politics.

There are black Pentecostal scholars among our authors. David Daniels, Leonard Lovett, William Turner, and Frederick Ware have not only contributed extensively to the scholarship on Afro-Pentecostalism but have also been faithfully involved in various aspects across the spectrum of its ecclesial life for several decades. Valerie Cooper, Clarence Hardy, Cheryl Sanders, and the late Ogbu Kalu represent scholars who stand outside the tradition, although their dialogue with and viable critiques offered to those within it and their work in Pentecostal studies have been no less passionate and insightful because they are not adherents. As African American scholars (perhaps with the exception of Kalu, who was Nigerian, although he lived in the States for the last part of his life), their sensitivity to realities that impact the entire black community and the Black Church provide a foundation from which to assess the movement's specific contributions and opportunities. This volume also includes the work of a white Pentecostal scholar, Cecil Robeck, who has been a consistent champion for racial reconciliation within the movement, and is certainly one of the most knowledgeable scholars of modern Pentecostal history. Finally, this book also features three white scholars from outside the classical Pentecostal tradition. Louis Gallien, Craig Scandrett-Leatherman, and Dale Irvin share extensive experience with the African American community. Gallien is an educator who has taught for several years in historically black institutions of higher education. Scandrett-Leatherman has been involved with black Pentecostal congregations both as an observer and a participant. Dale Irvin, has conducted extensive work on the intersection of Pentecostal spirituality and the social realities of our day within the global context, and is especially interested in issues of race and justice.

Drawing on the disciplines of history, theology, ethics, missiology, religious studies, or cultural anthropology, each author brings his or her unique vantage point to bear in ways that enrich the discourse and highlight nuances in the strategies of the movement that might not be evident if viewed through a single lens. Of course, black Pentecostalism cannot be reduced to being only a religious movement; rather, it is also a social, political, cultural, and ethical movement that has personal and social implications for those who are within it as well as the broader black community and the

Christian church. The unique backgrounds each author brings to this book are channeled toward elucidating the overarching theme by moving the examination of the Afro-Pentecostal movement out of artificial isolation from the cultural realities with which every viable movement must wrestle. Instead, the authors place the beliefs and practices of African American Pentecostals in their historical and socio-economic context, not only illuminating how the movement has drawn on its particular religious and ethical outlook to enable its adherents to grapple with the race, gender/sexuality, and financial inequalities they have confronted, but also by shedding light on how the movement has grown to become a powerful force on the American and global religious landscape.

Part I sets the foundation for evaluating how Pentecostalism emerged out of the antecedent Holiness movement, with its dual emphasis on Christian perfection and right social ethic, to become a movement of, literally, global proportions. It allows us to conceive how, with numerical growth, the movement has expanded its discourse in ways that have given its followers strategies to engage the complex racial realities of modern society, within local, national, and global contexts.

In chapter 2 Cecil M. Robeck Jr. illuminates the complexity of the social and religious culture that newly arriving blacks found in Los Angeles in the early twentieth century. He shows that the Azusa Street Mission was the only congregation that attempted to meet the needs of blacks who were then migrating to the city in large numbers by providing comfortable worship patterns drawn on traditions of slave religion. He further details how, amid a largely middle-class black community that was accommodated (and accommodating) to the dominant white society, class and culture appear to have played a role in the broader African American church community's rejection of the early Pentecostal revival in Los Angeles. In this framework, the unique agency and praxis of early Afro-Pentecostals can be better appreciated.

In chapter 3 the historian David D. Daniels shifts the study of early Afro-Pentecostalism from a focus on beliefs and culture, which often dominate the discourse about the movement, to that of institutions. He shows how the discourse of African American Pentecostals that evolved within the early twentieth-century public arena differed from that of black mainline Protestant churches, arguing that Pentecostalism initially operated strategically within black vernacular society with antecedents in "slave society" rather than in black civil society. Daniels insists that while black civil society interacted with the state as a counter-public, early Afro-Pentecostalism functioned with little regard to the state; as the movement grew, though, some streams of Afro-

Pentecostalism lodged their institutions within vernacular society while others situated themselves in the terrain where civil and vernacular society overlap. What clearly emerges are the diversity of Afro-Pentecostal initiatives in developing their own civic institutions, structures, and networks.

In Part II, four scholars explore Pentecostalism and its antecedent Holiness movement through the lens of gender and sexuality. In this framework, they explore how Pentecostal men and women have drawn on the movement's worldview to craft strategies for living out of their spirituality and community, and to redefine its self-understandings. These new strategies and discourses have allowed them to make sense of and survive not only the racial realities but also the challenges of gender within American society.

In chapter 4 Valerie Cooper traces two movements that unfolded two centuries before Azusa Street—American Evangelicalism and Wesleyan Holiness—and how changing understandings of women's appropriate place in public life created unprecedented opportunities for women's leadership. These changes allowed nineteenth-century, black Evangelical women to wrestle with expectations about their roles in ministry and public life, construct biblically based, pneumatological arguments for women's religious leadership, and preach with eschatological expectancy in ways that foreshadowed what subsequently emerged at the Azusa Street Revival. Cooper contends that it was upon this foundation that the largely egalitarian ethos of early Pentecostalism was established. This egalitarian ethos understood the movement of the passage in Joel 2:28 that the Spirit was being "poured out" equally on "all flesh." Early leaders made no distinction in race, culture, gender, or social class regarding who was fit and useful for the ministry, and thus gave freedom to women as well as men, poor as well as rich, the uneducated as well as the educated to participate in what God was doing. Within this understanding, the fact that the revival unfolded under the leadership of a largely self-educated black evangelist cannot be overlooked.

Clarence Hardy's discussion in chapter 5 reviews the groundbreaking work of early religionist Arthur Fauset. Hardy draws on Fauset's work on Pentecostalist and esoteric sects to look at how black Pentecostal women eschewed the categories immediately available to them while establishing new religious communities that provided alternative conceptions and creative forms of discourse about religious experience and the divine. In doing this, these women were able to reshape fading concepts of Victorian respectability and to reimagine new possibilities for religious leadership. In remaking the "politics of respectability," they replaced discourse about the (black) nation with the physical body as the principal site to imagine the divine and shifted to a religious modernism better suited to the demands of twenti-eth-century black urban life. In many respects, Hardy's chapter shows how Afro-Pentecostalism has developed its own forms of what might be called proto-feminist and proto-Womanist discursive practices, long before these movements appeared on the horizon.

The anthropologist Craig Scandrett-Leatherman's chapter 6 considers how early African societies used rites of passage that first lowered the sta-tus of boys into liminality and then elevated and reincorporated them into the community as men. Scandrett-Leatherman asserts that the "middle pas-sage" and American slavery were also rituals of status decline, though they lacked the final element of elevating black males, serving instead essentially violent purposes that kept them in the status of boys. For Scandrett-Leather-man, during the period before the civil rights movement, this violence was ritualized by the thousands of lynchings that occurred throughout the South. However, he sees in Charles Mason, founder of the Church of God in Christ, an attempt to ameliorate the emasculation of black men and the disempow-erment of the black community by strategically developing rituals of revision that helped black men resist these dehumanizing rites while promoting lib-eration of their tongues and bodies. What emerges is the undeniable agency of Afro-Pentecostals in an era and during a period when they were expected to be passively resigned to the conventions of the dominant (white) classes.

In chapter 7 Louis B. Gallien Jr. explores the Pentecostal foundations of three secular music icons with deep roots in African American Pentecostal-ism: Sam Cooke, Marvin Gaye, and Donny Hathaway. In this provocative chapter, Gallien relates the experience of these superstars' crossover from the gospel music that was an integral part of their young lives in the church to rhythm and blues, which catapulted them to success in the secular arena. He uses the stories of their experiences to shed light on the complicated themes of sexuality and spirituality within the black Pentecostal movement. Drawing on the scholarship of Michael Eric Dyson, Gallien contends that other schol-ars have often neglected these issues and thereby failed to critically address the intersection of these two themes. He further suggests that healthy dia-logue in this area is essential for developing strategies to ensure the life and relevancy of the movement. This chapter allows us to see how Afro-Pentecos-tal beliefs—in this case about "the world" and about culture—here were chal-lenged and expanded through the social and upward mobility of its members.

Part III addresses ethical concerns that black Pentecostal culture and spirituality raise within contemporary American society. By grappling with the often taboo subjects of sexuality, money, and race, the two contributors in this section deal candidly with an integral part of the human reality that black Pentecostals, like all other Christians as well as every human person, must navigate. Their insights suggest that even deeper discussions in these areas would be enormously fruitful for further scholarship.

The ethicist Cheryl J. Sanders's chapter 8 speaks to the ethical, political, and ecclesiological significance of Pentecostal preaching with particular attention to two perceived polarities: the prosperity gospel and the social gospel. It looks at the role of ethics in African American Pentecostal preaching's embrace and promotion of the prosperity gospel, which emphasizes God's will for the believer to become wealthy through faith. Sanders questions whether pastors who nurture their flocks with this message have neglected the social ethical message of the biblical prophets as advocates for the rights of the poor. If so, many African American Pentecostal preachers are abandoning the struggle for social justice, accepting the strings attached to faith-based government funding for their community development programs, and buying into the divisive family values discourse crafted by political conservatives. She further points to signs that the discourse is changing and strategies are shifting through a resurgence of prophetic activism among some black Pentecostal pastors, ministers, and community leaders who have maintained their theological conservatism while adapting a more effective, liberal social ethic, which is attractive to younger Pentecostals who desire a more socially relevant spirituality. Finally, Sanders implores African American Pentecostals to retrieve the biblically based message of advocacy for the poor and to resist conforming themselves to the worldly strategies of consumerism, simplistic multiculturalism, and political conservatism implicit in the prosperity gospel. Thus this chapter attempts to retrieve the prophetic praxis of a previous generation while calling attention to contemporary discursive practices, which are deemed to be a departure from and at odds with the more historic Black Church tradition.

Another ethicist, Leonard Lovett, uses the theological genre of the autobiographical essay to look back over his long career as a Pentecostal scholar, churchman, and social activist. Chapter 9 highlights the influence of the scholars who helped shape Lovett's socio-political thought in order to shed light on how racial dynamics within the Pentecostal academy have mirrored concerns found in other segments of the movement. It also provides insight into how some Afro-Pentecostal scholars were able to appropriate the guidance received through mentoring relationships with prominent scholars, and through studying the works of more liberal scholars, were enabled to engage in intellectual dialogue in the classroom and be involved in academic consultations to help frame a response to the racism they encountered within the movement. At the same time, Lovett candidly forces open a discourse that compels those within the movement to confront questions regarding the racial injustice still visible within the Pentecostal church and academy, as reflected in his rejection by white Pentecostal scholars and exclusion from recent reference works on the movement. Lovett's chapter is itself an illuminating discussion of the shifting discourses of Afro-Pentecostalism even when limited to the generation since its emergence in the theological academy.

Part IV examines Pentecostal approaches to the task of theology, paying special attention to two interrelated areas at the core of black religious thought—pneumatology, the study of the work of the Holy Spirit, and eschatology, a concern with the end of the world or of the ultimate destiny of humanity and liberation—as they relate to providing a religious framework for the struggle for social justice. These chapters contend that these themes are at the heart of Pentecostalism itself and explore how they might be used as vehicles for expanding the conversation between often isolated black Pentecostals and the broader Black Church and academic community.

The theologian, historian, and homiletician William C. Turner Jr. advances the thesis in chapter 10 that good pneumatology is liberation theology, and good liberation theology is pneumatology. Turner explores the gap between the African American Church's worship, service, prophetic-liberative social consciousness, and the underdevelopment of pneumatology in major scholarly projects. He laments that since this gap developed among the first generation of black theologians, there has been little sustained effort to close it, and suggests that there are grave consequences for both the Pentecostal movement and the larger church. For Turner, when fervor is without the guidance of such reflection, and when efforts to remedy the neglect in pneumatology are undertaken without sufficient sensitivity to concrete issues of liberation, the result is a discourse that is woefully inadequate for developing strategies to address the authentic spiritual and social needs of either black Pentecostals or the wider black community. Herein is a constructive proposal, both seeking to further Afro-Pentecostal self-understanding and to contribute to the wider theological academy.

Frederick L. Ware's chapter 11 suggests that shifting the discourse within eschatology, which he sees as a principal focus of both Pentecostal thought and black theology, could potentially form a powerful intersection between the two seemingly disparate ideologies. Ware contends, however, that African American Pentecostalism's tendency toward premillennialism (the belief that Christ will physically return to earth to reign for one thousand years at the end of an apocalyptic period of tribulation before the end of the world), is incompatible with black theology and that it fosters political, social, and economic indifference. He recommends a strategy that replaces premillennialism with an eschatology rooted in black folk sources and black Christian millennialism, and suggests that such reorientation is both liberative and promotes new possibilities for a constructive black Pentecostal theological discourse. Ware's chapter can thus be read both as highlighting the disparity between black slave and classical Afro-Pentecostal eschatologies, and as urging further adjustment and innovation in order to more adequately address the contemporary task of Afro-Pentecostal and black theology.

In Part V, two scholars with broad expertise in both global Christianity and varieties of Pentecostal spirituality explore ways in which Afro-Pentecostalism has enriched and been enriched by engagement in the global Pentecostal context. Their essays open the reader to two arenas—missiology and liberation theology—in which Afro-Pentecostalism has made a substantial contribution, while suggesting ways in which these contributions could be better appreciated.

The missiologist Ogbu Kalu was one of the most prolific and yet unheralded scholars of Afro-Pentecostalism until his death in early 2009. His chapter 12 first explores the strategies African Americans employed to evangelize the African motherland from the eighteenth century on. He then turns his attention to a comparison of the missionary achievements of two of the largest black Pentecostal denominations—the Church of God in Christ and the Pentecostal Assemblies of the World—between 1920 and 1950, examining specifically the Liberian context. He then explores contemporary linkages, networks, and blockages of the Afro-Pentecostal mission and the impact of those mid-century African American Pentecostals on contemporary African Pentecostalism. Kalu's chapter, one of the first scholarly overviews of Afro-Pentecostal missions history, clarifies the ways in which missions within black Pentecostal denominations have evolved from a monologue dominated by the American context to a discursive give-and-take between American and African cultures. The distinctive contributions of Afro-Pentecostal missionaries across their first century can be better appreciated against the broader religious and political landscape.

Picking up again on the intersection between pneumatology and liberation, Dale Irvin's chapter 13 suggests that a fully engaged discourse between black Pentecostal theology and black liberation theology has yet to be attempted. While Irvin sees the work of fellow contributor, Leonard Lovett, as laying the foundation for such a fuller discourse, he also avers that the conversation between the two disciplines is still in its infancy because the potential benefit of such dialogue often has been overlooked. Irvin's contention, as a historian of world Christianity, is that both have something specific to offer—not only to each other but to the global Christian community—and he suggests several ways they can serve to mutually critique and correct each other, while outlining the specific contributions each makes to this broader context. This emphasis on the diverse beliefs and practices of the global Afro-Pentecostal movement and the potential of its encounter with black liberation theology fittingly concludes the volume.

Taken together, the essays in this book provide a lens through which to move from simple reductionist characterizations of African American Pentecostalism to a more intricate understanding of this movement, whose reach and impact are still unfolding and expanding into every arena of American and global culture. They demonstrate that this expansion has already made significant contributions and enriched the theology, spirituality, praxis, and social realities of American and global religious life. At the same time, they highlight areas where further discussion is warranted, and suggest that these conversations can be made even richer when engaged with the breadth of both Pentecostalism and the broader Christian tradition.

NOTES TO CHAPTER 1

1. The argument for Parham has been most extensively laid out by James R. Goff Jr., *Fields White unto Harvest: Charles Fox Parham and the Missionary Origins of Pentecostalism* (Fayetteville, Ark.: University of Arkansas Press, 1988). The role of Seymour has been argued by Iain MacRobert, *The Black Roots and White Racism of Early Pentecostalism in the USA* (New York: St Martin's Press, 1988). And the supernaturalist paradigm remains as a holdover from earlier Pentecostal literature—e.g., Carl Brumback, *Suddenly . . . From Heaven: A History of the Assemblies of God* (Springfield, Mo.: Gospel Publishing House, 1961).

2. The literature on African American Pentecostalism is only recently emerging. See, for example, the selected bibliography at the end of this book.

3. See Cecil M. Robeck Jr., *The Azusa Street Mission: The Birth of the Global Pentecostal Movement* (Nashville, Tenn.: Nelson Reference, 2006).

4. Both these denominations began as interracial bodies but now have essentially African American constituencies.

5. See, for example, Arthur H. Fauset, *Black Gods of the Metropolis: Negro Religious Cults of the Urban North* (Philadelphia: University of Pennsylvania Press, 1944); Elmer T. Clark, *The Small Sects in America* (New York: Abingdon-Cokesbury Press, 1949); and Joseph R. Washington, *Black Sects and Cults* (Garden City, N.Y.: Doubleday, 1972).

6. The term "sanctified church" is the nomenclature many scholars of religion use to speak collectively about the black Holiness and Pentecostal tradition.

7. See Albert G. Miller, "Pentecostalism as a Social Movement: Beyond the Theory of Deprivation," *Journal of Pentecostal Theology* 9 (1996): 97–114.

8. See Karen Kossie-Chernyshev, "Looking Beyond the Pulpit: Social Ministries and African-American Pentecostal-Charismatic Women in Leadership," in Estrelda L. Alexander and Amos Yong, eds., *Philips Daughters: Women in Pentecostal-Charismatic Leadership* (Eugene, Ore.: Pickwick Publications, 2008), 61–73; cf. "Lucy Farrow," "Julia Hutchins," and "Ophelia Wiley," in Estrelda Y. Alexander, *The Women of Azusa Street* (Cleveland: Pilgrim Press, 2005), and *Limited Liberty: The Legacy of Four Pentecostal Women Pioneers* (Cleveland, Ohio: Pilgrim Press, 2008).

9. The example of Jakes's Potter's House is discussed in Amos Yong, *In the Days of Caesar: Pentecostalism and Political Theology: The Cadbury Lectures 2009* (Grand Rapids, Mich.: Eerdmans, 2010), ch. 6.1.3.

10. See, for example, Cheryl Townsend Gilkes, "'You've Got a Right to the Tree of Life': The Biblical Foundations of an Empowered Attitude among Black Women in the Sanctified Church," in Alexander and Yong, *Philips Daughters*, 152–69, and Estrelda Y. Alexander, "Recovering Black Theological Thought in Writings of Early African-American Holiness-Pentecostal Leaders," in Steven Studebaker and Michael Wilkinson, eds., *The Liberating Spirit: Pentecostals and Social Action in North America* (Eugene, Ore.: Pickwick, 2010), 23-52.

11. Representative works include Robert Beckford, *Jesus is Dread: Black Theology and Black Culture in Britain* (London: Darton, Longman and Todd, 1998); *Dread and Pentecostal: A Political Theology for the Black Church in Britain* (London: SPCK, 2000); and *Jesus Dub: Theology, Music, and Social Change* (New York: Routledge, 2006); Joseph Aldred, *Respect: Understanding Caribbean British Christianity* (Peterborough, UK: Epworth, 2005).

12. See, e.g., Amos Yong, "Justice Deprived, Justice Demanded: Afro-Pentecostalisms and the Task of World Pentecostal Theology Today," *Journal of Pentecostal Theology* 15.1 (2006): 127–47.

Origins

The essays in this section shed light on how African Americans within the earliest period of the Pentecostal movement engaged the racially complicated social context of early twentieth-century America out of which the movement arose. Two noted historians of Pentecostalism bring their collective knowledge to bear on unearthing the racial milieu through which African American Pentecostals were forced to navigate in order to birth a seemingly insignificant religious revival, which would by that century's end grow to influence every segment of the Christian church. Their essays place the movement's early development against the background of both race and class stratification, and the struggle of working-class African Americans who initially made up its the bulk to gain personal and social agency within American society. These essays also complement each other, with one (Robeck) providing a regional, historical focus on Afro-Pentecostal beginnings in the greater Los Angeles area, the heart of the early Pentecostal revival, and the second (Daniels) deploying a broader, socio-historical perspective. Together they add to existing historical accounts of the early history of black Pentecostal Christianity in the United States as well as help us see how black Holiness-Pentecostal adherents fused their social environment and religious sensibilities into resources for engaging the culture.

gian/Danish speakers, six Chinese language congregations, three Japanese congregations, five Spanish language congregations, ten African American congregations, and four synagogues.[10] More than 23 percent of the city's 226 congregations in 1906 fell into these ethnic categories.

Much of the African American growth in Los Angeles during this time occurred as African Americans from the South arrived in search of the promise of a healthy climate and mounting economic opportunity.[11] It came at a time when such opportunities actually existed for nearly everyone coming to Los Angeles, regardless of race or ethnicity, the exception being the Mexican community, which comprised less than 15 percent of the total population.[12] As many as 35 percent of the Mexicans were employed as day laborers, most of them by the Southern Pacific Railroad, where they undertook the most difficult work of ground clearance and track grading. Many others were unemployed.

The African American community grew slowly but steadily until April 1903, when it experienced a sudden growth surge. This increase came at the expense of the Mexican railroad workers. Work had been underway on Henry E. Huntington's Pacific Electric Company, which would carry passengers throughout the downtown Los Angeles area and to a number of outlying communities. In 1903 President Theodore Roosevelt announced that he would visit Los Angeles in time to participate in La Fiesta de Los Angeles, a holiday celebrated around Cinco de Mayo. As a result, Huntington's railway project would be given national attention.

With the encouragement of union organizers from outside the area, the Mexican laborers working for Huntington took this critical moment to establish the Unión Federal Mexicanos and strike for higher wages. They walked out less than two weeks before the Roosevelt's scheduled arrival. They were convinced that they would win; but they did not know their opponent.

Vowing never to submit to any union demands, the enterprising Huntington fired all of the Mexican workers who struck, and virtually overnight he recruited two thousand (mostly African American) railroad workers from throughout the southwest at wages higher than those being demanded by the Mexican union.[13] With the aid of police protection, these African American laborers began working around the clock on Huntington's tracks.[14] Within a week, this newly recruited work crew had displaced the Mexican workers, nearly doubled the African American population in Los Angeles, broken the labor strike, and completed the tracks down Main Street in time for the president's visit. Ironically, its completion came just in time for the celebration of the Los Angeles' Mexican Fiesta.[15] By 1910, Los Angeles would include the largest African American urban community west of Texas.[16]

African Americans who made their way to Los Angeles found a relatively safe and open city. Many of them were soon able to purchase property. As land prices increased around them, some of them became very effective speculators, compounding their land holdings and improving their economic standing in the community. By the beginning of the twentieth century many of them found themselves firmly in the city's middle and upper-middle classes.[17]

Prior to 1920, Los Angeles managed to avoid most of the Jim Crow laws that made life so impossible for African Americans around the country.[18] Among the earliest African American neighborhoods in Los Angeles is the area bounded on the north by East First Street, on the south by East Third Street, on the west by Los Angeles Street, and on the east by San Pedro Street. A cursory examination reveals that this neighborhood was in transition from a mostly Jewish population to one that would be dominated by African Americans for the next few years.[19] It already included a few African American businesses on Weller Street and, two or three blocks away, some railroad housing along Alameda and East Fifth Street.[20] That neighborhood slowly expanded south to Ninth Street and was bounded on the west by San Pedro Street and on the east by Alameda Street.[21] The majority of the African American community made their homes within walking distance of the railroad tracks.

Despite the many opportunities the city afforded to blacks, racism did exist. There were neighborhoods where residents made it clear that they did not want African Americans to purchase land or obtain housing.[22] Thus, racism and lower paying jobs sometimes required that many blacks "buy, build or rent a home in the poorer district in the city."[23] Still, people like Richard and Ruth Asberry and Jennie Evans Moore, who came to Los Angeles before the turn of the twentieth century, were property owners in a racially mixed neighborhood northwest of downtown.[24] While the Asberrys and Jennie Evans Moore held some economic advantages as property owners and were clearly part the Los Angeles middle class of African Americans in 1906, they functioned on the "blue collar" level through the jobs they held.[25] Furthermore, Frank Cummings (plasterer), William "Bud" Traynor (track layer), Willis (gardener) and Julia Hutchins (laundress), and Edward Lee (janitor) were clearly part of the lower-middle class, most of them having arrived in the city around 1903. Once the Azusa Street Mission opened, they would be joined by many others.

In spite of what racism there was in the city, a large number of African American Angelinos contributed substantially to the city and received much in return. The fact that Los Angeles had racially integrated schools and California had civil rights legislation as early as the 1880s did much to alleviate gross tensions in the day-to-day relations that existed between the races at that time.[26]

Discrimination could be found mostly at more basic levels in Los Angeles. In August 1906, for instance, several restaurants and hotels refused to provide services to African Americans.[27] Over the next nine months, others joined them, making it clear that African American trade would not be welcomed. In May 1907, however, Mayor A. C. Harper and the city council had had enough. They passed an ordinance prohibiting "objectionable signs in saloons, restaurants and other places of public convenience, aimed at Negroes as a race and discriminating against them as a class." The Reverend William H. Peck, pastor of First AME Church, greeted the action, on behalf of his congregation, with strong appreciation.[28] In spite of the clear incidents of racial discrimination that had taken place against African Americans in Los Angeles during these years, when compared to the forms of racism in much of the rest of the nation at that time, African Americans seemed to have had a privileged life.[29] Still the press continued to report on issues surrounding segregation,[30] African colonization efforts,[31] crime in the African American community,[32] and ethnic responses to the political landscape.[33]

The African American Churches in 1906 Los Angeles

In 1905, there were 180 churches and synagogues listed in the *Los Angeles City Directory*.[34] The following year, 1906, the number had grown to 226 churches and synagogues, an increase of 46, or 25.5 percent, in just one year.[35] The number of churches and synagogues listed in the *Los Angeles City Directory* in 1907 would be 254, including the Apostolic Faith Mission known popularly as the Azusa Street Mission.[36] In addition to the congregations listed, there were undoubtedly others that had sprung up too recently to be included in the count. And there were always a variety of tent and street meetings around the town, especially on Seventh Street between Spring and Broadway.[37]

If the full history of African Americans in Los Angeles has not yet been written, the same can be said of its African American churches. Those churches have long played a major role in the ongoing life of Los Angeles' African American community, as well as to the community at large. According to the *Los Angeles City Directory* for 1906, the city was already home to nine African American congregations: five were Baptist congregations, one was part of the Christian Church (Disciples of Christ), one was African Methodist Episcopal (AME), one was an African Methodist Episcopal Zion (AMEZ) church, and one was a Methodist church.[38]

The oldest of these churches is Second Baptist Church, established in 1885.[39] Located between Seventh and Eighth Streets on Maple Avenue, it had five hundred members. Through a series of splits, it had given birth to Tabernacle Baptist Church in 1898 with three hundred members and Mount Zion Baptist Church in 1902 with two hundred members, and, in December 1907, it would give birth to New Hope Baptist Church at Third and Stevenson with another one hundred members.[40] In addition, Mount Olive Baptist Church, founded in 1905, stood on the southwest corner of Santa Fe and Alamo streets and St. Paul's Baptist Church (1901) was located at 1818 Santa Fe Street. Between them, their membership accounted for 20.4 percent of the African American community.

An even larger percentage, roughly 27.7 percent, of the African American community held membership in the various Methodist churches of Los Angeles. Four Methodist denominations served the community in January 1906. First African Methodist Episcopal (FAME) Church was the oldest of these congregations, and it represented the overall interests of the AME Church in Los Angeles. Established in Los Angeles in 1870, in the home of former African American slave Biddy Mason,[41] its first building was located on East Third Street.[42] Originally known as Stevens African Methodist Episcopal Church, it had constructed a new wood frame sanctuary in 1888, at 312 Azusa Street. In February 1904, it changed its name to First African Methodist Episcopal Church and moved from these quarters, leaving behind a structure destined to become a center of the city's attention in the summer of 1906. The AME congregation, led by the Reverend Jarrett E. Edwards, occupied a beautiful, new, brick sanctuary valued at $20,000 and seating seven hundred people. It was located at 752 Towne, and while it took the official name of First AME, the congregation was typically called "Eighth and Towne."[43] From there, the congregation expected to provide a broader range of community services.[44]

The new facility was dedicated Sunday morning, February 21, 1904.[45] Two weeks later, on March 6, a Sunday afternoon service was held to dedicate two windows, one depicting the Good Shepherd and the other to memorialize the woman who had first organized the church, Biddy Mason.[46] The honorable Meredith P. Snyder, mayor of Los Angeles, the Reverend C. H. Anderson, pastor of Second Baptist Church, and the Reverend Peter Green, a venerable AME patriarch and church planter, were all featured speakers.[47] By 1906, the congregation had grown to eight hundred members.[48]

First AME Church in Los Angeles was clearly the most influential of the historic black churches in Los Angeles. Its congregation was also among the wealthiest in the city. In 1903, the church gave birth to a formal institution known as "The Los Angeles Forum." While this forum began in the church, it quickly separated, gaining a life of its own. As a result, participation was open to "any man or woman of good character."[49] The forum was a place where issues could be addressed by and within the African American community, where African Americans could be self-consciously African American at a sophisticated level, a place that provided community empowerment as much as it became a haven for seeking solutions to everyday problems and concerns.[50]

The conference meeting for the AME churches in Oregon and California was held in Los Angeles in October 1906. It seemed to provide a similar platform for local African Americans of the AME. Dr. Melvin Sykes, a local African American physician who specialized in blood and skin diseases,[51] and a member of First AME Church, gave the keynote address on the evening of October 3 of that year. In deeply moving terms, he described the "degradations . . . daily heaped upon the heads" of African Americans. His speech was followed by a second one, in which an African American attorney, Paul M. Nash, depicted the treatment of African Americans in the United States as being worse than the experience of the persecuted Jews in czarist Russia. Of particular note was his criticism of derogatory terms such as "darky," "nigger," "negro," and "coon" so prevalent in the local newspapers. He called on his hearers to advocate the use of "African" in their description of black people.[52]

Other discussions of significance in Los Angeles' African American community at the time included the question of miscegenation. When Bishop John W. Hamilton preached at the dedication of Wesley Methodist Church in July 1906, in the context of seeing the end of discrimination, he mentioned the ultimate possibility of a "union of the races." In a fascinating interview, a reporter later pressed him on the issue of whether the bishop supported interracial marriages. While Bishop Hamilton was willing to affirm "the right of any individual to marry whom he pleases, without regard to race or color," he refused to say whether or not he personally favored interracial marriage.[53]

About the same time, the African Methodist Episcopal Zion Church (AMEZ) established a congregation at 622 East Fourth Street (1905), and in August 1906 it sponsored the Afro-American Congress in its new facility at Pico Street and Paloma Avenue.[54] During 1906, division rocked this congregation and a number of its members left the congregation to join the First AME Church. A new pastor was appointed to the AMEZ congregation and the church began to rebuild. By early 1909 it was still under the oversight of the Reverend W. D. Speight; by then it was reportedly doing well.[55]

First Methodist Church, the well-to-do, mostly white, historic Methodist congregation at Sixth and Hill, was responsible for giving birth to two African American congregations in Los Angeles. First, it established Wesley Chapel in 1888. By 1906 the chapel was a vital "colored" congregation of five hundred members, and it had dedicated a new facility on the northeast corner of Eighth and San Julian.[56] In 1903, First Methodist Church established a second African American congregation, Mason Chapel. By early 1909, Mason Chapel boasted one hundred members. Still, as late as 1907, the Methodists of Southern California debated the questions of whether African Americans were yet capable of governing their own churches.[57]

The Colored (now Christian) Methodist Episcopal (CME) Church was the latest Methodist denomination to arrive in Los Angeles. In January 1906, it established a congregation of forty-five members next to the home of the pastor, the Reverend G. W. Pinkney, at 622 East Fourth Street.[58]

The African American community in Los Angeles was also served by a variety of other congregations. Westminster Presbyterian Church had been established "for the negro people" in October 1904, funded partially by the Presbyterian Church and partly by the Freedmen's Aid society. Built on the corner of Thirty-seventh and Denker, it was touted as "the only Negro Presbyterian church in California" and possibly "on the Pacific Coast."[59] It was the only African American congregation "west of Main Street" in Los Angeles as late as 1909, when it consisted of forty members.

A small, African American Christian Church, pastored by William Z. Hopper, held meetings on the northeast corner of Eighth and Wall streets. Mr. Coulter, the owner of Coulter's dry goods store on Broadway, later gave a building at Eighth and Central to the congregation.

An African American congregation taking the name St. Philip the Evangelist Episcopal Church was founded in 1907. In February 1909, it still had only twenty members.[60]

Many African Americans also attended other racially integrated churches in the city. Most of the African American Roman Catholics worshiped at Our Lady of the Angels Church on La Placita, then the central plaza of the city.[61] The number of African American Roman Catholics was sizable, most of them having come to California from southern Louisiana.[62] While First Baptist Church and First New Testament Church were predominantly white congregations, both of them had African American members.

The Holiness Church of Southern California also had a large African American constituency and frequently highlighted African American preachers in its services and camp meetings.[63] The first Holiness Church, organized by African Americans, was set in order in a hall located at 427 San Pedro Street on October 5, 1899. The first pastor of that congregation, H.

M. Spiller, led services in which many Caucasians also participated. He was granted full credentials with the Holiness Church on April 10, 1900.[64]

Other African Americans attended smaller independent missions, churches, storefronts, cottage prayer meetings, and tent meetings throughout the city in the early years of the twentieth century.[65] Such African American preachers holding meetings in Los Angeles frequently received extensive press coverage of these gatherings. During the summer of 1907, the African American evangelist J. L. Griffin ministered widely throughout the African American churches of the city, crossing denominational boundaries and distributing the offerings he received to various rescue charities in the city. His services at Mount Zion Baptist Church were said to include "the wild excitement and weird scenes of the old slave-day revivals among the colored people," and like other revivalists of the period, Griffin's presentations were animated, even performances in themselves. One imaginative reporter wrote, "Griffin is a perfect dynamo, and has a flow of language that would worry a phonograph to death."[66]

Following his services at Mount Zion, Griffin set up a tent at the corner of East Ninth and Mateo Streets where he held services throughout the month of September. A range of prominent people around the country, including several mayors and at least one governor, endorsed his ministry.[67] He was given special permission to baptize his converts in the lake at Echo Park, where he baptized a "cosmopolitan" group, including African Americans, whites, and at least one Native American.[68] As late as October, the *Herald* reported that he was holding new revival meetings in the Volunteers' Hall on Main Street, had purchased the tent now erected at Ninth and Mateo where meetings were still going on, and he was continuing his work for the needy of Los Angeles, regardless of their race.[69] Yet by year's end, announcement had been made that an interdenominational group of African American ministers would now endorse the work of Mrs. Mamie F. Turner to establish the Sheltering Arms Home at the corner of Dayton and Cypress Streets.[70] Dr. Griffin's name was not among them.

The Azusa Street Mission and the African American Mainstream

When the small congregation that would become the core of the Azusa Street Mission first met at the Asberry home on North Bonnie Brae Street in 1906, it was composed largely of African Americans. There were the occasional Caucasian visitors who attended those meetings, people like Emma Osterberg and her son, Arthur, and possibly W. G. and May Evans, but on the whole, the group was African American. On the evening of April 9, 1906, when members of this group first spoke in tongues, only African Americans were present. The group moved its meetings to Azusa Street where it quickly attracted not only African Americans but also Caucasians from the Wesleyan Holiness Movement who were searching for their baptism in the Spirit, Mexicans who were relatively new to the area, and an assortment of Russians, Armenians, Chinese, Japanese, and Native Americans. Because the dominant ethnic and racial makeup of the members was African American, and the congregation was led by an African American, it was no surprise that the dominant worship style would reflect an African American tradition. But it was a specific type of African American worship tradition.

The African American Christian community was and still is comprised of at least two very different worship traditions, often following lines drawn by their respective social classes. The historic African American churches—the African Methodist Episcopal (AME) Church (founded 1787), the African Methodist Episcopal Church, Zion (AMEZ) (founded 1820), the Colored Methodist Episcopal (CME) Church (founded 1870), and the National Baptist Convention (founded 1880)—that emerged following the American Civil War, stood as symbolic of the one tradition. They constituted the historic mainline that dominated the African American Christian community in Los Angeles at that time. While they were clearly dominated by their African American membership, in some significant ways they had chosen to lean toward the dominant Caucasian culture among which they lived.

Even a quick glance at the news accounts regarding the activities and affiliations of these churches demonstrates their position as an African American expression of the dominant culture as they adopted the same types of activities and affiliations their white counterparts enjoyed.[71] They built imposing, multipurpose structures of brick and stained glass. They adopted a level of sophistication and formality that rivaled what was found in the white community. They functioned as well-run organizations, with clearly defined, formal authority structures. They donned the same robes, pursued the same degrees, and sought the same titles as their white counterparts had. They embraced the Scriptures, often appealing to higher critical methods to interpret them, and they gave little credence to prophetic words, visions, dreams, or other phenomena such as dancing or falling in the Spirit with demonstrated parallels in their African past. They invested in large pipe organs and developed choirs, choral ensembles, and musicians as sophisticated and professional as any in the country. They sponsored concerts that highlighted African American talent. They founded African American clubs and societies, and aided the formation of African American labor unions. They held public forums on civic and social topics thought to be relevant to their African American membership. They lifted up education and encouraged their young to seek both that education and the advantages that it promised. Their members entered the professions, became home-owning pillars of the community, and in Los Angeles, they appealed to the African American majority that had made the city their home for nearly half a century, those who belonged largely to the middle and upper classes of the African American community.

Standing in opposition to their more refined neighbors, there were the congregations that found their center in what has been described as the African American "folk church."[72] They tended to embrace the "folk church" tradition, without the formal expressions and trappings of their more affluent African American neighbors in the historic black churches. They could frequently be found worshipping in Wesleyan Holiness churches, in tents, in cottage prayer meetings, or in storefront facilities such as the one founded by Mrs. Julia W. Hutchins at Ninth and Santa Fe, instead of in modern facilities. Often they adopted informal operating structures and informal styles of worship. They embraced the Scriptures, but did not entrust them to any higher critical analysis to determine their meaning. They also gave willing credence to prophetic words, visions, and dreams, and they made space for other phenomena such as dancing or falling in the Spirit that they shared with their African past, and which they discerned to be consistent with the Scriptures as they understood them.

Within this "folk church" tradition pipe organs were displaced by exuberant a cappella singing that was frequently accompanied by hand clapping, foot tapping, or some other form of rhythm making such as drums, spoons, washboards, and the occasional tambourine. The whole congregation served as the choir, and it was common for this tradition to worship without hymnals, with a person lining out the melody while others followed with improvisational harmonies. Their pastors seldom, if ever, donned robes, rarely held advanced educational degrees, and often eschewed all titles, except "Brother" or "Sister," or in some cases, "Pastor" or "Elder." Frequently, they criticized those African Americans who sought such things, as though they had somehow compromised their true identity as African Americans in exchange for the hope of greater cultural acceptance by the white majority culture.[73]

The vast majority of the African folk church members did not belong to any social club or organization or even to labor unions. In fact, such things were often thought to be "trappings of the world" and thus, were to be avoided. While they could appreciate the need for a basic education, they believed wholeheartedly that formal education did not really hold many answers to life's ultimate questions, especially when it came to God. Therefore, formal education was frequently kept at arms length as lived experience and lessons learned from the "school of hard knocks" were valued more.

In Los Angeles, the lower and lower middle classes of African Americans who were or who would become part of the "folk church" tradition were relatively new to the city. Roughly half of the people who were representative of these classes came to Los Angeles in 1903 or later. Most of them had come from rural locations in the South, though some had already experienced life at the low economic end of other towns or cities. Many of them lacked a basic education, let alone a college degree. Most of the men were employed in positions of manual labor, whether they were in the building construction trade or tracklayers or cooks or porters for the local, regional, and national railroads then under construction. Many of the women found work as domestics, as cooks, or as washerwomen. Most of them rented their homes or rooms, some living in company owned, substandard housing, but they still hoped that they would one day own a piece of property they could call their own.

For the most part, their members did not have access to the professions. They took honest labor in the blue collar community, fulfilling an honorable role but without many of the trappings embraced by the higher classes. Still, probably without realizing it, they were also accommodating themselves within their new urban reality, in much the same way that the lower classes of white Protestants were doing throughout the country. It is little wonder that Pastor Seymour could preach the following:

> Many people today think we need new churches, (that is to say church buildings,) stone structures, brick structures, modern improvements, new choirs, trained singers right from the conservatories, paying from seven to fifteen hundred dollars a year for singing, fine pews, fine chandeliers, everything that could attract the human heart to win souls to the meeting house is used in this twentieth century. We find that they have reached the climax, but all of that had failed to bring divine power and salvation to precious souls. Sinners have gone to the meeting house, heard a nice, fine, eloquent oration on Jesus, or on some particular church, or on some noted man. The people have been made glad to go because they have seen great wealth, they have seen people in the very latest styles, in different costumes, and loaded down with jewelry, decorated from head to foot with diamonds, gold and silver. The music in the church has been sweet, and it is found that a good many of the church people seem to be full of love,

but there has always been a lack of power. We wonder why sinners are not being converted, and why it is that the church is always making improvements, and failing to do the work that Christ called her to do. It is because men have taken the place of Christ and the Holy Spirit. . . . The church had the right idea that we need bishops and elders, but they must be given authority by our Lord and Savior Jesus Christ, and their qualifications for these offices must be the enduement of the power of the Holy Ghost.[74]

When these two groups, the more formal historic black congregations and the informal, newer, storefront, independent black congregations of Los Angeles, are compared, it is clear that the "folk church" tradition was closer to the older religious slave communities that had dominated the old South. Some of the elements found in "slave religion" could be found in both types of churches, particularly in the dialogical ways that sermons were conducted, as a conversation between preacher and congregation. The "call and response" style of preaching is common throughout the African American community. But when pipe organs replaced rhythm makers, when hymn books replaced memories, when Spirituals were replaced by chorales, when titles were adopted that seemed to participate in the mentality held by plantation owners, when secular concerns seemed to outweigh spiritual concerns, and when products of the mind seemed to vilify products of the hands, it seemed clear to members of the "folk church" that their African American sisters and brothers in the historic churches had lost their way.[75] It seemed to them that their African American sisters and brothers were embarrassed by their African and African American slave past as they embraced the things that would put distance between them and that past.

The Asberrys, Moores, Cummings', Traynors, and Hutchins' held a great deal more in common with the African American "folk church" tradition than they did with their counterparts in the historic African American churches of Los Angeles. As a result, the impact of the African American "folk church" tradition would make a significant contribution to worship at the Azusa Street Mission.

From the outside, the African American community in Los Angeles during the first decade of the twentieth century may have looked homogeneous. It was not. Los Angeles did draw a large percentage of African Americans from the American middle class who were clearly moving up the social scale. On February 12, 1909, the *Los Angeles Daily Times* broke with tradition and issued a special eight-page section of the newspaper devoted to the story of the African American community in Los Angeles. It was a marvel of liberal thinking in its day, but it revealed a basic uneasiness about the nature of the African American community. While many, if not all of the articles found in this section were by and about African Americans, it told only one side of the story. It was the story of the middle and upper-middle classes within the African American community, the story of those who had already made it. It was a collection of community member success stories, woven together in the many tales that chronicled their move from rags to riches, and it was a story perpetuated by the editors of the African American newspaper, the *California Eagle*, as well.

Issues between the African American community and the white community in Los Angeles were complicated not only by issues of race and a wide range of ethnicities but also by the presence of class struggles in both of these communities. Many of the earliest African Americans in Los Angeles were well established in the region whose fortunes grew as the community grew. They were often property owners who had made long-term investments in the community and had already established themselves. Many of them had attended colleges or universities, some were professionals, and they tended to belong to the more established mainstream Protestant churches, to First African Methodist Episcopal, to Second Baptist Church, to Wesley Chapel, even to the forty-member Westminster Presbyterian Church. Indeed, the section of the *Los Angeles Daily Times* that celebrated the presence of the African American community in Los Angeles in February 1909 clearly represented the concerns and interests of the middle to upper-middle class of African Americans in Los Angeles. All of the churches mentioned in that newspaper's pages represented this group of African Americans, while other churches such as the Azusa Street Mission, with its much larger attendance but generally lower class of members, and its clear ties to the "folk church" tradition, were not. No such church was even mentioned in the 1909 African American section of the *Los Angeles Daily Times*.

The coverage of African American churches in Los Angeles in these papers provides a stunning example of the story that was not told. The story of the Azusa Street Mission was never mentioned. The pastor, William Joseph Seymour was not named. The revival that had provided so much fodder for newspaper headlines for three years, and that bucked established societal norms regarding the role of women in the church or the intermingling of races, did not receive even an allusion.[76] That as many as fifteen hundred people were worshipping each weekend at the Azusa Street Mission between 1906 and 1909, potentially making it the largest African American oriented congregation in the city, was not mentioned.[77] One can only wonder at the reasons for this silence. Was it shame, or disgust? Was it a reminder of things past, things that those who envisioned these pages would just as soon forget? Was it sending a message to the newer African American immigrants to the city, reminding them that they should "pay their dues" and not rock the boat that had resulted in such economic success as at least half of the Los Angeles African American community already enjoyed? Or was it simply intended to show the dominant white community that African Americans were every bit as capable of success as their white counterparts—a separate, but equal world? Perhaps the answers will become clearer as the story of the Azusa Street Mission and its many less-than-successful parishioners unfolds. What is clear, however, is that there were really two African American worlds in Los Angeles in the first decade of the twentieth century. These two worlds were reflected also in the city's black churches, and at some levels they collided with one another. As a result, the Azusa Street Mission never became part of the ecclesial power structure in the African American community but was treated as a "fraudulent, low-class cult" by its more affluent black neighbors.[78]

Concluding Thoughts

In contrast to many other cities in United States of 1906, Los Angeles provided a significant freedom to its African American citizens. For a quarter century, their fortunes had risen alongside most other Angelenos. The same upward mobility had marked their churches. Most pastors were well educated. Most African American church buildings would have matched most of the church buildings used by Caucasians dollar for dollar. Stained glass, organs, robes, and liturgical formality was a mark of most of these churches. Black storefront churches simply did not exist.

The Azusa Street Mission, an African American congregation at its founding and at the time of its closing in 1931, was nonetheless quite different from nearly all other existing African American congregations in the city. Its differences lay in the fact that it attracted participation from more Caucasians than did any other African American congregation in the city, and its worship style was not consistent with that shared by the upwardly mobile majority of African Americans. In fact, it represented more the style of slave churches in the African American past, the style of frontier rather than urban worship, a style from which much of Los Angeles' African American population had attempted to distance itself.

It is not surprising that rhetoric developed between them that maintained their striking distinctions in culture and class. The city would have to wait until

1920 before a new wave of African American migration, a migration dominated by poor blacks, would begin to change this in any substantial way. Following the "Great Migration" of the late teens and early twenties, a new kind of African American church would come to dominate in Los Angeles, a church much closer to that which William J. Seymour had led at the Azusa Street Mission.

NOTES TO CHAPTER 2

1. Larry Martin, *The Life and Ministry of William J. Seymour and a History of the Azusa Street Revival* (Joplin, Mo.: Christian Life Books, 1999); Douglas J. Nelson, "For Such a Time as This: The Story of Bishop William J. Seymour and the Azusa Street Revival, A Search for Pentecostal/Charismatic Roots" (PhD diss., University of Birmingham, UK, 1981); Robert R. Owens, *Speak to the Rock: The Azusa Street Revival—Its Roots and Its Message* (Lanham, Md.: University Press of America, 1998); and Cecil M. Robeck Jr., *The Azusa Street Mission and Revival: The Birth of the Global Pentecostal Movement* (Nashville, Tenn.: Nelson Reference and Electronic, 2006).

2. "The Same Old Way," *Apostolic Faith* [Los Angeles, CA] 1.1, September 1906, 3.2.

3. "Bible Pentecost," *Apostolic Faith* [Los Angeles, CA] 1.3, November 1906, 1.1.

4. "Religious Fanaticism Creates Wild Scenes," *Los Angeles Record,* July 14, 1906, 1; William F. Manley, "True Pentecostal Power, with Signs Following," *Household of God* 2.9 (September 1906), 6, states that there were about twenty-five "colored" and three hundred "white" people present when he visited the church in late August or early September 1906.

5. Douglas Flamming, *Bound for Freedom: Black Los Angeles in Jim Crow America* (Berkeley, Calif.: University of California Press, 2005), 115.

6. The two best treatments of African Americans in Los Angeles to date are the 1936 University of Southern California PhD diss. (now in book form) by J. Max Bond, *The Negro in Los Angeles* (San Francisco: R and E. Research Associates, 1972), and Flamming, *Bound for Freedom,* though the latter work contains many errors of fact regarding the early black congregations in Los Angeles, especially on Azusa Street. Mark Wild, *Street Meeting: Multiethnic Neighborhoods in Early Twentieth-Century Los Angeles* (Berkeley, Calif.: University of California Press, 2005), begins his study in 1925 but mentions Azusa Street twice, 24 and 68; and R. J. Smith, *The Great Black Way: L.A. in the 1940s and the Lost African American Renaissance* (New York: Public Affairs Books, 2006), emphasizes the 1940s but covers Azusa Street on 157–66.

7. Jack D. Forbes, "The Early African Heritage of California," in Lawrence B. De Graaf, Kevin Mulroy, and Quintard Taylor, eds., *Seeking El Dorado: African Americans in California* (Los Angeles: Autry Museum of Western Heritage, 2001), 79–80.

8. Quintard Taylor, *In Search of the Racial Frontier: African Americans in the American West, 1528–1990* (New York: W. W. Norton and Company, 1998), 34; Bond, *Negro in Los Angeles,* 1–4.

9. "Population Is Past 230,000," *Los Angeles Herald,* April 15, 1906, 5; Nils Bloch-Hoell, *The Pentecostal Movement* (London: Allen and Unwin, 1964), 30, rightly notes that half the population was "fresh immigrants." The description of Los Angeles as a "metropolis of two million people" in James R. Goff Jr., *Fields White unto Harvest: Charles F. Parham and the Missionary Origins of Pentecostalism* (Fayetteville, Ark.: University of Arkansas Press,

1988), 131, is wide of the mark, although Goff's point regarding the city's cosmopolitan character is well taken. Most towns within thirty miles of Los Angeles, such as Long Beach, Pasadena, and Whittier averaged fewer than five thousand residents each in 1906.

10. *International Directory of Los Angeles 1906–1907* (Los Angeles: International Publishing Company, 1907). For the German language congregations, see pp. 131–32, for the Russian congregation, see p. 975. For the Scandinavian congregations, see p. 1000, and for the Spanish language congregations, see p. 1102. A more inclusive list may be found in the *Los Angeles City Directory 1907* (Los Angeles: Los Angeles City Directory Company, Inc., 1907), 37–41.

11. Lawrence B. De Graaf, "The City of Black Angels: Emergence of the Los Angeles Ghetto, 1890–1930," *Pacific Historical Review* 39 (1970): 330–31.

12. On the Mexican population, see Ricardo Romo, *East Los Angeles: History of a Barrio* (Austin: University of Texas Press, 1983), 29. On the percentage for whom Spanish was the first language, see Antonio Ríos-Bustamante, "The Barrioization of Nineteenth-Century Mexican Californians: From Landowners to Laborers," in Manuel G. Gonzales and Cynthia M. Gonzales, eds., *En Aquel Entonces [In Years Gone By]: Readings in Mexican-American History* (Bloomington: Indiana University Press, 2000), 78. This article was originally published in *Masterkey: Anthropology of the Americas* 60 (Summer/Fall 1986): 26–35.

13. For the Union's accounting of the size and racial makeup of the labor imported from El Paso by Huntington, see "Mexican Laborers Are on Strike," *Los Angeles Record*, April 24, 1903, 1, and "Police and Council Aid Street Railway in Contest with Mexicans," *Los Angeles Record*, April 25, 1903, 1. For Huntington's side of the story, see "Peons' Fool Strike Is Broken, Track-Laying Kept Up All Night," *Los Angeles Daily Times*, April 25, 1903, 2:1.

14. De Graaf, "City of Black Angels," 330.

15. Charles Wollenberg, "Working on *El Traque*: The Pacific Electric Strike of 1903," in Norris Hundley Jr., ed., *The Chicano* (Santa Barbara, Calif.: Clio Books, 1975), 96–107, especially 103. Cf. William B. Friedricks, *Henry E. Huntington and the Creation of Southern California* (Columbus: Ohio State University Press, 1992), 140; and Romo, *East Los Angeles*, 68–69.

16. Taylor, *In Search of the Racial Frontier*, 206.

17. Robert Lewis Williams Jr., "The Negro's Migration to Los Angeles, 1900–1946," *Negro History Bulletin* 19 (February 1956): 102–3, suggests that the majority who came to Los Angeles were already part of the middle class.

18. On the other hand, William Deverell, *Whitewashed Adobe: The Rise of Los Angeles and the Remaking of Its Mexican Past* (Berkeley, Calif.: University of California Press, 2004), tells a powerful story about anti-Mexican and Mexican American racism during these years. At the same time, both Chinese and Japanese Americans in California were the objects of highly restrictive legislation. One important limitation that no African American ever shared was the prohibition against owning land in California.

19. *Los Angeles City Directory 1903* (Los Angeles: General Directory Publishers, 1903), 1402 and 1598, include a number of Jewish names such as Harris, Epps, Maxwell, James, Dauchy, Sameshimes, Lichter, Laietsky, and Wolff. The *Los Angeles City Directory 1904* (Los Angeles: General Directory Publishers, 1904), 1446 and 1640–42, still reveal the names of Harris, Maxwell, James, and Dauchy. But Morton has replaced Epps, Foruchi has replaced Sameshimes, Farrand has replaced Lichter, Leake and Martinez have replaced Laietsky, and Robb has replaced Wolff.

20. De Graaf, "City of Black Angels," 328–29.

21. J. McFarline Ervin, "The Participation of the Negro in the Community Life of Los Angeles" (master's thesis, University of Southern California, 1931; repr., San Francisco: R. and E. Research Associates, 1973), 12. McFarline, who completed his work in 1931, suggests that the southernmost line was Slauson Avenue, but in 1906, the extremity of the community was still considerably north of that line.

22. "Edendale Indignant over Negro Neighbors," *Los Angeles Express,* October 2, 1907, 2.11.

23. "Colony of Negro Families," *Los Angeles Express*, July 8, 1905, 14.

24. The Asberrys purchased a home at 222 North Bonnie Brae Street, where they lived between 1899 and 1901. By 1903 they had purchased their home at 214 North Bonnie Brae Street, but they continued to own the earlier property, which contained two houses. Jennie Evans Moore owned her home at 217 North Bonnie Brae Street.

25. Richard Asberry had made his money working for the Pullman Company. Upon moving to Los Angeles, however, he was employed as a janitor. Jenny Evans Moore purchased a home for $500 in gold coin, November 9, 1896, while employed as a cook. See, *Maxwell's Los Angeles City Directory and Gazetteer of Southern California 1896* (Los Angeles: Los Angeles Directory Co., Publishers, 1896), 980.

26. De Graaf, "City of Black Angels," 329.

27. "Negroes Turned Down," *Pasadena Evening Star*, August 21, 1906, 1.

28. "Negroes Thank Mayor Harper," *Los Angeles Herald*, May 12, 1907, 2.5.

29. Lonnie G. Bunch, "A Past Not Necessarily Prologue: The Afro-American in Los Angeles," in Norman M. Klein and Martin J. Schiesl, eds., *20th Century Los Angeles: Power, Promotion, and Social Conflict* (Claremont, Calif.: Regina Books, 1990), 104–5.

30. "Rights of Negroes," *Los Angeles Herald*, July 12, 1907, 4.

31. "Negro Holds His Race Is Fast Retrograding," *Los Angeles Herald*, October 4, 1907, 2.

32. "May Charge Arson against a Gang of Negroes," *Los Angeles Examiner*, June 27, 1906, 9; "Porter Nearly Beaten to Death by Negroes," *Los Angeles Examiner*, July 24, 1906, 12; "Negroes Quarrelsome and One Is Stabbed," *Los Angeles Herald*, July 30, 1907, 12.

33. "Colored Republicans Form Organization," *Los Angeles Examiner*, October 5, 1906, 3; "Negroes Will Be Organized into League," *Los Angeles Herald*, May 19, 1907, 6; "Negroes Organize a League," *Los Angeles Express*, August 30, 1907, 8.

34. *Dana Burks' Los Angeles City Directory 1905* (Los Angeles: Los Angeles City Directory Co., Inc. 1905), 32–35.

35. *Dana Burks' Los Angeles City Directory 1906* (Los Angeles: Los Angeles City Directory Co., Inc., 1906), 37–41.

36. Ibid., The Apostolic Faith Mission at 312 Azusa Street is listed on p. 40.

37. Among those holding such meetings in 1905 were the Holiness Church and the Household of God. The regular use of tents by preachers in the Holiness Church is well documented in Josephine M. Washburn, *History and Reminiscences of the Holiness Church Work in Southern California and Arizona* (1912; repr., New York: Garland Publishing, Inc., 1985). William Francis Manley's Household of God met regularly in a tent in Los Angeles. Frank Bartleman, *How Pentecost Came to Los Angeles* (Los Angeles: F. Bartleman, ca. 1926), 17, repr. in *Witness to Pentecost: The Life of Frank Bartleman* (New York: Garland Publishing, Inc., 1985), mentions that he attended one of Manley's tent meetings in June 1905.

38. *Dana Burks' Los Angeles City Directory 1906*, 37–39. The directory list included: *Baptist:* Mount Olive Baptist Church (colored), 2003 Santa Fe Av, Rev. G. W. Shields; pastor, h.

2473 Leonard; Mount Zion Baptist Church (colored) 719 Stephenson Av. Rev. S. E. Piercy, pastor, h. 2901 Pennsylvania Av; St. Paul's Baptist Church (colored) 1808 Santa Fe Av, Rev. David Evans, pastor, h. 2933 New Jersey; Second Baptist Church (colored), 740 Maple Av. C. H. Anderson, pastor, h. 2934 Pennsylvania Av.; Tabernacle Baptist Church (colored), 952 Hemlock, Rev. J. D. Gordon, pastor. res 1619 E. 14th; *AME Zion:* African M. E. Zion, 622 E. 4th, S. W. Hawkins, pastor, h. 620 same; African M. E. Zion., Pico nw cor Paloma Av. Rev. W. D. Speight, pastor, h. 959 E. Pico; *AME:* First African Methodist Episcopal Church E. 8th sw cor Towne Av. W. H. Peck, pastor, h. 1520 Griffith Av; and *Methodist:* Wesley Chapel (colored), San Julian ne cor. 8th, G. R. Bryant, pastor, h. 607 E 8th.

39. Leland D. Hine, *Baptists in Southern California* (Valley Forge, Pa.: Judson Press, 1966), 51.

40. "Troubles of Negro Congregation Reach Court of Justice Austin," *Los Angeles Express*, November 14, 1907, 4.

41. Dolores Hayden, "Biddy Mason's Los Angeles, 1856–1891," *California History* 68 (Fall 1989): 97.

42. "New Church," *Daily Los Angeles Star* 1:76, August 28, 1870, 2.1; "New Church," *Daily Los Angeles Star* 1:84, September 7, 1870, 3.2.

43. G. R. Bryant, "Religious Life of Los Angeles Negroes," *Los Angeles Daily Times*, February 12, 1909, 3.7. The move and name change are documented also in the *Los Angeles City Directory* (1904 and 1905). On the nickname see Flamming, *Bound for Freedom*, 113.

44. "New Colored Church Will Be Dedicated Early in February," *Los Angeles Herald*, January 30, 1904, 10; "African Methodist Church Is Dedicated by Bishop Lee," *Los Angeles Herald*, February 23, 1904, 7.

45. "African Methodist Church Is Dedicated by Bishop Lee," *Los Angeles Herald*, February 23, 1904, 7.

46. On the contribution of this woman to the history of Southern California, see Hayden, "Biddy Mason's Los Angeles," 86–99, and DeEtta Demaratus, *The Force of a Feather: The Search for a Lost Story of Slavery and Freedom* (Salt Lake City: University of Utah Press, 2002).

47. "Memorial to Biddy Mason, Mayor Snyder in Pulpit," *Los Angeles Daily Times*, March 7, 1904, 5.

48. "New Colored Church Will Be Dedicated Early in February," *Los Angeles Herald*, January 30, 1904, 10.

49. Theodore W. Troy, "The Forum," *Los Angeles Daily Times*, February 12, 1909, 3.2; Emory Joel Tolbert, "The Universal Negro Improvement Association in Los Angeles: A Study of Western Garveyism" (PhD diss., University of California, Los Angeles, 1975), 91–92.

50. Bunch, "A Past Not Necessarily Prologue," 107.

51. One of many advertisements that published his services can be found under the title "Blood and Skin Diseases a Specialty," *Los Angeles Daily Times*, July 6, 1907, 2.9.

52. "Only 'African' Will Do," *Los Angeles Daily Times*, October 4, 1906, 2.1.

53. "Marry Any Color," *Evening News*, July 23, 1906, 1.

54. "Afro-American State Conference in Session," *Los Angeles Examiner*, August 28, 1906, 4.

55. *Dana Burks' Los Angeles City Directory 1906*, 37–39.

56. "New Wesley Chapel M. E. Church Is Dedicated," *Los Angeles Examiner*, July 23, 1906, 7.

57. "Color Line Will Not Be Drawn by Methodist of Los Angeles," *Los Angeles Record*, September 27, 1907, 3.

58. G. R. Bryant, "Religious Life of Los Angeles Negroes," *Los Angeles Daily Times*, February 12, 1909, 3.4.

59. "Exclusively for Negroes," *Los Angeles Daily Times*. June 29, 1907, 2.8; "Exclusively for Negroes," *Los Angeles Express*, June 29, 1907, 15; "Negroes Dedicate New Presbyterian Church," *Los Angeles Examiner*, July 1, 1907, 12.

60. G. R. Bryant, "Religious Life of Los Angeles Negroes," *Los Angeles Daily Times*, February 12, 1909, 3.2.

61. Michael E. Engh, *Frontier Faiths: Church, Temple and Synagogue in Los Angeles, 1846–1888* (Albuquerque, N.M.: University of New Mexico Press, 1992), 106.

62. Bond, *Negro in Los Angeles*, 105.

63. Washburn, *History and Reminiscences*, 138. The photographs (between p. 160 and p. 161) identify George A. Goings, William Washington, and Frank Chapman and their spouses, as African American ministers in the Holiness Church. See also Charles Edwin Jones, "The 'Color Line' Washed Away in the Blood? In the Holiness Church, At Azusa Street, and Afterward," *Wesleyan Theological Journal* 34.2 (Fall 1999): 257.

64. Washburn, *History and Reminiscences*, 266, 277.

65. William F. Manley held interracial "Household of God" tent meetings in 1905; cf. Nelson, "For Such a Time as This," 186.

66. "Scenes Wild and Weird," *Los Angeles Daily Times*, August 11, 1907, 6; "Negro Evangelist to Hold Tent Meetings," *Los Angeles Herald*, August 14, 1907, 3.

67. "Baptizer of 8000 Here," *Los Angeles Herald*, September 2, 1907, 5; "Evangelist Feeds 5000 Children," *Los Angeles Herald*, September 8, 1907, 3.

68. "Dr. J. L. Griffin to Baptize at Echo Park," *Los Angeles Herald*, September 22, 1907, 3; "Baptizer in Lake Bumped by Boats," *Los Angeles Herald*, September 23, 1907, 6; "Baptized in Echo Lake," *Los Angeles Express*, September 23, 1907, 6.

69. "J. L. Griffin Will Open Revival," *Los Angeles Herald*, October 20, 1907, 3; "Dr. Griffin Preaches Straight from Shoulder," *Los Angeles Herald*, October 21, 1907, 3.

70. "Home for Unfortunate Colored Girls Founded," *Los Angeles Express*, December 12, 1907, 8.

71. The *California Eagle*, which began publication in 1891, was the preeminent African American newspaper for the people of Southern California. Cf. Julia Norton McCorkle, "A History of Los Angeles Journalism," *Annual Publications*, vol. 10 (Los Angeles: Historical Society of Southern California 1915–1916), 35. It featured articles on prosperous African Americans, eminent speakers such as Booker T. Washington, noted Divines who preached at specific churches, concerts that featured professional musicians specializing in classical music and opera, public discussion forums, African American lodges, and literary societies. Unfortunately, virtually all issues published prior to February 1914 are currently missing. Drawing from the pages of the *California Eagle*, however, the former editor of the paper wrote a short account of William J. Seymour and the Azusa Street Mission in Charlotta A. Bass, *40 Years: Memoirs from the Pages of a Newspaper* (Los Angeles: privately published, 1960), 25–26.

72. Pearl Williams Jones, "The Musical Quality of Black Religious Folk Ritual," *Spirit: A Journal Incident to Black Pentecostalism* 1.1 (1977): 23, summarizes the "black Folk Church" as including, (1) worship services that are freely structured around "prayers, praise, and preaching" that is not heavily influenced by their "white counterparts"; (2)

"improvisational music" that is "integral" to all aspects of its services and rituals; (3) "testimonies, prayers and praise, and in any manner the individual feels led to express" is encouraged; (4) "the responsorial style of religious worship involves the preacher, congregation, choir and everyone in communal worship [sic.]"; and (5) a "historical lineage that reaches back to the slave's praise houses which were autonomous provinces not formally associated with independent or white denominations."

73. See the complaint, "We may be turned out of the big wood and brick structures. . .," which refers to the historic churches of Los Angeles in "Spreads the Fire," *Apostolic Faith* [Los Angeles, CA] 1.2, October 1906, 4.2. Similarly, there is innuendo in the claim, "Many times we do not need these song books of earth, but the Lord simply touches us by His mighty Spirit and we have no need of organs or pianos, for the Holy Ghost plays the piano in all our hearts, and then gives the interpretation of the song and sings it in the English language"; untitled entry, *Apostolic Faith* [Los Angeles, CA] 1.4, December 1906, 2.5.

74. William J. Seymour, "The Holy Spirit: Bishop of the Church," *Apostolic Faith* [Los Angeles, CA] 1.9, July—September 1907, 3.1. While these same criticisms could have been leveled at both the historic black and white churches in Los Angeles, the criticisms leveled were precisely the points on which the historic black churches seem to have demonstrated their ability to join the city's mainstream as evidenced by the newspaper articles and ads of the day.

75. Pearl Williams Jones ("The Musical Quality of Black Religious Folk Ritual," 21) claims that "The traditional liturgical forms of plainchant, chorales, and anthems do not fulfill the needs of traditional Black folk religious worship and ritual. They are unrelated and inappropriate as vehicles for folk-style religious worship services because liturgical musical forms do not represent the dominant cultural values of the black community." Her criticism of the older, independent black denominations that used these liturgical forms is that these churches had merely "attempted to impress European musical forms onto their congregations," and the result was a violation of black culture and community.

76. G. R. Bryant simply wrote, "The African Methodists were the first of these to organize. More than twenty years ago they started out with a small membership and labored under many disadvantages to pay for the old church property on Azusa Street. They were at one time in such straitened circumstances for the payment of the property that one of the bishops advised the officials of the church to give up the property, but some of the faithful band held on until all could see the possibilities of paying the debt, which was done in 1902 under the pastorate of the Reverend J. E. Edwards. A new and better location for a church on the corner of Eighth street and Town avenue was purchased and a large and beautiful house of worship was erected at a cost of over $20,000. In 1907, the pastor, Dr. W. H. Peck, and the official board sold the old Azusa street property for enough money to finish paying for the new church on Eighth street and Town avenue." G. R. Bryant, "Religious Life of Los Angeles Negroes," *Los Angeles Daily Times*, February 12, 1909, 3.4.

77. Arthur Osterberg, "I Was There," Full Gospel Business Men's Fellowship International, *Voice*, May 1966, 18. Second runner up was First AME with its eight hundred members in 1906 and nine hundred members in 1909.

78. Flamming, *Bound for Freedom*, 116.

Navigating the Territory

Early Afro-Pentecostalism as a
Movement within Black Civil Society

DAVID D. DANIELS III

Introduction

Just prior to the advent of Pentecostalism among African American Holiness Christians in 1906, the Black Church was a predominately Baptist and Methodist entity. Nearly all African American Christians were Protestant, and 96 percent were either Baptist or Methodist. The membership of the four major black Protestant denominations—the National Baptist Convention, Inc., African Methodist Episcopal Church, African Methodist Episcopal Zion Church, and Colored Methodist Episcopal Church—accounted for approximately 84 percent of the total all African American Christians, representing 3,113,625 out of a total of 3,685,097.[1]

Within a generation, Afro-Pentecostalism would attract more than 500,000 adherents, becoming the largest religious family among black denominations after the Baptists (3,782,464) and Methodists (1,099,375) by 1936. During this period, black Pentecostals would emerge as the third largest religious family within the overall Black Church, surpassing not only black Roman Catholics (137,684), but other Protestant groups including Episcopalians (32,172), Congregationalists (20,434), and Presbyterians (13,983). The growth of Afro-Pentecostalism would change the religious landscape of black Protestantism, making it a predominately Baptist, Methodist, and Pentecostal phenomenon rather than the Baptist and Methodist phenomenon that held at the advent of the twentieth century. Organizationally, by 1940, Afro-Pentecostalism consisted of more than fifty denominations and many independent congregations. Geographically, it covered all the regions of United States and, through its geographically overlapping networks, created a national organizational base for the Afro-Pentecostal public posture in black civil society.[2]

Mapping early Afro-Pentecostalism onto the African American civil landscape allows us to identify the key ways this movement engaged black civil society, which, during the early twentieth century, was central to the campaigns for racial justice and the efforts toward racial progress. Among African Americans, the institutions of black civil society were responsible for various initiatives such as increasing literacy and college education rates, providing employment for the professional and working class, producing networks that connected people across the country, establishing a media system for communication, and organizing venues, both secular and sacred, for artists to mount cultural performances.

As a concept, civil society serves as an alternative lens through which to interpret early Afro-Pentecostalism, and an alternative to theories about church-sect or social-deprivation theories. Scholars who utilize the sociological distinctions of church and sect designate early Afro-Pentecostalism as a sect because of its rejection of the role of the church in legitimizing the political state, reproducing dominant middle-class culture, and sanctioning dominant social morals and manners. Those who employ social-deprivation theories contend that early Afro-Pentecostalism avoided direct involvement in the public arena because it is a movement of the poor, which compensates for such involvement by focusing on personal behavior and otherworldly pursuits such as a future life in heaven. These sociological approaches characterize Afro-Pentecostalism as practicing more emotional worship styles, possessing more leaders with a low educational level, occupying more storefront sanctuaries, and having fewer relationships with the white Protestant establishment than such mainstream black Protestant denominations as the National Baptist Convention, Inc., and the African Methodist Episcopal Church.

For the sake of our discussion, the era of early Afro-Pentecostalism extends from the advent of the movement in 1906 to the inauguration of the Second Great Migration in 1942. This chapter explores this thirty-six-year period as the era of the first generation of Afro-Pentecostalism as a movement. It first introduces concepts of civil society and maps early Afro-Pentecostalism on the civil landscape from the perspective of how significant sectors within early Afro-Pentecostalism utilized formal means to form public opinion, foster trust, educate its members, and express culture and, consequently, participate in the construction of black civil society. The focus here is on how early Afro-Pentecostalism engaged the four types of key institutions—communicative, associative, educative, and expressive—that constitute civil society. Second, this chapter examines how pivotal sectors within early Afro-Pentecostalism interacted with a network of three primary entities—church, school, and lodge—while contesting alliances between the black church and electoral politics as well as the black church and the white establishment. This network and these alliances structured black civil society during the first part of the twentieth century. Finally, we explore the content of civil engagement of dominant social systems within U.S. society—patriotism, patriarchy, racial segregation—by major sectors within early Afro-Pentecostalism. In each of these discussions, we place Afro-Pentecostalism within the religious context crafted by the five major black denominations.[3]

Across the spectrum of black religious groups during the early twentieth century, major denominations, such as the AME Church, employed a vast array of formal means to participate in the construction of black civil society, while minor denominations, such as the National Primitive Baptist Convention, opted to utilize a limited array of formal means to do the same. A key question shaping this inquiry is where to plot early Afro-Pentecostalism along this continuum. The question here is whether the civil engagement of early Afro-Pentecostalism reinforces or undermines the model of civil engagement of the major black denominations. I argue that Afro-Pentecostalism plays a dual role: supportive and subversive. It supports the reigning model of civil engagement in certain sectors and contributes to the strengthening of black civil society on the one hand while on the other hand it undermines the dominant model by adopting cultural styles, values, and norms which were at odds with this model's middle-class orientation. In this way, we see that early Afro-Pentecostalism's various discursive practices both supported and at the same time challenged the project of forming black civil society during the first half of the twentieth century.

Early Afro-Pentecostalism as a Constituent of (Black) Civil Society

The tradition of sociological scholarship drawing from Robert Wuthnow and Jeffrey Alexander characterizes civil society as constituted by four types of institutions: communicative, associative, educative, and expressive. *Communicative institutions*, such as newspapers, influence public opinion through their informational articles. They frame debates and develop perspectives on social issues along with setting social agenda. *Associative institutions*, such as sororities and fraternities, foster trust and civility through internal group interactions. Trust and tolerance are learned through group activities of deliberation, consensus-building, cooperation, and project implementation. *Educative institutions*, such as schools, produce and disseminate knowledge, creating an informed population. And *expressive institutions*, such as choirs that produce music that set values and beliefs to song, utilize the arts (visual, musical, literary, culinary) to display values and beliefs. Collectively, these four institutions of civil society produce visions, collective aims, and the social fabric of the common good.

Civil society stands between the family on one hand, and the government and the economy on the other. Noting this distinction, the sociologist Robert Wuthnow suggests that the majority of conversations about civil society stress five interrelated topics:

> First, it is defined negatively as that which is not formally governmental, meaning that it is composed of the civilian population and does not depend on coercive powers of government as the primary means by which conformity to social norms is enforced. Second, it is also defined negatively as excluding those aspects of individual behavior that may be considered private, such as matters of intimacy, sexuality, and other relations within the family, or the leisure activities of individuals, or many of their personal convictions, beliefs, and opinions. Third, it is defined positively as the secondary groups, associations, and organizations through which citizens develop and express their collective aims and aspirations, and through which they either enlist the government's assistance to realize their aims or successfully pursue them on their own. Fourth, because of the aims of civil society are taken to be public or collective goods that require cooperation or the tempering of self-interest in favor of the good of all, purely economic activities are generally excluded, as are organizations oriented toward these activities (especially for-profit firms). And, finally, civil society also presupposes and includes a certain kind of individual or civic person, particularly one who can instinctively or through training behave responsibly and civilly toward fellow citizens, make informed decisions, participate rationally in public discussions about collective goals, and conform to conventional norms of moral decency and public propriety.[4]

Wuthnow's general definition of civil society emphasizes conformity to social norms fostered by nongovernmental entities; public behavior of tolerance, trust, and civility; associational life that generates collective aims and aspirations; public or collective goods produced through cooperation; and the civic person as product of civility, informed decision making, and rational public deliberations. This general definition spotlights the interpersonal dimensions that constitute civil society and privileges the role of associations in sustaining that society. Wuthnow offers this general definition in order to critique it and expand it to incorporate into the conception of civil society the role of institutions.

For the sociologist Jeffrey Alexander, black civil society was a site built within the black community by African Americans who were excluded from participating in the larger civil society for most of the history of the United States up until 1965 by slavery and by legalized racial segregation.[5] According to Alexander, black civil society emerges in the Great Migration in 1917 with the shifting of the U.S. black population from being residentially rural and economically agrarian toward being residentially urban and economically located within the service and industrial sectors. Racial segregation within the urban societies of the South and North to which rural African Americans relocated during the Great Migration deepened their isolation from the majority society and their subordination to the white majority. Within these urban societies were racial ghettoes where African Americans cultivated "dense, cross-class interactions" that fostered a new racial "solidarity and collective identity."[6] Alexander contends that black civil society emerged from African Americans drawing upon the "universalizing representations and practices" of the larger American civil society or "black identification with white civil society" as well as resources internal to African American life in marshalling their opposition to racial segregation and subordination and in their campaigns for full inclusion into larger American society.[7] Within Alexander's conception, the black church plays a pivotal role in constructing black civil society.

Instead of opting out of the communicative, associative, educative, and expressive institutions that constitute civil society as some smaller black denominations did, major sectors within Afro-Pentecostalism followed the example of the five major black denominations and inserted Afro-Pentecostalism as a constituent of black civil society. Afro-Pentecostal denominations joined the major black Baptist and Methodist denominations in making the religious newspaper the primary communicative institution. For all three religious families, opinion making would be the key outcome. Alongside the various secular newspapers such as the *Chicago Defender, New Amsterdam News*, the *Pittsburgh Courier*, and dozens of other local black dailies and weeklies, there were a host of black Baptist and Methodist newspapers such as the *Arkansas Baptist Vanguard*, the *Christian Recorder* (AME), the *Christian Index* (CME) and the *Star of Zion* (AMEZ). The largest sector was among the black Baptist media, which included forty-three different news publications; black Methodist denominations and congregations produced at least four news publications.

Afro-Pentecostal denominations did not publish religious magazines and academic journals as the major black Baptist and Methodist denominations did. Afro-Pentecostal denominations, however, did join in publishing religious newspapers. These included *The Whole Truth* (Church of God in Christ), *Voice in the Wilderness* and *Christian Outlook* magazines (Pentecostal Assemblies of the World), *The Present Truth Gospel Preacher* (Church of the Living God, the Pillar and Ground of the Truth), *The Holiness Union* (United Holy Church of America), *The True Witness* (Fire Baptized Holiness Church of God of the Americas), *The People's Mouthpiece* (Apostolic Overcoming Holy Church of God), the *Contender for the Faith* (Church of our Lord Jesus Christ of the Apostolic Faith), the *Pentecostal Ensign* (All Nations Pentecostal Church), *The Word of Truth* (King's Apostle Holiness Church of God), and the *Latter Day Messenger* (Mount Sinai Holy Church of America). These media allowed the various Afro-Pentecostal perspectives, interests, and agendas to be communicated and debated as well as to inform and shape black public opinion. Such periodicals also supplemented black Baptist and Methodist media in ensuring that black public opinion, which is crucial to civil society, was crafted in formal ways by more than the media of the white majority, which tended to promote black inferiority.[8]

Afro-Pentecostal denominations followed the major black Baptist and Methodist denominations to a degree in organizing various auxiliaries for women, children, and young people as their primary associative institutions. The major black Baptist and Methodist denominations, however, included congregations that sponsored literary societies, lyceums, and athletic teams as well as mutual aid societies and educational fund-raising societies. This latter set of associative groups was uncommon among Afro-Pentecostal congregations during the era. Although the kinds of associative groups differed, all three traditions participated in associative institutions. Consequently, all three traditions fostered trust and civility as key behaviors crucial to civil society.[9]

For black Baptist, Methodist, and Pentecostal denominations, the primary educative institution was the school, with its production of knowledge as the fundamental agenda. Education was a major institution within black civil society, and the black denominations were one of its major sponsors and funders. By 1906, black congregations and denominations funded, partially or totally, approximately 348 black schools in the United States, including 57 post-secondary institutions across twenty states and two territories (Indian Territory and the District of Columbia). While the majority of black colleges were initially funded and controlled by white missionary societies, African

American denominations and congregations were pivotal in the establishment of 15 black colleges.[10]

While black Baptist and Methodists included colleges and seminaries in their educational continuum, black Pentecostals added Bible institutes. The schools established by black Pentecostals during this era included Saints Industrial and Literary School (Mississippi), Faith Home and Industrial School (Arkansas), Page Normal and Bible Institute (Texas), and Holiness Bible Institute and School (Tennessee), all of which were sponsored by the Church of God in Christ. The United Holy Church of America operated the Bible Training School (North Carolina) and the Boynton Institute (Virginia). The Church of our Lord Jesus Christ of the Apostolic Faith sponsored Christ Bible Institute (New York), and Christ's Holy Sanctified Church organized Christ Holy Sanctified Industrial School (Louisiana).[11]

The worship service and the religious program—musicale, Christmas pageant, and Easter performance—were the primary expressive institutions of black Baptist, Methodist, and Pentecostal denominations, and their key behavior was culture making. Early Afro-Pentecostalism opted to draw from folk and popular culture and produced a sanctified sound. Black Pentecostal women and men were also instrumental in the development of a forerunner of gospel music called "sanctified music." Sanctified music became the major carrier of black religious folk music associated with slave and West African culture, which was noted for its call-and-response, improvisation, polyrhythms, and diatonic harmonies.[12]

Established black Pentecostal recording artists like Sallie Sanders, Ford McGee, and Arizona Dranes added the new gospel songs to their repertoire. In their recordings of the 1920s, black Pentecostal recording artists introduced to the broader religious community their musical culture, which incorporated the New Orleans jazz style and ragtime-style piano accompaniment and was impervious to distinctions between sacred and secular music. This musical culture prepared the black religious community for Thomas Dorsey's choral and solo compositions that he began distributing in the late 1920s. Finally, during the 1930s, the radio broadcasts of Eva Lambert in New York City along with Lucy Smith's and William Roberts's in Chicago, introduced the new gospel compositions to thousands of homes. Consequently, the Afro-Pentecostal and black Baptist musical tradition together developed gospel choir music.[13]

Sectors within the five major black denominations, however, sponsored literary, musical, and dramatic societies, which promoted elite Western literature, classical music, operas, marching band repertoires, and anglicized spirituals along with other African American artistic works. This created an alternative cultural trajectory to the one promoted by the Afro-Pentecostal denominations as well as the sector within the two major black Baptist denominations that embraced gospel music.

Thus, major sectors in Afro-Pentecostalism produced communicative, associative, educative, and expressive institutions that variously inserted Afro-Pentecostalism into black civil society. While black Pentecostal participation in black civil society failed to mirror totally participation of the major black denominations, it was a vital and constitutive element of early Afro-Pentecostal development.

Early Afro-Pentecostalism, Major Black Denominations, and Dominant Civil Network and Alliances

Pivotal sectors within early Afro-Pentecostalism interacted with the network of three primary entities—church, school, and lodge—which formed the organizational base of black civil society. The Afro-Pentecostal critique of lodges led to them becoming prohibited sites for black Pentecostals. During the early twentieth century, Afro-Pentecostalism contested alliances between the black church and electoral politics as well as the black church and the white establishment, to the extent that the organizational base and partnerships of black civil society would be challenged and undermined by the growth of Afro-Pentecostalism.

For many early twentieth-century leaders, the civil network of the church, school, and lodge formed the organizational base of the four (at that time) major black denominations and constituted the organizational base of black civil society. Some contended that "schools, churches, and secret organizations have contributed in the greatest degree to the uplift of the Negro race."[14] Black fraternal orders, which included male and female organizations, were the next largest sector of nationally organized entities within black civil society. The leading national associations were the Odd Fellows, Pythians, Masons, and Elks. Black fraternal associations included United Brethren of Friendship, the Sisters of the Mysterious Ten, the Independent Order of St. Luke, and the Grand United Order of True Reformers. During the early twentieth century, the largest four black male and female national lodges counted nearly 800,000 members. As an entity, they would be larger than the membership of the second largest black denomination, the AME Church.[15]

Lodges also provided "health and burial insurances, employment opportunities, social functions, and ritual life."[16] They exercised a role in burial rites for their deceased members who belonged to the church. These rites were enacted around the casket after the eulogy and final blessing at the church and later at the gravesite. Lodges also engaged in the ritual ceremony of laying a cornerstone at newly built church edifices. Along with these ceremonies conducted at congregations associated with the major black denominations during this era, lodges developed secret rituals. These ranged from secret handshakes to rites of admissions and rituals of bonding. Lodges such as the Masonic orders included secret mythologies about origins of civilization and the different races that generated new racial identities for African Americans as well as means of socialization.[17]

Lodges were primary sites for black men to exercise leadership, participate in male bonding, engage in intergenerational mentorship, and raise funds to provide loans for business ventures. It was pivotal to black civil society during the early twentieth century; there were even lodges that could offer small loans and life insurance policies, which yielded up to $1000.00 in 1910. In some cities and towns, the lodge building rented space to local businesses ranging from insurance companies, pharmacies, banks, printing establishments, movie theaters, restaurants, newspaper offices, and barber shops as well as churches. In cities like Chicago, all elected officials had joint membership in churches and lodges.[18]

None of this implies that Baptists, Methodists, or other black denominations accepted involvement in lodges without discussion. There were debates about the role of funeral and other rites, and even about the possibility of joint church and lodge memberships. However, embrace of the lodge—at least in certain segments of the black church—motivated the Afro-Pentecostal response.

Whereas major Afro-Pentecostal denominations joined the major black denominations in networking with schools, they disagreed with them in the appropriateness of the church partnering with the lodge, especially those secret societies like the Masonic orders. Afro-Pentecostalism dismissed lodges because of their members' pledges of secrecy. Masonic teachings were deemed as pagan and competition for the time and money of churches. While some black Pentecostals "disapprove[d] of [C]hristians connecting themselves with secret, oath-bound societies, [seeing them] as being needless, profitless . . . and not conducive to piety or Christian usefulness," other black Pentecostals contended it was wrong for Christians to belong to "secret societies or any other organization or body wherein is a fellowship with unbelievers bound by an oath."[19]

Black Baptist, Methodist, and Pentecostal denominations competed with lodges by adopting what they deemed as the "good" within fraternal orders.

They inaugurated "programs to care for their sick and bury their dead and to design pins and emblems publicizing denominational identity."[20] The Church of God in Christ, for instance, established a national benevolent burial association that was open to its members.[21] The House of God which is Church of the Living God, the Pillar and Ground of the Truth sponsored a Benevolent Helping Hand Club to support "sick, distressed and destitute members."[22] That club would also defray some of the burial expenses for club members.

The refusal of Afro-Pentecostal denominations to support the lodge undermined the organizational base of black civil society in two ways. On the one hand, this rejection of the lodge blocked black Pentecostal women and, especially, men from utilizing the array of resources provided by lodges for personal and racial advancement. On the other hand, even as Afro-Pentecostalism grew organizationally during its first generation, the lodge depended less on that segment of the black church and more on the major black denominations for personnel, talent, and resources.

In early twentieth-century debates about the appropriate relationship between the church and electoral politics, and about the relationship between the black denominations and the white establishment, some sectors in the black Baptist, Methodist, and Pentecostal denominations rejected political involvement of black clergy and churches while other sectors promoted it. These debates found expression in the secular and religious newspapers. The use of churches as sites of political meetings was described by critics in negative terms. According to *The Broad Ax*, a Chicago weekly newspaper, "The Negro race is the only race in the world to have their churches turned into political halls for faking preachers and the small-headed base White Republican politicians who contend that they can buy any 'Darkey preacher and a whole church full of N[egroes] for ten dollars.'"[23] In 1912 the *Chicago Defender* castigated black churches for allowing their space to be used for political meetings. The editorial charged that political partisanship led to discrimination against Democratic candidates by Republican interests.[24]

In a number of cities, black clergy and leaders played an influential role in electoral politics, more often in the Republican Party and, by 1910, even in the Democratic Party. African Americans retained their voting rights in the black towns of such states as Arkansas, Florida, Mississippi, Oklahoma, and Kansas. The small number of black elected officials in these cities and towns was supported by the Black Church across the United States. For the most part, however, the church was excluded from direct involvement in electoral politics during the early twentieth century because of the disenfranchisement due to racial segregation. Yet the political activity of clergy like Reverdy

Ransom and Archibald J. Carey Sr., both of the AME Church, set the course that activist clergy would pursue. This course did not create black politics but rather created a public space for the Black Church to play a pivotal role in the electoral process. Additionally, local clergy associations connected to one of the five major black denominations passed resolutions to endorse specific political candidates during the early twentieth century. For instance, in 1914 the Chicago Colored Baptist Churches and the AME Preachers' Union endorsed the aldermanic candidacy of Oscar DePriest.[25]

Early black Pentecostals counted within their ranks activist leaders like E. R. Driver and Emma Cotton, both pastors in California, who endorsed political candidates during the 1930s. Robert Clarence Lawson, founder of the Church of Our Lord Jesus Christ of the Apostolic Faith, of New York City, was heavily involved in Harlem politics. Smallwood Williams, a leader in Lawson's denomination and pastor in Washington, D.C., also participated in local politics. When American women received voting rights in 1928, black Pentecostals debated whether it was biblical for Christian women to vote; many sectors within Afro-Pentecostalism, like the Church of God in Christ, approved the right of their women to exercise this new privilege in electoral politics. Lillian Brooks Coffey, a leader in the Women's Department of the Church of God in Christ, remarked in a 1941 address to the National Convocation of her denomination, "[a]vail yourself of the necessary preparation to fight the Battle for Democracy in which all of the people may share. I firmly believe that the church should take an active part in the affairs of the government."[26] While a large sector within the five major black denominations and Afro-Pentecostalism rejected the involvement of the church in politics, there were a minority of leaders like Driver, Cotton, Lawson, Williams, and Coffey.[27]

The relationship between the five major black denominations with the white establishment—that is, major white Protestant denominations and philanthropic foundations—ranged from close to distant. For instance, there were partnerships between the National Baptist Convention, Inc., and American Baptist Churches around secondary and college education as well as between the Christian Methodist Episcopal and the Methodist Episcopal Church, South, around education and global missions. Local white Baptist associations like those in Chicago occasionally loaned congregations (such as Olivet Baptist Church) funds to help pay the cost of purchased church complexes. Philanthropic foundations like the Elizabeth McCormick Memorial Fund provided funds to Olivet Baptist Church to open a free health clinic for poor children.[28]

On the other hand, some Afro-Pentecostal denominations, like the Church of God in Christ, prided themselves on supporting their religious activities without funding from white educational foundations, churches, or philanthropists. In order to avoid the grip of white paternalism, Afro-Pentecostalism defined itself as being "owned, organized, operated, and controlled solely by Negroes" and identified itself as possessing an "independent, self-helping attitude."[29]As Afro-Pentecostalism grew in size and influence during its first generation, the hesitancy of those denominations to engage the white religious and philanthropic establishment encouraged black self-determination and self-reliance. This stance differed slightly from the self-determination and self-reliance of the major black denominations. These denominations had to wrestle with white paternalism and against the quest for control by the white establishment because of their involvement with the white religious and philanthropic organizations.

Three trajectories of congregational relationships to the community existed among the major black denominations. First, there were congregations that utilized evangelism as the exclusive way to relate to the community. Second, there were congregations that related to the community through evangelism and charity. Third, there were congregations, informed by social Christianity, that served the community as community centers, which sponsored social services such as employment and housing information, gymnasiums, health clinics, parish nursing, day and night training schools, kindergartens, schools of music, consumer cooperatives, boys and girls clubs, and parents' meeting; these congregations were called institutional churches. Many of these institutional churches were open every day of the week, and some were open twenty-four hours a day.

Among the five major black denominations, the institutional congregations included Olivet Baptist Church and Institutional AME Church in Chicago, Bethel AME Church in Philadelphia, Mount Gilead Baptist Church (Institutional) in Fort Worth, Tabernacle Baptist Church Memphis, and Bethel Institutional Baptist Church in Jacksonville (Florida). All of these institutional congregations became community hubs of black civil society. They were vital community centers that not only intersected with social service agencies but in some instances became providers of educational, informational, recreational, health care, and consumer services themselves.[30]

Afro-Pentecostalism adopted the trajectory of congregations as sites that related to the community through evangelism and charity, especially in the distribution of free meals and free, or low-cost, clothing. While the leading congregations of Afro-Pentecostal denominations resisted becoming institutional churches during this era, they did sponsor rescue homes for children and retirement homes for the aged, free meals and clothing for the poor, and a series of "Poor Saints Homes" for the homeless in various cities across the United States.[31]

By prohibiting black Pentecostals from joining lodges, there was a personal and collective loss that undermined the organizational base of black civil society. Further, since the major black denominations were divided over the alliances between the black church and electoral politics, Afro-Pentecostal denominations in general tilted the scale toward a separation between church and politics, although there was a significant group of black Pentecostal leaders who advocated the church's political involvement in the society. Last but not least, the relationship between Afro-Pentecostalism and the white religious and philanthropic establishment encouraged black self-determination and self-reliance that differed somewhat from the self-determination and self-reliance of the major black denominations. The absence of the small, yet prominent, trajectory of institutional congregations within Afro-Pentecostalism that existed in the major black denominations thus left Afro-Pentecostalism to adopt the larger trajectory of congregations as independent sites which related to the community through evangelism and charity. It is clear how the role that Afro-Pentecostalism crafted for itself within the civil network and alliances of black civil society at times undermined the organizational base and at other times strengthened aspects of black civil society.

Afro-Pentecostalism, the Major Black Denominations, Civil Ruptures, and Civil Repairs

Black civil society was ruptured by racial segregation, patriarchy, and patriotism. Afro-Pentecostalism made various attempts to bring about a civil repair of the relationship between blacks and whites, black men and women, and the black citizenry and federal government.

Legal racial segregation structured the relationship between blacks and whites during this era. The major black denominations and Afro-Pentecostalism were forced to work within legalized system of racial segregation in constructing black civil society. Major black denominations chose between an activist racial integrationism of leaders such as W. E. B. DuBois, who espoused the overthrow of legalized racial segregation, and critical racial accommodationism of leaders such as Booker T. Washington, who advocated the organization and development of African Americans into citizens capable of proving their ability to earn racial equality. Afro-Pentecostalism inserted interracialism as an alternative to both by focusing on constructing black-led interracial organizations, whereas both the immediacy of racial integrationist and the gradualism of the critical accommodationist worked in the present, both had to wait on the future for their options to be materialized.[32]

The Azusa Street Revival led by William J. Seymour and his Apostolic Faith Mission provided Afro-Pentecostalism's model of race relations. From 1906 to 1908 blacks, whites, Latinos/Latinas, and Asians worshipped together at the mission. White Pentecostal leaders such as Florence Crawford, Glenn Cook, Clara Lum, Hiram Smith, and Frank Bartleman worked alongside Seymour and other African Americans. During an era in American Christianity and society when most institutions and movements espoused racial segregation, early Afro-Pentecostalism struggled with its interracial identity. Outside of Pentecostalism, the few interracial congregations in American religion were predominately those white congregations with black members within the Holiness movement, Christian Science churches, Roman Catholic parishes, or the Peace Mission of Father Divine. The major black denominations remained almost entirely African American because whites declined to join. Interracialism within early Afro-Pentecostalism shaped interracial congregations and denominations. While interracial congregations existed within Afro-Pentecostalism, they were a very small percentage of the total number of churches (this despite the interracial character of the Azusa Street Mission). The two leading interracial early Afro-Pentecostal denominations were the Church of God in Christ and the Pentecostal Assemblies of the World.[33]

Interracial congregations within Afro-Pentecostalism during this era included majority African American congregations with white members; multiracial congregations with African American, white, and Latino members; and majority white congregations with African American members. Afro-Pentecostalism also created within black civil society black-led interracial denominations: the Pentecostal Assemblies of the World, and the Church of God in Christ. The Pentecostal Assemblies of the World, established in 1907, was predominately white until 1924 when it became majority African American but retained a number of white clergy and congregations throughout the early twentieth century. While the majority of white clergy left the denomination in 1924, a critical group remained. In 1924 the then predominately African American, albeit interracial, denomination elected the Garfield T. Haywood, a black man, as presiding bishop. By 1931 the bishopric of the Pentecostal Assemblies of the World was interracial: four African Americans and three white Americans. The denomination sponsored interracial national conventions in northern cities but also included white delegates from the South as well. After Haywood's death in 1931, a group of the African Americans agreed to merge with a white group of clergy and churches in 1932, leaving the Pentecostal Assemblies of the World a smaller religious body. Although the predominately black denomination possessed fewer overall churches and even fewer white churches, it remained interracial and initiated the practice of consecrating a white clergyman every time an African American clergyman was elevated to the bishopric in order to preserve its ideal of interracial leadership. In 1937, almost all the African Americans who left in 1932 had returned.[34]

In 1907 a faction of the churches affiliated with the Church of God in Christ as an African American holiness fellowship embraced the Pentecostal message and was disfellowshipped from the parent body. Between 1909 and 1924, four groups of white clergy and churches would join the black-led Church of God in Christ, while a large group of whites withdrew from the Church of God in Christ. The African American leadership of the denomination tried three different ecclesial experiments to sustain interracialism. From 1909 to 1914, the Church of God in Christ functioned as a federation of three clergy networks: the original religious body led by Charles Harrison Mason, a nearly all-white religious body led by Howard Goss and E. N. Bell, and a nearly all-white religious body with a few Latinos led by Leonard P. Adams. In 1914 the Goss-Bell network would leave and join other white groups of clergy and churches to organize the Assemblies of God. Adams's group would be joined by a small white group of clergy who left the newly formed Assemblies of God in 1916 led by William Holt. Holt would be instrumental in the second and third interracial experiment. In the second experiment (1916–24), Holt, Adams, and other whites would integrate the leadership of the original religious body led by Mason with Adams being recognized as a member of the bishopric (called the board of overseers) and Holt becoming the first general secretary; during the second phase at least four Latino congregations joined the denomination.

In the third phase, from 1924 to 1932, the Church of God in Christ adopted a Protestant model of establishing a minority—white—conference, specifically to unite congregations across the United States that belonged to the predominately black denomination. This development was in response to the argument of those who questioned the anomaly of white congregations in a black denomination as a racial minority within the larger system, but sought to maximize their presence by uniting under a common administrative unit. The conference existed until around 1932 when the predominately black leadership abolished it, accusing its white leadership of attempting to form a denomination with white members of the Church of God in Christ. For the remainder of the early Afro-Pentecostal era, the Church of God in

Christ would continue to attract white clergy and laity as members as well as periodically including whites as speakers at the national convocation. Whites would regularly attend not only the national convocation held in Memphis but also the state convocation held in Texas.[35]

While the five major black denominations were able to remain minorities in ecumenical bodies such as the Federal Council of Churches (which were white-led and majority white in membership), during its formative years sectors within Afro-Pentecostalism created black-led and, often, black majority, interracial congregations and denominations. These institutions provided an alternative, organized space in the black and general civil society to legalize racial segregation, modeling a way for the races to practice interracialism in the South and North. At the height of legalized racial segregation, sectors within Afro-Pentecostalism risked establishing new interracial organizations and projected an interracial identity.[36]

During those formative years, Afro-Pentecostalism challenged patriarchy with more than 50 percent of the denominations embracing the ordination of women clergy and 20 percent being headed by women. Among the denominations that ordained women but reserved the bishopric to male clergy were the United Holy Church of America and the Pentecostal Assemblies of the World. In The House of the Lord, an initially male-led denomination, a woman succeeded the founder as presiding bishop. Nearly all women bishops in either the black or white church during this era were elevated to the bishopric in Afro-Pentecostal denominations founded by women: Church of the Living God, the Pillar and Ground of the Truth; Holy Nazarene Tabernacle Church of the Apostolic Faith; Kings Apostle Holiness Church of God; Mount Sinai Holy Church of America; All Nations Pentecostal Church; and Mt. Calvary Pentecostal Faith Church.[37]

During World War I, the five major black denominations joined their white counterparts in supporting the war. While there were a few dissenters, these black denominations defined their patriotism in terms of their support. Some major black Pentecostal leaders challenged the U.S. entry into World War I through adopting pacifism and engaging in antiwar preaching. According to the historian Theodore Kornweibel Jr., the Church of God in Christ and the Pentecostal Assemblies of the World articulated their opposition to the war.[38] The most prominent Pentecostal pacifist during this time was Charles Harrison Mason.

According to a federal agent, Mason preached throughout the United States that World War I was "a rich man's war and a poor man's fight," basing his objection to the war on the biblical injunction against "shedding human blood or taking human life."[39] After Congress passed the draft act, Mason directed his assistants to apply for conscientious objector status for draft-age males in the Church of God in Christ. Federal agents placed Mason and others under surveillance and had them arrested for obstruction of the draft in various states for their pacifist activities. Mason, however, would express his loyalty to the U.S. government by encouraging members of his denomination to buy U.S. bonds. The Church of God in Christ crafted its conception of patriotism by affirming "loyalty to magistrates, civil laws, the constitution, president, and flag, all God-given institutions," and insisting that "Church members could perform any other service which did not conflict with these principles [against shedding blood]."[40] The leadership exclaimed that they "admonish and exhort out members to honor magistrates and . . . obey the civil laws."[41]

Additionally, within Afro-Pentecostalism there were sectors that embraced the black nationalism of the Pan-Africanist movement, the Universal Negro Improvement Association (UNIA), led by Marcus Garvey. Among Afro-Pentecostal denominations that supported the UNIA were Triumph the Church and Kingdom of God in Christ, and the African Universal Church. In 1919 Triumph the Church and Kingdom of God in Christ would host Marcus Garvey at its national meeting. The African Universal Church hosted the UNIA meetings in its Miami congregation. However, the major black denominations along with most national black civic and religious leaders refused to support Garvey or the UNIA.

We have seen that Afro-Pentecostalism emphasized a counter-set of values and actual racial options than that of the major black denominations. It did this while working within the same systems of racial segregation, patriarchy, and patriotism as the major black denominations. These values and racial options thus shaped Afro-Pentecostalism as a distinctive movement within the larger black church community.

Conclusion

With black civil society Afro-Pentecostalism crafted resistance to the racial arrangement of segregation even as it also formed an alternative response to the racial plight of black people. On the one hand, Afro-Pentecostalism joined the major black denominations in the United States in contributing to the construction of black civil society during the early twentieth-century. Yet, instead of embracing the dominant values and norms of white society that black civil society adopted, Afro-Pentecostalism challenged these values and norms at their core. Hence Afro-Pentecostalism was both a part of, and yet also separate from, the wider black community. Through its participation in and distinctive contributions to the construction of the black civil society, Afro-Pentecostalism blazed a familiar but yet fresh trail for the black church into the second half of the twentieth century.

NOTES TO CHAPTER 3

1. *Religious Bodies Census: 1906* (Washington, D.C.: Department of Commerce and Labor/Bureau of the Census, 1910), 137.

2. R. R. Wright Jr. "The Church and Religious Work among Negroes," in Jessie Parkhurst Guzman, Vera Chandler Foster, and William Hardin Hughes, eds., *The Negro Year Book: A Review of Events Affecting Negro Life, 1941–1946*, 10th ed. (Tuskegee, Ala.: Department of Records and Research, Tuskegee Institute, 1947); Wright includes statistics from the 1936 religious census. The statistics on Afro-Pentecostals are drawn from Wright and supplemented by other sources.

3. "Major" as defined in terms of the membership size and public influence. Those designated are the National Baptist Convention, Inc., National Baptist Convention of America, African Methodist Episcopal (AME) Church, African Methodist Episcopal Church Zion (AMEZ), and Christian Methodist Episcopal Church (CME), originally titled the Colored Methodist Episcopal Church. There were only four major black denominations until 1915 when the National Baptist Convention of America was organized by a faction that withdrew from the National Baptist Convention, Inc.

4. Robert Wuthnow, "Can Religion Revitalize Civil Society? An Institutional Perspective," in Corwin Smidt, ed., *Religion as Social Capital: Producing the Common Good* (Waco, Tex.: Baylor University Press, 2003), 193.

5. Jeffrey Alexander, *The Civil Sphere* (New York: Oxford University Press, 2006).

6. Alexander, *Civil Sphere*, 279.

7. Ibid., 277 and 279.

8. W. E. B. Du Bois, ed., *The Negro Church* (1903; repr., Walnut Creek, Calif.: AltaMira Press, 2003), 111, 128, and 133.

9. Lillian Brooks Coffey, ed., *Yearbook of The Church of God in Christ for the Year 1926* (n.p., ca. 1926), 108–24; Anthea Butler, *Women in the Church of God in Christ: Making a Sanctified World* (Chapel Hill, N.C.: University of North Carolina Press, 2007), 45–48.

10. The African Methodist Episcopal Church founded Wilberforce College (now University) in 1856, Allen University in 1880, Morris Brown College in 1881, Paul Quinn in 1881, Shorter College in 1886, and Edward Waters in 1888. The Christian Methodist Episcopal Church organized Lane College in 1879, Paine College in 1884, Texas College in 1895, and Miles Memorial College in 1907. Black Baptists founded Arkansas Baptist College in 1885, Selma University in 1878, and Virginia College and Seminary in 1888. The African Methodist Episcopal Zion established Livingstone College in 1882. The Church of God in Christ founded the predecessor institution to Saints College in 1914.

11. C. E. Jones, *Black Holiness: A Guide to Black Participation in Wesleyan, Perfectionistic, and Glossolalic Pentecostal Movements* (Methuen, N.J.: Scarecrow Press, 1987).

12. See David D. Daniels III, "'Gotta Moan Sometime:' A Sonic Exploration of Earwitnesses to Early Pentecostal Sound in North America," in *Pneuma: Journal of the Society for Pentecostal Studies* 30.1 (2008): 5–32.

13. Cheryl J. Sanders, *Saints in Exile: The Holiness-Pentecostal Experience in African American Relgion and Culture* (New York: Oxford University Press), 71–78, 86–90.

14. I. W. Crawford and P. H. Thompson, *Multum in Parvo: An Authenticated History of Progressive Negroes in Pleasing and Graphic Biographical Style*, 2nd ed. (Natchez, Miss.: Consumers Printing Co., 1912), 12.

15. Joe Trotter, "African American Fraternal Associations in American History: An Introduction," *Social Science History* 28.3 (2004): 356.

16. John M. Giggie, *After Redemption: Jim Crow and the Transformation of African American Religion in the Delta 1875–1915* (New York: Oxford University Press, 2008), 20.

17. St. Clair Drake, *Churches and Voluntary Associations in the Chicago Negro Community* (Chicago: W. P. A. District 3, 1940), 110.

18. Giggie, *After Redemption*, 93; Crawford and Thompson, *Multum in Parvo*, 122–23. See also Clement Richardson et al., eds.; *The National Cyclopedia of The Colored Race*, vol. 1 (Montgomery, Ala.: National Publishing Company, Inc., 1919), 592–93.

19. Charles Pleas, *Fifty Years of Achievement from 1906 to 1956: A Period in the History of the Church of God in Christ* (Memphis, Tenn.: Church of God in Christ, 1956), 78, cited in Giggie, *After Redemption*, 184 (brackets original to Giggie); "Secret Societies, etc.," *2000 Organizational Manual Pentecostal Assemblies of the World, Inc.* (Indianapolis: 2000), 103.

20. Giggie, *After Redemption*, 91.

21. Coffey, ed., *Yearbook of the Church of God in Christ for the Year 1926*, 64, 65.

22. *Discipline of the House of God which is Church of the Living God, The Pillar and Ground of the Truth* (1956; rev. ed., Philadelphia: The Church of the Living God Publishing House, 1979), 92–93.

23. Ralph Davis, "The History of the Negro Newspaper in Chicago" (master's thesis, University of Chicago, no year given), 59, cited in Drake, *Churches and Voluntary Associations in the Chicago Negro Community*, 110.

24. *Chicago Defender*, July 22, 1913, 7, cited in Joseph A. Logsdon, "The Rev. Archibald J. Carey and the Negro in Chicago Politics" (master's thesis, University of Chicago, 1961), 30.

25. On Chicago's Black Baptist Clergy and AME Preachers' Union endorsing political candidates see *Broad Ax*, November 28, 1914, cited in Drake, *Churches and Voluntary Associations in the Chicago Negro Community*, 111. Cf. Miles Mark Fisher, "The History of the Olivet Baptist Church of Chicago" (master's thesis, University of Chicago, 1922), 92.

26. As cited in James H. Purdy Jr., "Churches of God in Christ Hold Session," *Chicago Defender*, December 13, 1941, 10.

27. David D. Daniels III, "Doing All The Good We Can: The Political Witness of African American Holiness and Pentecostal Churches During the Post-Civil Rights Era," in Maryann N. Weidt and R. Drew Smith, eds., *New Day Begun: African American Churches and Civic Culture in the Post-Civil Rights America* (Durham, N.C.: Duke University Press, 2003), 168–69; on Driver and Cotton see "Endorsers," *Los Angeles Sentinel*, November 1, 1934, 5.

28. Fisher, "The History of the Olivet Baptist Church of Chicago," 95.

29. "Thousands Converge On Memphis To Attend 31st Convocation of 'Saints,'" *Atlanta Daily World*, November 29, 1938, 2.

30. Carter G. Woodson, *The History of the Negro Church*, 2nd ed. (Washington, D.C.: The Associated Publishers, 1921), 273–78.

31. J. E. Campbell, "Holiness Speakers Bestir Followers at Convocation," *Atlanta Daily World*, December 5, 1938, 3.

32. Evelyn Brooks Higginbotham, *Righteous Discontent: The Women's Movement in the Black Baptist Church 1880–1920* (Cambridge, Mass.: Harvard University Press, 1993), 193.

33. Douglas J. Nelson, "For Such a Time as This: The Story of Bishop William J. Seymour and the Azusa Street Revival, a Search for Pentecostal/Charismatic Roots" (PhD diss., University of Birmingham, UK, 1981). The few multiracial congregations existed in the southwestern states: Apostolic Faith Mission and Saints Home Church of God in Christ in Los Angeles; and the Pilgrim Mission (predecessor to Phoenix's first Church of God in Christ congregation). The majority African American congregations with white members included Holy Nazarene Tabernacle and All Nations Pentecostal Church in Chicago, Christ Temple Pentecostal Assemblies of the World in Indianapolis, Church of God in Christ in Detroit, Mount Calvary Pentecostal Faith Church in New York City, First Church of God in Christ in Brooklyn (New York), and Holy Temple Church of God in Christ in Springfield (Massachusetts). The majority white congregations with black members included the Stone Church in Chicago, Glad Tidings Assemblies of God in New York City, and Hopkinsville (Kentucky) Church of God in Christ.

34. Morris E. Golder, *History of the Pentecostal Assemblies of the World* (1973; repr., Birmingham, Ala.: Faith Apostolic Church, 1993), 58–59, 70–72, 85.

35. David D. Daniels, "Charles Harrison Mason: The Interracial Impulse of Early Pentecostalism," in James R. Goff Jr. and Grant Wacker, eds., *Portraits of A Generation: Early Pentecostal Leaders* (Fayetteville, Ark.: The University of Arkansas Press, 2002), 264–69.

36. David D. Daniels, "'Everybody Bids You Welcome': A Multicultural Approach to North American Pentecostalism," in Murray W. Dempster, Byron D. Klaus, and Douglas Petersen, eds., *The Globalization of Pentecostalism: A Religion Made To Travel* (Oxford: Regnum Books International, 1999), 227–31.

37. Daniels, "'Everybody Bids You Welcome,'" 235; Sanders, *Saints in Exile*, 32–33.

38. Theodore Kornweibel Jr., "Bishop C. H. Mason and the Church of God in Christ during World War I: The Perils of Conscientious Objection," *Southern Studies: An Interdisciplinary Journal of the South* 26.4 (Winter 1987): 261–81.

39. Ibid., 266, 265.

40. Ibid., 269.

41. Ibid., 277.

II

Gender and Culture

One of the most engaging aspects of African American Pentecostalism has been its ability to infuse the black religious context with new models of how gender, race, and class can be construed in ways that empower, rather than denigrate, black people. The essays in this section highlight the specific contribution Pentecostal spirituality has made in helping individual women and men, as well as the larger black male and female subcultures, negotiate the issues of gender within the larger culture to gain a sense of agency within limitations imposed by segregation. These essay address ways that men and women within the Holiness and Pentecostal movements drew on its resources to redefine themselves as fully human and deserving of human dignity, and broached barriers imposed on them from the broader society. But they also expose how issues of gender and sexuality are worked out within Pentecostal culture and link that culture to the issues of everyday existence. These essays reveal how responses of Afro-Pentecostals to the contested issues of gender are distinctive from those of white evangelical and Pentecostal traditions (the essays by Cooper, Hardy, and Scandrett-Leatherman), and illuminate the unique Afro-Pentecostal interface with secular culture (Gallien's discussion of crossover artists). What emerges is a feminism and masculinity peculiar to black Pentecostal and charismatic Christianity, one that displays a complicated set of responses to "the world." Such responses highlight how the usual (white) discussions of "Christ-and-culture" are potentially overturned when the racial dimension is factored in.

4

Laying the Foundations for Azusa

Black Women and Public Ministry
in the Nineteenth Century

VALERIE C. COOPER

Once, while lecturing in a course on Pentecostalism, I was struck by a student's question.[1] The student asked simply, "Why Azusa?" In a sense, this young person was asking if phenomena like glossolalia had reoccurred at various times during history, why did these experiences come together so powerfully in the Pentecostal Revival at Azusa Street that began in 1906?[2] What particular circumstances—social, theological, political, or other—coalesced at Azusa to produce the wide-ranging, rapidly expanding movement we call Pentecostalism, the fastest growing Christian movement on earth, "accounting for one in every four Christians"?[3]

Azusa Street was unique in many ways. Media sources noted, often disdainfully, the leadership roles that blacks held in the movement.[4] William J. Seymour, the African American who headed the Azusa Street Mission during its most influential early years, was surrounded by women—both black and white—who preached, operated in multiple gifts of the Spirit, and enthusiastically carried the message of Azusa and Pentecostalism around the globe. According to the Pentecostal scholar Cecil M. Robeck Jr., "From the outset, the leadership that surrounded Seymour was racially mixed and included both women and men."[5] Coming as it did during a period in the United States marked by the expansion of de jure Jim Crow segregation, Azusa Street represented a remarkable—even *miraculous*—period of religious racial integration that is quite unique in American history, even into the present. Although, as scholars like Iain MacRobert have documented, this period of integration was under constant assault and ultimately gave way to the formation of racially separated but nearly theologically identical Pentecostal confederations and denominations very early on, the Azusa Street Mission was nonetheless an amazing moment in American religious history.[6]

In addressing the question, why Azusa? we must not only examine the complexity that attended the emergence of Pentecostalism but also consider various influences, including the effect that women's increasingly public ministries had on the precursor Evangelical and Wesleyan Holiness movements.[7] One of the circumstances producing the critical mass that contributed to Azusa as a phenomenon was the changing role of women in Evangelicalism and in the African American community in the years just prior to the 1906 origins of the Revival. In addition to the dynamic leadership of men like Seymour, black women brought to their involvement in Azusa changing expectations about their roles in ministry and public life, biblically based arguments for women's religious leadership, a developing pneumatology, and eschatological expectancy. These women's views about public activism and theology had been shaped by debates over slavery, the Civil War, and the subsequent collapse of Reconstruction, and contributed to the dynamic sociological and historical factors that produced Azusa Street.

The Pentecostal scholar, Joe Creech, has argued that the Azusa Street Revival of 1906 to 1909 has been mythologized as the "central point from which the worldwide Pentecostal movement emerged" and that such understanding presents a distorted picture of early Pentecostalism as having universally shared Azusa's "unique social and religious dynamics—spontaneity, charismatic leadership, ecstasy, and the subversion of race, class, and gender categories."[8] Far from having shared such a "common sectarian, egalitarian ethos," Creech argues that "Pentecostalism arose from multiple pockets of revival that retained their preexisting institutional structures, theological tendencies, and social dynamics,"[9] Azusa came to represent a myth of origin for Pentecostalism, despite the fact that the movement's origins were not that precise historically or geographically.

Creech's analysis helps to explain the existence and significance of competing movements before, during, and after Azusa. It also argues for an understanding of Pentecostalism as a movement that evolved gradually from Holiness and other religious and social movements rather than abruptly at a single point in 1906. Pentecostalism's Holiness precursors thus take on added significance as legitimate contributors to the theology and practice of what would later be labeled as Pentecostal. Indeed, even the use of the term "Pentecostal" predates Azusa in Holiness circles.[10]

Even if the characteristics that distinguished Azusa were not universally experienced throughout early Pentecostalism, they have nonetheless fascinated historians and theologians. How did Azusa come to be defined by Creech's description as "unique social and religious dynamics—spontaneity, charismatic leadership, ecstasy, and the subversion of race, class, and gender categories"?[11] Again, why Azusa—why was Azusa so uniquely egalitarian? Azusa's characteristic subversion of race, class, and gender categories resulted, in part, from the participation of black Holiness women whose theological imaginations had been shaped by similar experiences from the battle against slavery through the collapse of Reconstruction.

During the nineteenth century, several African American women emerged into the public sphere in association with their work for the abolition of slavery, or in Holiness churches. These pioneering public ministries laid the groundwork for later Pentecostal understandings of charismatic ministry, particularly among women. Their apocalyptic pronouncements about slavery and its swiftly approaching judgment set the stage for Pentecostalism's eschatological expectancy. In the midst of both pro- and antislavery camps that used scripture to shape their arguments, these women also used the Bible and fashioned a biblical aesthetic centered on issues of justice and equality. At least one woman, Jarena Lee, was constructing a kind of theology of experience that would closely resemble later Pentecostal theology.

Iain MacRobert suggests that racism is directly to blame for the underreporting by some whites within the movement of black involvement and leadership in the early days of Pentecostalism.[12] Fortunately, recent scholarship has sought to rediscover the significance of African Americans like the Azusa Street revivalist William J. Seymour and the Church of God in Christ founder C. H. Mason. However, while scholars have recovered the names and roles of several of the black men who shaped Pentecostalism, they have to date been less successful in recalling the names of black women who also contributed to the theology and practice of the nascent movement. Happily, recent publications like Anthea D. Butler's *Women in the Church of God in Christ: Making a Sanctified World,* Estrelda Alexander's *The Women of Azusa Street,* and Cheryl Townsend Gilkes's *If It Wasn't For the Women,* are reversing this trend by focusing upon the role of black women in shaping early Pentecostalism.[13] We further these investigations here by highlighting the significant contributions of several nineteenth-century African American women who, although not Pentecostals themselves, nonetheless laid a foundation for the later Pentecostal movement in their preaching, teaching, and public activism.

In the eighteenth and nineteenth centuries, Evangelical Christianity began to provide American women with theologically legitimated, but limited, access to the public sphere. The historian Christine Heyrman argues that Evangelicalism both undermined white male privilege and empowered disenfranchised blacks, women, and others because it challenged the social status quo in the antebellum South.[14]

In her study of New England Baptists from the colonial period, Susan Juster suggests that Evangelicalism's emphasis upon a personal experience of salvation provided points of liminality, which she defines as those experiences that pull people out of their own time and space, and create new social orders and relationships.[15] The African American literary scholar Nellie Y. McKay would agree, pointing out the effect that the conversion experience had on black women, and how nineteenth-century black women understood Evangelical conversion to bestow a kind of "democracy of saved souls" where all "were on an equal spiritual standing with them before the Lord."[16] In her study of Holiness women, Nancy Hardesty extends this democratizing tendency beyond salvation to include sanctification as well: "Revivalism stressed experience and encouraged activity. All are sinners in need of salvation and sanctification. All are welcome and able to repent and believe, to consecrate themselves to lives of holiness."[17] Further, notes Hardesty, sanctification was understood as "a gift of power" to speak and act on God's behalf, and even to overcome prejudice.[18]

Chronicling the emergence of black and white women preachers and exhorters, the church historian Catherine A. Brekus notes that "between 1740, when the revivals of the First Great Awakening began in New England, and 1845, when a second wave of revivals ended with the collapse of the Millerite movement, several generations of women struggled to invent an enduring tradition of female religious leadership."[19] Although these women were often attacked or belittled, they nonetheless insisted that they had been sent by God. Brekus documents the itinerant ministries of nineteenth-century white women like Harriet Livermore and Nancy Towle, and nineteenth-century black women like Jarena Lee, Sojourner Truth, Zilpha Elaw, Rebecca Jackson, and Julia Foote, who were "part of a larger evangelical culture—both black and white—that sanctioned women's religious leadership" (5). Brekus argues that such women were "'biblical' rather than secular feminists, and they based their claims to female equality on the grounds of scriptural revelation, not natural rights" (6–7).

Brekus states that "in many ways, the presence of large numbers of white and black women in the pulpit [between 1740 and 1845] seems to offer evidence of the democratization of American Christianity . . . [and] that the distinctions of race, class, and sex were less important than whether or not one had been 'saved'" (11). However, Brekus observes that this "evangelical democratization" which seemed to permit women to preach was most visible among northern Evangelicals, and least visible among those in the south (16). She indicates that central to the "more than twenty female evangelists' . . . stories . . . told in print during the first decades of the nineteenth century" (167) was a description of the woman's salvation experience or calling to ministry as a sovereign and irresistible act of God to which the only appropriate and proper response was obedience. Nancy Hardesty notes that when their calling to preach (often received as a dream or vision) conflicted against religious authorities' admonitions, Holiness women like Jarena Lee and Amanda Berry Smith felt compelled to obey God's call rather than humans' restrictions.[20]

So by the nineteenth century, Evangelical women had made significant forays into the public sphere. Women like Phoebe Palmer propagated Holiness theology and significantly expanded frontier Methodism with their small prayer groups and "Holy Clubs," which resembled the home churches and Bible studies by which Pentecostalism grows today, in that they were home based and frequently female led. By the middle and end of the nineteenth century, several Holiness women had expanded these modest, home-based beginnings into Holiness camp meetings, or multistate, itinerant, healing, and proto-Pentecostal ministries. For example, Maria Woodworth-Etter records her barnstorming healing crusades across the Midwest in her journal, *Signs and Wonders*.[21]

Evangelical women also made significant inroads into popular culture during the nineteenth century, as when Harriet Beecher Stowe penned the influential antislavery novel, *Uncle Tom's Cabin*, or when Julia Ward Howe put lyrics to the popular folk melody "John Brown's Body" to create "The Battle Hymn of the Republic." The abolitionist movement provided many women with powerful theological motivations for their social action and public engagement. Energized by the fight against slavery, African American women, in particular, pioneered social engagement, which would anticipate later Pentecostal women's preaching and teaching ministries. Black women wrestled with the nebulous place that society accorded them and, in battling race oppression and slavery, also tended to battle the gender oppression that sought to lock them out of public discourse.

One woman who pioneered a leadership role was black Holiness preacher Jarena Lee. Lee received what she believed was a divine call to ministry in 1807, when she heard a voice telling her to "Go preach the Gospel."[22] However, as a member of the newly formed African Methodist Episcopal (AME) Church, the first independent African American denomination, she was unable to convince its first bishop, Richard Allen, to confirm her calling by granting her permission to be ordained. Allen, who left the predominantly white Methodist Episcopal Church because of its racism, would not agree to Lee's protest against the sexism that Lee had identified in the new AME denomination. Instead, Allen noted that the Methodist Episcopal Church's *Book of Discipline* "did not call for women preachers" (36).

Lee was not slowed by Allen's rebuff, reasoning instead, "And why should it be thought impossible, heterodox, or improper, for a woman to preach? [S]eeing the Saviour died for the woman as well as the man" (ibid.). However, Lee reported that Allen's opposition did have an immediate dampening effect upon her ardor for the work of the gospel. She notes, "that holy energy which burned within me, as a fire, began to be smothered" (ibid.). Lee concluded that anything that threatened to put out the fire of God within her had to be opposed. Interestingly, by describing this "holy energy" as a fire, she appropriates language that would have been familiar to nineteenth century readers as biblical images of the Word of God and the Spirit of God.[23]

Nevertheless, Jarena Lee conducted a wide ranging and very dangerous ministry, traveling back and forth across the Mason-Dixon line and subjecting herself to the possibility that although she was a free woman, she could be captured and enslaved. Her audiences were frequently integrated. According to the historian William Andrews, who included Lee's autobiography in his edited anthology, *Sisters of the Spirit*, "in 1827 . . . at the age of forty-four, [Lee] traveled 2,325 miles and delivered 178 sermons. Much of the distance she covered by foot, the rest by wagon, ferryboat, and carriage."[24] At one point, Lee was so consumed with the desire to preach that she dreamed that she "took a [scripture] text and preached it in [her] sleep," ultimately becoming so animated and so loud that she woke herself up and also woke up the rest of the household (35).

Lee faced the agonizing double jeopardy that confounds the lives of African American women: she was inconveniently black and female in a social order that valued neither very highly, and more frequently undermined and underestimated both. The success of her ministry, despite the obstacles of patriarchy and racism, demonstrates both the abundance of her charismatic gifts and the force of her personality. Nevertheless, Lee was constantly required by doubters to give an account of her calling. In her 1836 apologia, Lee explains her right to preach as a consequence of her personal experiences of God.

When Lee wrote that "I have never found [the Spirit of God] to lead me contrary to the Scriptures of truth, as I understand them" (48), she was in fact laying the groundwork for an appeal to life experience as the interpretive key to scripture.[25] Lee's life became, in effect, the second prism through which she could filter the biblical witness, and effectively disregard those materials that would seem to call into question her desire to be a preacher. She stated, in effect, that she knew better, because she knew God so well. This explains her repetition throughout the narrative of the efficacy of her ministry—her frequent references to effects such as salvations, or emotive responses from her ad hoc congregants. Having stated that it was her experience of God that gave her higher understanding, Lee was compelled to prove by the effects of her experiences that it was indeed God, and not "Satan . . . [having] transform[ed] himself into an angel of light, for the purpose of deception," on whose behalf she worked.[26] As evidence of the divine origins of her power, she repeatedly stated her positive results. In Lee's theology, her experiences of ministry function pneumatologically—they are the proof of the Holy Spirit working in and through her. Like many Pentecostals after her, Lee used experience as a means of encountering and interpreting the Holy Spirit.[27]

Lee developed a theologically complex argument for women's ordination based upon a close reading of scripture. She saw no reason why women could not preach the gospel since the first person to have proclaimed Jesus' resurrection was a woman, Mary Magdalene. At one point, perhaps frustrated by the limitations placed upon her preaching ministry by men (but certainly, as she tells it, inspired by the Holy Spirit), Lee stood up when a man who was preaching during a Sunday service faltered. She took up his text from where she was standing in the congregation and proceeded to outpreach the man, finishing his sermon for him. Bishop Richard Allen, who was present at the time, was impressed with Lee's preaching ability and sanctioned her for a limited itinerant preaching ministry, but he never allowed her to be ordained.[28]

Jarena Lee was not the only African American woman making a sophisticated, audacious, personal, and ultimately biblically based argument in favor of women's public ministries. In her autobiography, *A Brand Plucked from the Fire*, Julia Foote details the process by which she herself converted to the view that women had as much right to preach as men did. From the New Testament, she notes that the same Greek word is rendered in English translations as "servant of the church" when referring to a woman, but "minister" when referring to a man (Rom. 16:1 and Eph. 6:21).[29] Convinced that the New Testament modeled women's active participation in ministry, she wrote, "When Paul said, 'Help those women who labor with me in the Gospel,' he certainly meant that they did more than to pour out tea."[30] When no pastor in her denomination, the AMEZ Church, would open his pulpit to her, Foote held meetings in her home. In the latter part of the nineteenth century, she enjoyed a second career in the burgeoning Holiness movement. Unlike Jarena Lee, Julia Foote did achieve her goal: eventually, the AMEZ Church did ordain her, first as a deacon, and finally, shortly before her death, as an elder.

Another black Evangelical woman who had a well-known public ministry in the nineteenth century was Sojourner Truth. Truth was a nineteenth-century African American woman whose public activism and itinerant preaching very closely resembles that of Pentecostal women in the twentieth century. In her biography of Truth, Nell Painter argues that Truth was a Pentecostal.[31] While I suspect that she is probably better described as Holiness, I do agree with Painter that Sojourner Truth represents a category of black women who pioneered what would later come to characterize Pentecostalism in their commitment to a kind of Evangelical Christianity and publicly engaged ministry.

According to the racial and social hierarchies of the nineteenth century, black women were barely considered to be human, certainly never to be treated as ladies. Evelyn Brooks Higginbotham demonstrates that during the antebellum period, black women were held to be so far below white women that even rape laws were not regarded as applying to them or providing them legal protection from sexual assault. So the logic went, since black women were incapable of the moral reasoning necessary to refuse sex, and since they were in fact property, it was not possible to rape one.[32] Rather than accept this nebulous social space, black women of the nineteenth century went on to create an alternative social identity, emerging more audaciously than contemporaneous white women, into the public sphere. After all, what did they have to lose?

Marilyn Richardson, a scholar of African American intellectual history, stated that in "September 1832, in Boston, Massachusetts, Maria W. Stewart, a black woman, did what no American-born woman, black or white" is recorded to have done before: "She mounted a lecture platform and raised a political argument before a 'promiscuous' audience, that is, [an audience] composed of both men and women."[33] A student of the radical black abolitionist David Walker, Stewart's public speaking career began in the same year that Walker died mysteriously after publishing a revolutionary, apocalyptic but also deeply biblical tract on the sinfulness of slavery. Her public speaking ended three years later, perhaps as a consequence of the sometimes violent opposition she faced. In her speeches, Stewart laced heavy doses of Scripture with abolitionist rhetoric, predicting a coming apocalypse for America if it did not quickly repent of the evil of slavery.

Stewart's speeches point to divine approbation toward blacks as evidence of the coming judgment of whites. If America denies blacks the very "liberty and independence" it demanded from the British, how can it be a free nation? If God gives black people the gift of the Holy Spirit,[34] "the greatest of all blessings," how can whites who do not even give blacks the fair wages of their labors avoid judgment? Stewart declared judgment to be only fitting for the oppressors her words and world-view prophesied against. Moreover, she invokes American republican rhetoric, contrasting the promised, "liberty and independence" against the lowest biblical image of sin and judgment, Babylon, to make her case for a reconstructed social order where "many of the sable-skinned Africans . . . now despise[d], will shine in the kingdom of heaven as the stars forever and ever."[35]

The elegance of Stewart's rhetoric is clear in five little words with which she powerfully framed a new exegetical paradigm. She states simply, "you . . . fare sumptuously every day."[36] The biblical allusion is apparent: Stewart is quoting Luke 16:19–31, the parable of Lazarus and the rich man. The text itself is subversive, and Stewart's use of it doubly subversive. In a reversal of the usual way of things, the parable discards the rich man's name and records only the name of the poor man. In a further reversal of the men's stations in life, the poor man is comforted in heaven after a miserable life on earth, and the rich man is tormented in hell after a comfortable life on earth. Moreover, the rich man believes, even in hell, that Lazarus will still fetch and carry for him as poor men did while he was on earth. Even in hell, he doesn't fully comprehend that his and Lazarus's circumstances have radically changed. The rich man doesn't comprehend that in this new world order, Lazarus is no longer his servant, Lazarus is no longer available to fetch him a drink. But Stewart's adaptation of the parable, in context, does not merely describe a rich man punished and a poor man rewarded, but rather blacks in heaven and whites in hell. Indeed, it declares the coming apocalypse of judgment that Stewart and Walker before her had often prophesied. This interpretation is both revolutionary and deeply subversive: it is, in essence, classic counter-hegemonic discourse. The experience of black people is the key to interpreting the parable, and the point of the story. All it took was five little words: "you . . . fare sumptuously every day."

Stewart's use of Luke 16 was also apocalyptic, suggesting that judgment was coming to the United States for its sin of slavery. In this line of reasoning, she was contributing to eschatological expectations around Emancipation. Such eschatological expectations intensified for many African Americans when Reconstruction collapsed, and later fed into Azusa Street.

By the Civil War, the apocalypticism of abolitionists like Maria Stewart had soaked into popular culture. That many Americans had come to understand the war as judgment for the sin of slavery is attested to by the fact that even

President Lincoln proclaimed this in his second inaugural address. Lincoln, who was not a particularly avid churchman, seems to have begun a quiet but intense study of the Bible, perhaps as a response to the mounting pressures the Civil War placed upon his shoulders. At least one scholar has suggested that the "Four score and seven years ago" that begins the Gettysburg Address represents Lincoln's invocation of biblical-sounding terminology. Certainly, by his Second Inaugural Address, Lincoln is overtly biblical and theological as he considers the cost the war has wrought in blood and treasure. Although he notes that both North and South were persuaded of their righteousness in the conflict, both have suffered as a result of it. Lincoln declared:

> Both read the same Bible and pray to the same God, and each invokes His aid against the other. It may seem strange that any men should dare to ask a just God's assistance in wringing their bread from the sweat of other men's faces, but let us judge not, that we be not judged. The prayers of both could not be answered. That of neither has been answered fully. The Almighty has His own purposes. . . . Fondly do we hope, fervently do we pray, that this mighty scourge of war may speedily pass away. Yet, if God wills that it continue until all the wealth piled by the bondsman's two hundred and fifty years of unrequited toil shall be sunk, and until every drop of blood drawn with the lash shall be paid by another drawn with the sword, as was said three thousand years ago, so still it must be said "the judgments of the Lord are true and righteous altogether."[37]

Lincoln framed the Civil War as a sovereign act of God's judgment in which the "unrequited toil" of slavery has been recompensed by "every drop of blood . . . drawn with the sword" of war. Indeed, according to this interpretation of events, the war has dragged on precisely because God intended it to repay slavery's every slight. African Americans' high hopes for full inclusion in American democracy were soon dashed, however, by the collapse of Reconstruction in 1877, just twelve years after the end of the war. The period between 1877 and 1920 is sometimes called "the Nadir" for blacks because it was attended by marked increases in lynchings and other forms of terrorism and violence, nearly universal economic disenfranchisement, and the establishment of Jim Crow codes across the South.[38] The African American religion scholar Timothy Fulop describes it this way:

> The last twenty-five years of the nineteenth century have appropriately gone down in African-American history as "the Nadir." Disenfranchise-

ment and Jim Crow laws clouded out any rays of hope that Reconstruction had bestowed in the American South. Darwinism and phrenology passed on new "scientific" theories of black inferiority, and the old racial stereotypes of blacks as beasts abounded in American society. The civil, political, and educational rights of black Americans were greatly curtailed, and lynching reached all-time highs in the 1890s. . . . The Nadir was accompanied by a cacophony of black voices seeking to make sense of the history and destiny of African Americans. One strand of these voices proclaimed in song, sermon, and theological treatise that the millennial reign of God was coming to earth.[39]

Given the volatile mix of apocalyptic expectations and cruelly thwarted hopes in the period leading up to Reconstruction and its abrupt end, it is not surprising that many blacks lapsed into escapist, otherworldly musings and the despair of dark and millennial broodings about a soon-coming warrior Jesus bringing judgment in his wake. This sense, that America had been chastened by war and had nevertheless refused to repent, filled many, especially those in the Holiness camp, with a near-certainty that the end was coming soon. This eschatological expectancy was particularly poignant among African Americans; given their frustrations with the federal government's failed promises of justice and protection, they longed for the justice that King Jesus would bring on his return.

Fulop concludes that three types of millennialism characterized African American millennial eschatology during the Nadir: cultural millennialism, millennial Ethiopianism, and progressive millennialism. While proponents of cultural millennialism saw the United States as a "redeemer nation of the world," millennial Ethiopianism "posits a Pan-African millennium, a future golden age continuous with a glorious African past accompanied by God's judgment of white society and Western civilization."[40] Progressive millennialism, while a more traditional type of millennialism "is not without notes of Pan-Africanism and strong social criticism concerning race relations" although it also "reveals an optimism that the millennium will be marked by racial equality and harmony."[41] All three types of African American millennialism of the Nadir were also characterized by a belief in a kind of "black exceptionalism," which argued that people of African descent were particularly spiritual people and of particular concern to God.[42]

William J. Seymour was heavily influenced by one such eschatologically focused Holiness group that called itself the "Evening Light Saints," because its members believed that a literal, spiritual night was soon about to fall on humanity, during which the church would provide the only light. The Evening Light Saints, a Holiness group founded in 1880 by Daniel S. Warner, subsequently developed into the Church of God (Anderson, Indiana). Contemporaneous reports link William J. Seymour with the group while he lived in Indianapolis, prior to taking up the leadership of the Azusa Street Revival. Premilliennialist in their eschatology, the Evening Light Saints taught that a "new age of the Christian church, the Evening Light (named for Zech. 14:7 'at evening time it shall be light'), was restoring the church of the apostles."[43] The group stressed racial and gender inclusiveness: all members were addressed simply as "Saints." According to Robeck, "In the 1890s the Evening Light Saints was one of the few groups in which blacks and whites were treated equally and gifted women were encouraged to preach. . . . When William J. Seymour ultimately arrived in Los Angeles [Azusa], he was as committed to a policy of non-sectarianism, the equality of the races, and the equality of women and men as Warner was."[44]

Although the period immediately preceding the emergence of Pentecostalism was indeed a nadir for blacks, the period between 1880 and 1920 was in some ways a boom time for women; some historians even refer to it as the Women's Era. With the end of the Civil War, Evangelical, Holiness, and other women turned their attention to other social projects, such as fighting for woman's suffrage and Prohibition, and caring for the waves of European immigrants flooding onto North American shores. In some ways, though, African American women's dual concerns of race and gender sometimes produced a more socially transgressive radicalism; at the same time, white women, particularly white Evangelical women, were also active on the growing edge of ministry in the public arena.

Higginbotham describes the activism of black Baptist women at the turn of the century. She argues that although the women were denied ordination in the largest black Baptist denomination, the National Baptist Convention (a privilege that they are still, in the main, denied), they nevertheless exercised a proto-feminist consciousness regarding their importance both to the Convention and the wider black community. Paradoxically, by organizing a separate Women's Convention, the women were able to counter the power of the ordained male hierarchy of the general convention, and to exercise less restrained policy-making power in their own right. Higginbotham documents how the women organized Bible Bands, which taught a kind of feminist Bible interpretation (although the women certainly would never have called it that). Moreover, their fund-raising became essential to the financial health of the whole denomination and several black colleges and schools, their evangelistic efforts built the congregations of many a local church, and their social activism enabled many blacks to make a smoother transition from slave to paid worker.

When the Pentecostal movement finally dawned, women (particularly black women) regarded the urgency of the hour as all the justification they needed to engage in very public preaching, teaching, evangelistic, and healing ministries. After all, they reasoned, Jesus was coming soon. Within the new movement, the apocalypticism born of the nadir of black hopes combined with black and Evangelical women's strong, biblically informed, proto-feminist social activism to fuel a radical women's engagement. As they had done with regard to the abolition of slavery, women spoke out—they preached and prophesied. When their right to ordination was questioned, they formed separate, often home-based Bible studies or missions and grew them into churches where their authority as leaders was less likely to be questioned. When the religious hierarchy in one region hardened against them, they moved out in missions, or established separate Women's conventions to consolidate their own political power within their own churches. Or, they simply married a pastor and assumed active leadership as the first lady of the congregation in question.

In this context, then, we return to our initial question: Why Azusa Street? What happened at the Azusa Street Mission was the consequence of many factors, which converged "in the fullness of time."[45] Among those factors that came to shape that amazing revival, we have highlighted the role of African American Evangelical women. Black women brought changing expectations about their roles in ministry and public life, a developing pneumatology based upon experience, and eschatological expectancy to their involvement in Azusa. In the century preceding Azusa Street, women like Sojourner Truth had been itinerant preachers, while women like Jarena Lee and Julia Foote had constructed biblical arguments for women's religious leadership. The apocalyptic predictions of women like Maria Stewart stoked eschatological expectations, which were later evident in Pentecostalism's millennialism, and Jarena Lee had pioneered a pneumatology, which emphasized experience as a means of interpreting the work of the Holy Spirit in the world.

The ministries of women like Jarena Lee, Julia Foote, Sojourner Truth, and Maria Stewart were the beginning trickle that, by Azusa Street, had became a flood. Fortunately, neither their stories, nor their contributions to the century preceding Azusa Street, are lost to us. Hopefully, future scholarship will understand their ministries as part of the many streams that flowed to produce the Azusa Street Revival.

1. I use the term "Pentecostal" to encompass those churches and groups in this country and abroad that call themselves "Pentecostal," "Charismatic," "Neo-Pentecostal" and/or "Third-Wave," as well as those churches and parachurch organizations that share a similar emphasis upon the gifts of the Holy Spirit, such as speaking in tongues, healing, and prophecy.

2. For a discussion of the history of the phenomenon of speaking in tongues throughout Christian history, see, for example, "the Charismatic Tradition," in Robert Mapes Anderson, *Vision of the Disinherited: The Making of American Pentecostalism* (Peabody, Mass.: Hendrickson, 1992), 10–27. Anderson notes, "[T]he Pentecostals have maintained that speaking in tongues has had a continuous history from the Apostolic Age to the present" (25).

3. Harvey Gallagher Cox, *Fire from Heaven: The Rise of Pentecostal Spirituality and the Reshaping of Religion in the Twenty-First Century* (Reading, Mass.: Addison-Wesley, 1995), 15.

4. See, for example, *Larry E. Martin, Skeptics and Scoffers: The Religious World Looks as Azusa Street: 1906–1907, The Complete Azusa Street Library* (Pensacola, Fla.: Christian Life Books, 2004), 116, 38. Here racist cartoons demean the black revivalist William J. Seymour and contrast him, disparagingly, against Charles Fox Parham, who was white.

5. Cecil M. Robeck Jr., *The Azusa Street Mission and Revival: The Birth of the Global Pentecostal Movement* (Nashville: Nelson Reference and Electronic, 2006), 14.

6. Iain MacRobert, *The Black Roots and White Racism of Early Pentecostalism in the USA* (New York: St. Martin's Press, 1988). MacRobert argues quite persuasively that the chief reason motivating many whites in nascent Pentecostalism was the perceived need to eliminate black leaders and, occasionally, black congregants as well from their churches. Thus theological excuses were given to explain what were probably, primarily segregationist motivations.

7. Hereafter simply "Holiness."

8. Joe Creech, "Visions of Glory: The Place of the Azusa Street Revival in Pentecostal History," *Church History* 65.3 (1996): 406.

9. Ibid.

10. Robeck, *Azusa Street Mission and Revival*, 31–33.

11. Creech, "Visions of Glory," 406.

12. MacRobert, *Black Roots and White Racism*.

13. Anthea D. Butler, *Women in the Church of God in Christ: Making a Sanctified World* (Chapel Hill, N.C.: University of North Carolina Press, 2007); Estrelda Alexander, *The Women of Azusa Street* (Cleveland, Ohio: Pilgrim Press, 2005); Cheryl Townsend Gilkes, *If It Wasn't for the Women: Black Women's Experience and Womanist Culture in Church and Community* (Maryknoll, N.Y.: Orbis Books, 2001).

14. Christine Leigh Heyrman, *Southern Cross: The Beginnings of the Bible Belt* (New York: Knopf/Random House, 1997), 26: "Taken together, what they tell is why southern whites of all classes so long kept their distance from evangelicals. Present, although not predominant, in those pages are disgruntled laymen and -women who complain of Baptist preachers insulting local grandees or Methodist ministers condemning slavery. But far more common are middle-aged farmers who storm that young Methodist preachers

have disputed their authority over the household or turned the heads of their wives, and distraught matrons who fret that their newly pious daughters now shun unconverted kin, or that their once boisterous, swaggering sons have sunk into seeming madness from fear of hellfire and the devil. In sum, what held the center of lay concern, what aroused their sharpest fears, were the ways in which Baptists and Methodists struck at those hierarchies that lent stability to their daily lives: the deference of youth to age; the submission of children to parents and women to men; the loyalties of individuals to family and kin above any other group; and the rule of reserve over emotion within each person."

15. Susan Juster, *Disorderly Women: Sexual Politics and Evangelicalism in Revolutionary New England* (Ithaca, N.Y.: Cornell University Press, 1994).

16. Nellie Y. McKay, "Nineteenth-Century Black Women's Spiritual Autobiographies: Religious Faith and Self-Empowerment," in Joy Webster Barbre and Personal Narratives Group, eds., *Interpreting Women's Lives: Feminist Theory and Personal Narratives* (Bloomington: Indiana University Press, 1989), 152.

17. Nancy Hardesty, *Women Called to Witness: Evangelical Feminism in the Nineteenth Century*, 2nd ed. (Knoxville: University of Tennessee Press, 1999), 48.

28. Ibid., 49–52.

19. Catherine A. Brekus, *Strangers and Pilgrims: Female Preaching in America, 1740–1845* (Chapel Hill: University of North Carolina Press, 1998), 3. Hereafter cited in text.

20. Hardesty, *Women Called to Witness*, 76–77.

21. Maria Beulah Woodworth-Etter, *Signs and Wonders* (1916; repr., New Kensington, Penn.: Whitaker House, 1997).

22. William L. Andrews, ed., *Sisters of the Spirit: Three Black Women's Autobiographies of the Nineteenth Century* (Bloomington: Indiana University Press, 1986), 35, 38. Hereafter cited in text.

23. This image of holy fire is quite common in the Bible. One text that might best exemplify such imagery is Jer. 20:9, "Then I said, I will not make mention of him, nor speak any more in his name. But *his word was in mine heart as a burning fire shut up in my bones*, and I was weary with forbearing, and I could not stay" (King James Version, emphasis mine). However, while Jeremiah's fire was kindled when he attempted to stop preaching, Lee's is quenched when Richard Allen attempts to stop her from preaching. Nevertheless, Lee uses this sensation of fire and its consequences as proof to her own vocation as preacher. Elsewhere, in Acts 2:3–4, a text of particular importance to Pentecostals, fire is symbolic of the Holy Spirit: "And there appeared unto them cloven tongues like as of fire, and it sat upon each of them. And they were all filled with the Holy Ghost, and began to speak with other tongues, as the Spirit gave them utterance."

24. Andrews, ed., Sisters of the Spirit, ix.

25. Lee's description of the "holy energy" which diminished when Richard Allen refused her request for ordination, is an excellent example of Lee's appeal to her own life experiences for guidance and direction. She seems to have interpreted this diminution as a sign from God. She also builds an argument from scripture for women preachers, but in her narrative, this pneumatological evidence precedes her scriptural justification for her ministry.

26. Lee, in Andrews, *Sisters of the Spirit*, 168.

27. Donald W. Dayton, *Theological Roots of Pentecostalism*, Studies in Evangelicalism 5 (Metuchen, N.J.: Scarecrow Press, 1987), 24, argues that Pentecostalism's focus upon experience is, in part, a consequence of its Lukan emphasis, rather than the centrality of

Pauline theology as is predominant elsewhere in Protestant churches. Pentecostals read their faith through Luke/Acts and the central experience of Pentecost, in Acts 2: "This captures the key claim of Pentecostalism and indicates why it carries the name that it does. The movement's distinctive way of reading the New Testament leads it to the conclusion that, as in the early church, the modern believer becomes a disciple of Jesus Christ and receives the fullness of the Spirit's baptism in separate events or 'experiences.'" Here, the two democratizing experiences of the Holiness movement, salvation and sanctification, are replaced by the two democratizing experiences of Pentecostalism, salvation, and baptism in the Holy Spirit.

28. Andrews, *Sisters of the Spirit*, 44–45.

29. According to Hardesty, Holiness women often made such arguments in favor of their right to religious leadership—noting the leadership roles held by biblical women like Deborah or Phoebe. Further, she notes the use by Phoebe Palmer of "the Pentecostal argument" as spoken by Peter in Acts 2:17–18, while directly quoting Joel 2:28. Both texts note that "your daughters shall prophesy." Although Palmer began developing this theology as early as 1856—long before Azusa in 1906—it points to the belief that Pentecost was distinguished by radical gender equality. See Hardesty, *Women Called to Witness*, 63–65, and 143–45; cf. "Defenses of Woman's Ministry," in Nancy Hardesty, *Your Daughters Shall Prophesy: Revivalism and Feminism in the Age of Finney*, Chicago Studies in the History of American Religion 5 (Brooklyn, N.Y.: Carlson Publishing, 1991), 167–69.

30. Julia A. J. Foote, *A Brand Plucked from the Fire*, in Sue E. Houchins, ed., *Spiritual Narratives* (New York: Oxford University Press, 1988), 79.

31. Nell Irvin Painter, *Sojourner Truth: A Life, a Symbol* (New York: W. W. Norton, 1996).

32. In *State of Missouri v. Celia*, a slave woman was convicted in 1855 of murdering her master, who had regularly forced her to have sex with him and had even impregnated her. The prosecution's presentation turned on whether Celia, a black woman and a slave, was covered under Missouri law that prohibited rape against "any woman." The defense tried to prove that Celia had killed her owner in self-defense, since his property rights could not have extended to include rape. In convicting and ultimately executing Celia, the court upheld the owner's right to unimpeded sexual access to his slave property. Evelyn Brooks Higginbotham, "African-American Women's History and the Metalanguage of Race," in Darlene Clark Hine, Wilma King, and Linda Reed, eds., *"We Specialize in the Wholly Impossible": A Reader in Black Women's History* (Brooklyn, N.Y.: Carlson Publishing, 1995), 7.

33. Marilyn Richardson, ed., *Maria W. Stewart, America's First Black Woman Political Writer—Essays and Speeches* (Bloomington: Indiana University Press, 1987), xii.

34. Stewart does not identify the criteria by which she has judged that black people have received the Holy Spirit, but only states that they have indeed received it. Her religious formation appears to have been eclectic, in that she affiliated herself with "Methodist, Baptist, and Episcopal congregations" (see Richardson, *Maria W. Stewart*, 9). However, since she makes no references to Pentecostal phenomenology like speaking in tongues or even miracles, it can be surmised that she is referring to the work of the Holy Spirit in saving sinners and motivating them to confess Christ—both activities which she describes frequently.

35. Maria Stewart, "Productions of Mrs. Maria W. Stewart, Presented to the First African Baptist Church and Society in the City of Boston" in Sue E. Houchins, ed., *Spiritual Narratives* (New York: Oxford University Press, 1988), 19.

36. Ibid., 20.

37. Abraham Lincoln, "Second Inaugural Address" (March 4, 1865); available at http://www.bartleby.com/124/pres32.html (last accessed October 12, 2008). The biblical reference at the end of the quotation is from Ps. 19:9 (KJV).

38. The use of this term, the Nadir, to describe the period following the collapse of Reconstruction for African Americans was popularized by Rayford Whittingham Logan, *The Betrayal of the Negro, from Rutherford B. Hayes to Woodrow Wilson*, new enl. ed. (New York: Collier Books, 1965).

39. Timothy E. Fulop, "'The Future Golden Day of the Race': Millennialism and Black Americans in the Nadir, 1877–1901," in Timothy Earl Fulop and Albert J. Raboteau, eds., *African-American Religion: Interpretive Essays in History and Culture* (New York: Routledge, 1997), 230.

40. Ibid., 231.

41. Ibid.

42. Although she predates "the Nadir" in her public ministry from 1831 to 1833, I would characterize Maria Stewart's millennialism as millennial Ethiopianism.

43. Robeck, *Azusa Street Mission and Revival*, 29.

44. Ibid., 30. Undoubtedly, Seymour's ability to resist Charles Fox Parham's "Anglo-Israelite" theology and racial segregation is rooted in his earlier acceptance of the Evening Light Saints' racial and gender egalitarianism (Robeck, *Azusa Street Mission and Revival*, 39–50). It is likely that the racial equality stressed by the Evening Light Saints shaped the early theology of the Church of God, into which it developed. Massey concludes that the high percentage of African American members in the Church of God is due to the church's strong commitment to racial unity. "The reasons for this significant percentage are historical, theological, and social. It is due, in no small measure, to the appealing and promising unity ideal that is at the heart of the Church of God message, an ideal forever allied to the church's message with the call to scriptural holiness"; see James Earl Massey, *African Americans and the Church of God, Anderson, Indiana: Aspects of a Social History* (Anderson, Ind.: Anderson University Press, 2005), 20.

45. In the King James Version (also the New Revised Standard Version and the New American Bible, and indeed in the Anglican Book of Common Prayer), this phrase, "fullness of time" denotes that an event has occurred at a time of God's ordaining (see Gal. 4:4; Eph. 1:10).

5

Church Mothers and
Pentecostals in the Modern Age

CLARENCE E. HARDY III

What would it mean to place Pentecostals at the center of histories of black religious culture in the modern era? And what would it mean to place women's leadership at the center of our accounts of black Pentecostalism's evolution into an urban religion three decades after the black poet Frances Harper declared in 1893 the "threshold of [a] woman's era"?[1] From the testimonies of women he gathered for his seminal *Black Gods of the Metropolis*, Arthur Fauset provides an avenue for us to consider these questions. By comparing the testimony of two Philadelphia women, one prominent and the other not, Fauset helps illuminate the early contours of a black Pentecostalism in the 1930s and '40s that would come to dominate black Protestant piety by century's end.

In Virginia, a "middle-aged colored woman" Fauset calls Mrs. W had been a Baptist, but now when gambling threatened to overrun her neighborhood in Philadelphia she joined a local Pentecostal congregation for help and comfort in a world seemingly awash in sin. As Mrs. W explains:

> I had come to Philadelphia from Virginia. I knew I needed something, but I didn't know just what. I looked outside my house one day and there were some men gambling on the doorstep. I never had seen anything like that before and I couldn't get over it. I said to myself, "Oh, if only I had more power, I could keep men from gambling like that!"[2]

After a dream where a voice from heaven spoke to her and deepened her sense of restless anxiety, she went in search of divine power and was directed to a congregation where "some sanctified people" worshipped. Her faith, which had seemed adequate to her before, now was not. "When I walked in I felt the spirit," she remembered. "I said, 'I'm converted. I know I am. I'm leading a clean life in these times. But I need more power.'"[3]

In 1924 Ida Robinson, another migrant to Philadelphia who had been born in Georgia and reared in Florida, established a new confederation of churches, in part to preserve women's right to ordination. By including a portrait of Robinson's new Pentecostal group, Mount Sinai, among the five in his study, Fauset connects Pentecostalism to nontraditional religious groups and offers a broader map of the new religious terrain was then emerging in the early decades of the twentieth century. While Mount Sinai "deviated" from the "orthodox evangelical pattern" with its emphasis on glossolalia and music, what most distinguished Ida Robinson from the mainstream was her followers' singular devotion to her as a "charismatic leader."[4] The vibrant presence of women in both the pews and the pulpit was an arresting image for Fauset. As he writes in his portrait of Robinson's Philadelphia congregation: "Mt. Sinai is distinctive among the cults considered here in the extent and degree of female participation. Many of the elders are women, as are also a larger number of the preachers."[5]

When Mrs. W's story is viewed against Fauset's portrait of Robinson it is apparent that black women became increasingly visible as religious leaders in the early decades of the twentieth century. More and more black women began to assert their own rights to spiritual authority as black migrants, unsatisfied with the choices immediately available to them, began to create new kinds of religious communities. The two religious communities represented by Mrs. W and Mount Sinai provide a context for understanding the contours of an emerging black religious culture that challenged older claims of Victorian respectability and reconceived the very nature of (religious) community. While Mrs. W (apparently) never entered the ministry, Robinson was a woman who openly exercised spiritual power as a minister in the public square. Rooted in black Holiness and Pentecostal traditions, she was a "church mother" who represented, initiated, and participated in broad changes in black religious culture. While many studies in recent years have focused on black Pentecostal women as gospel singers and prominent church workers, planters, and builders, Fauset's work suggests that it is black women's emergence into the public square that best defines black Pentecostalism's flowering in those early years.[6] Just as the story of Pentecostals is at the center of the evolution of black religious culture in the interwar period, the story of black religious women's assertive entrance into the public square is at the center of black Pentecostalism's emergence as an urban religion from its beginnings in the Mississippi Delta and upper South.

The Dreams of Church Mothers

The same dream that had helped change Mrs. W into "an ardent worker in the Holiness group"[7] established within her the right to speak for God against the hidden vices now made much more visible in the city. After seeing men right outside her door gambling in open daylight, she had a dream that in the end would propel her into a new religious community. Remembering how she became an apostolic Pentecostal, Mrs. W told Fauset:

> Then one day I had a dream I felt myself lifted on a high mountain. It was so high I could look and see over the world. When I looked behind me it seemed as if the sun was going down right at my back. It looked like it does in the country. Looks like if you went to the end of the field you could touch it. Then a voice said to me, "This represents the son of God. It's almost down. You must warn men and women to be holy." I rushed down from the mountain crying. When I got down, there was a host of people waiting for me to listen to me. I talked to them. Then I woke up. Things went on so and so for two or three days. Then the same thing appeared in the kitchen while I was doing the dishes. I was wide awake. I clapped my hands. Then I went to a woman and asked here, "What shall I do?" She said, "Go down to one of these [sanctified] churches."[8]

The dreams she had, both waking and sleeping, recalled the rural life she had left behind. Established now in the city, she had visions of the fields and wide-open spaces of her life before. In her dream, as she came down from the mountain she felt the sun on her back just "like it does in the country." Caught between worlds—North and South, urban and rural—Mrs. W's dream lent her an authority she did not fully use in the waking world. On the mountain she had received a divine message of warning to share with others, and in her dream, at least, people were eager to hear her message. When she rushed down the mountain there "was a host of people waiting . . . to listen to me," she recalled. While we have no evidence that she would later embrace the life of a preacher or evangelist, others decades before had and others would continue to do so. When the popular evangelist and preacher, Ida Robinson, heard rumors in 1924 that the United Holy Church, the same Pentecostal denomination that had ordained her, would soon stop ordaining women (at least publicly), after a ten-day fast she received a divine vision that instructed her to "come out on Mount Sinai" and "loose the women." [9]

Robinson's vision motivated her to establish Mount Sinai to provide institutional space for women to exercise clerical leadership.

The seeds for Robinson's move out to Mount Sinai began, in fact, many decades before. Shortly after Emancipation, black Baptist observers from the North believed that the power some black women exercised within rural religious communities in the South was an unfortunate heritage from the days of bondage and undoubtedly among the "vices and irregularities inseparably attendant upon the state of slavery." Though these "church mothers" or "gospel mothers" were, according to the black missionary Charles Satchel in the late 1860s, "outside of the New Testament arrangement," these women nevertheless claimed "to be under the special influence of the Spirit" and began to "exercise an authority, greater in many cases, than that of ministers."[10] Whether this less formal expression of leadership actually had a more ancient pedigree that stretched beyond slavery to Africa is unclear, but after many black women found their influence waning in congregational settings after emancipation, black Holiness (and later Pentecostal) networks provided space for resurgence in women's power and influence over new congregations through the Bible Bands that Anthea Butler, a historian of the Church of God in Christ (COGIC), has so ably described.[11]

This new power would take shape as women led Pentecostal bands into northern cities under the jurisdiction of male-led denominations such as Charles Mason's COGIC, or established themselves as bishops and central overseers over entire regional and multiregional church bodies they founded, led, and controlled. Within COGIC, church mothers "dug out," that is, planted and nurtured, new churches as they established a parallel power structure to that of male clergy. They exercised separate spiritual authority over the women in the congregation, and they had profound influence over the entire congregation, often constraining the power of male pastors. Within the Women's Department of COGIC established in 1911, church mothers "defined the content of their own roles" without interference from men. And male pastors who wanted to make significant changes in a congregation's worship practice often had to reckon with a church mother's informal power over the entire parish.[12]

Women such as Rosa Horn of Harlem, Lucy Smith of Chicago, Mary Magdalena Tate of Tennessee, and Ida Robinson of Philadelphia were often addressed as "Mother," implicitly transforming the role of church mother as they built regional empires of faith, often with themselves at the center of power. Although they were addressed in a similar fashion as church mothers in the COGIC, they exercised far greater authority. Whereas church mothers within COGIC wielded informal power in individual congregations, these women served as clerical leaders over multiregional networks of churches. In addition, since traditional church mothers were, as the historian Wallace Best argues, "the most desexualized [category] in the black church tradition" reserved for older respected women, the "church mother" title "authenticated their calls to ministry" while "deflecting focus on her body or the nature of her personal relationships."[13] So while women like Robinson, Tate, and Smith were officially titled elders and bishops in their circles, their parishioners often called them mothers and, more importantly, when these women defended their clerical leadership, they expanded the church mother role.

In the 1890s, when black Methodists debated the ordination question for women, one minister asserted: "There is plenty of work for good women . . . to do in this world, without unsexing them by making them elders."[14] In this environment, defining their sacerdotal duties as mothering was a way women like Mrs. W. could actually preach in a world where men limited opportunities for women to preach and lead congregations. Two decades before Robinson established her group, Mary Magdalena Tate, the first woman in the United States to head a predominantly black denomination as chief overseer and bishop, founded her own group in 1903.[15] The Church of the Living God, the Pillar and Ground of the Truth, the denomination Tate established, was concentrated in the mid-South, Georgia, and Florida, but by the time of her death in 1930 spanned more than twenty states with churches spreading as far north as Connecticut and Pennsylvania.[16] In her longest surviving letter, written around 1928, she begins with the salutation, "Now, loving children," and then includes a wide range of teachings from how to keep the Sabbath to how both men and women were capable of becoming "sons of God." With maternal love and longing, Tate ends her correspondence to her broader church much as she began: "Bye, bye, from your own Dear Mother."[17]

Church Mothers Embrace a Wider World

Around the same time Tate was active as a church builder up and down the East Coast, Robinson had a vision that would establish the scope of her ministry as the leader of Mount Sinai. Robinson's vision anticipated the new modern cosmopolitan reality mass migration would engender in black religious culture. In that vision, which set the stage for her career first as an evangelist, and then as a preacher and denominational leader, she saw that "there was a great church being born in the city, with people coming from the North, South, East, and West."[18] The diasporic moments of dispersal and unity Robinson imagined and preached about were like joints in the body— points of separation that were also points of linkage and connection—which provided the possibility for collective coordination and movement from a broader basis than before.[19] In coping with the effects of mass migration in the early decades of the twentieth century, women Pentecostal leaders like Robinson adopted a perspective that embraced a more expansive view of religious community. Black Holiness rhetoric had been baptized in the fire of the Pentecostal revivals at Azusa Street in Los Angeles in 1906. It expanded as Pentecostal ministers and evangelists of both sexes spread the new faith from the South and West into the Northeast and Midwest over boundaries of territory and gender.[20]

Evangelism, of course, had provided an initial drive for much of this evolution, and women Pentecostal leaders in particular envisioned the entire world as their parish. Mother Rosa Horn of Harlem and Lucy Smith of Chicago found that radio evangelism not only made them more recognizable than Tate, but it also buttressed an imagined internationalism often unmoored from institutional demands and responsibilities. Horn, a South Carolina–born dressmaker-turned-preacher, founded the Mount Calvary Assembly Hall of the Pentecostal Faith Church for All Nations in 1926. The church of three thousand fed thousands more during the Depression even as the organization spread into five cities along the East Coast by 1934. The windows circling her original building in Harlem with the message "Jesus Saves" in English, French, and Spanish demonstrates how a more globally inflected vision flowed from evangelism and stamped the Holiness ranks with a more internationalist orientation.[21] Through the "instrument of the devil" that was radio, these church mothers knit together a new religious community that went beyond the categories of denominations and institutional church bodies. As Horn told one newspaper reporter:

> It is impossible to state accurately how many infidels have been converted and brought back to the church; how many healings have been wrought; how many estranged families have been reunited, and generally how much sunshine and cheer have been brought into the lives of many people. Even other ministers have told me that their lost members have returned to their churches.[22]

In the same year that Horn founded her congregation, Lucy Smith founded the influential All Nations Pentecostal Church in Chicago. Smith was a forerunner in live religious broadcasting and built her congregation out of the radio waves on her broadcast, *The Glorious Church of the Air,* beginning in 1933, with a persona as a "mother . . . to the drifting black masses."[23] Like Horn, her universal church was unmoored from institutional fixtures. When one Chicago scholar mentioned to Smith that he had heard her broadcasts, Smith replied: "my services are getting to be among all people, all over."[24]

Mrs. W's story illuminates, once again, how Pentecostals shaped black religion as a modern culture against a restrictive climate where racial uplift and group identity seemed more emphasized than individuality. In the past, joining a sanctified church was a risk Mrs. W would not take, but the city presented new problems and new opportunities for Philadelphia's newest arrivals. As she explained to Fauset:

> [I]n Virginia we would have been ashamed to go to a Holiness church. The people in the little towns down there all know each other and this makes them afraid to be different. But we were in Philadelphia now, and in this big city we didn't have to worry about what our friends might think.[25]

The anonymity of the city, coupled with the way urban life made old temptations like gambling new, now produced space for individuality and allowed for an embrace of a more globally inflected and expansive rhetoric of community. The space that allowed for individuality and difference for Mrs. W had also helped church mothers like Horn, Smith, Robinson, and Tate generate notions of religious community not tied to the borders of the American state. While evangelism in a newly variegated world certainly provided energy for these new communal conceptions, Tate, who did not have a radio ministry, demonstrates that it was mass migration itself that had not only provided the shield of anonymity to escape group expectations but also the basis for new expectations. Knowing that her parishioners were now less tied to their former homes in the South, Mother Tate was the first woman religious leader to reconfigure the religious language of holiness so as to knit together a religious community that bridged sharp regional divisions with language now possible after mass migration. Migration forced Tate and her church to consider their ties to one another instead of their connections— formal and otherwise—to the outside observers before whom they would need to be respectable. Tate urged her followers never to allow any regional division within her church family. In an evocative section titled, "Of United Universal Ones" which nearly concludes her central governing document, the *General Decree Book,* she wrote:

There shall never be a Mason-Dixon Line, nor a middle wall of petition, nor any division or separation or difference of any description between the Saints and Churches herein named. North, South, East and West, home or foreign in the United States of America or in the Isles thereof or in any and all other lands and countries and Isles thereof. . . . There shall never be anticipated, or indulged or otherwise practice or in any way at all acts of state or sectional prejudices and differences among any of the members.

"Satan shall never seduce the true Saints into such confusions," Tate argued, because they would not allow "various manners of educations and of languages used" or the "dispositions of some sections and people's [sic] . . . to stop the love and unity and ones [i.e., oneness] of the true people and Saints of God."[26]

Father Divine, who held such a prominent place in Fauset's book, was the apotheosis of the nonracialist promise only ephemerally realized in the idealized memories of Azusa Street among early Pentecostals. While Fauset linked Divine to "cults" defined by "faith healing" and "holiness" and not Pentecostalism, Divine's followers often practiced glossolalia. Father Divine, while still called George Baker, had attended the 1906 revival at Azusa Street, where he reportedly spoke in tongues.[27] Despite his stronger links to Charles Fillmore, Unity, and the New Thought movement of the prior century that Pentecostals did not embrace, Divine did seek, as Pentecostals did at Azusa, a new basis for religious community beyond American-defined racial identity, as did also these northern cults. With a stance that went far beyond simple "race neutrality" toward a perspective of determined nonracialism, Divine's ministry, which reached its height in Harlem during the 1930s and continued in Philadelphia in the 1940s, represented a radicalization of the sentiments for unity found in Tate's attempts to hold her church fellowship together. Nothing captured Divine's sentiments more than his simple refusal to describe people as white or black in an age obsessed with notions of racial purity. Rather, he described people instead as "dark-complected" and "light complected."[28] His rejection of race paralleled his rejection of national identity. "I am none of your nationalities," Divine once said in reference to his divine identity. "You don't have to think I AM an American. . . . I AM none of them."[29]

Yet, in truth, few ministers were more committed than Robinson, Tate, Smith, and Horn to new conceptions of religious community that would overtake boundaries of region and even nation. And perhaps no one of the four expressed this passion more bracingly than Robinson, directly in the teeth of an American nationalist sentiment unquestionably at its height. In 1942, not long after the Japanese attacked Pearl Harbor and the United States and Japan declared war on one another, an FBI report alleged that Robinson was an agitator because she had stated publicly that she had "nothing against the Japanese."[30] For Robinson, sworn enemies of the United States were not the enemies of the people of God.

Robinson, Horn, Smith, or Tate would not achieve the actual global dimensions as their contemporary Father Divine or their Pentecostal successors in the postwar period, but from the beginning these black Pentecostal women leaders were especially assertive in their embrace of an expansive notion of religious community. They had already crossed the boundaries of gender and territory, and in their entrance into the public square their very presence—more than any specific doctrine or practice—embodied the challenge black Pentecostalism represented to prior conceptions of respectability in the now more cosmopolitan world black people inhabited at the dawn of the modern age and "the threshold of [a] women's era."

NOTES TO CHAPTER 5

1. Frances E. W. Harper, quoted in Hazel V. Carby, "'On the Threshold of Women's Era': Lynching, Empire, and Sexuality in Black Feminist Theory," *Critical Inquiry* 12.1 (Autumn 1985): 262.

2. Arthur Huff Fauset Collection, Special Collections Department, Van Pelt Library, University of Pennsylvania, Philadelphia, Pa. Box 5, Folder, 96, unnumbered page; hereafter identified as "Fauset Collection."

3. Fauset Collection, unnumbered page.

4. Arthur Fauset, *Black Gods of the Metropolis: Negro Religious Cults of the Urban North* (1944; repr., Philadelphia: University of Pennsylvania Press, reprint 2001), 69.

5. Ibid., 14.

6. See, for example, Jerma A. Jackson, *Singing in my Soul: Black Gospel Music in a Secular Age* (Chapel Hill: University of North Carolina Press, 2004), and Anthea D. Butler, *Women in the Church of God in Christ: Making a Sanctified World* (Chapel Hill: University of North Carolina Press, 2007).

7. Fauset Collection, unnumbered page.

8. Ibid.

9. For an account of Ida Robinson's visions, see Harold Dean Trulear, "Reshaping Black Pastoral Theology: The Vision of Bishop Ida B. Robinson," *Journal of Religious Thought* 46.1 (Summer-Fall 1989): 21. For additional biographical information about her life, music, and sermons see Harold Dean Trulear, "Ida B. Robinson: The Mother as Symbolic Presence," in *Portraits of a Generation: Early Pentecostal Leaders,* ed. James R. Goff Jr. and Grant Wacker (Fayetteville: The University of Arkansas Press, 2002), 309–24; and Bettye Collier-Thomas, *Daughters of Thunder: Black Women Preachers and Their Sermons, 1850–1979* (San Francisco: Jossey-Bass Publishers, 1998), 194–210.

10. *American Baptist*, June 26, 1868, as quoted in James M. Washington, *Frustrated Fellowship: The Black Baptist Quest for Social Power* (Macon, Ga.: Mercer University Press, 1986), 109.

11. For the African legacy evident in female leadership roles, see Cheryl Townsend Gilkes, "The Politics of 'Silence': Dual-Sex Political Systems and Women's Traditions of Conflict in African-American Religion," in *African American Christianity: Essays in History*, ed. Paul E. Johnson (Berkeley: University of California Press, 1997), 80–110. For example of women's waning influence in congregational life during the later half of the nineteenth century, see Elsa Brown, "Negotiating and Transforming the Public Sphere: African American Political Life in the Transition from Slavery to Freedom," in *African American Religious Thought: An Anthology*, ed. Cornel West and Eddie S. Glaube (Louisville, Ky.: Westminster John Knox Press, 2003), 435–74.

12. Cheryl Townsend Gilkes, "'Together and in Harness': Women's Traditions in the Sanctified Church," in *African American Religious Thought: An Anthology*, ed. Cornel West and Eddie S. Glaube (Louisville, Ky.: Westminster John Knox Press, 2003), 636; Anthea D. Butler, "Church Mothers and Migration in the Church of God in Christ," in *Religion in the American South: Protestants and others in History and Culture*, ed. Beth Barton Schweiger and Donald G. Mathews (Chapel Hill: University of North Carolina Press, 2004), 195–218.

13. Wallace Best, "'The Spirit of the Holy Ghost is a Male Spirit': African American Preaching Women and the Paradoxes of Gender," in *Women and Religion in the African Diaspora: Knowledge, Power, and Performance*, ed. R. Marie Griffith and Barbara Dianne Savage (Baltimore, Md.: Johns Hopkins University Press, 2006), 117–18.

14. Quoted in Martha S. Jones, *All Bound Up Together: The Woman Question in African American Culture, 1830–1900* (Chapel Hill: University of North Carolina Press, 2007), 193.

15. Kelly Willis Mendiola, "The Hand of a Woman: Four Holiness-Pentecostal Evangelists and American Culture, 1840–1930" (PhD diss., University of Texas at Austin, 2002), 291–92.

16. Helen M. Lewis and Meharry H. Lewis, *Seventy-fifth Anniversary Yearbook of the Church of the Living God, Pillar and Ground of the Truth, 1903–1978* (Nashville, Tenn.: The New and Living Way, 1978), 9–10.

17. Mary Magdalena Tate, "A Special Message from Mother to Her Children," in *Mary Lena Lewis Tate: Collected Letters and Manuscripts*, ed. Meharry H. Lewis (Nashville, Tenn.: The New and Living Way Publishing Company, 2003), 36–41.

18. Quoted in Trulear, "Reshaping Black Pastoral Theology," 21; see also Trulear, "Ida B. Robinson."

19. I have adopted both the reading of Stuart Hall's ideas and the metaphor of joints from Brent Edwards, "The Uses of *Diaspora*," *Social Text* 66 (Spring 2001): 64–66.

20. For an account of the complicated place the Azusa Street Revival holds in Pentecostal origins, see Joe Creech, "Visions of Glory: The Place of the Azusa Street Revival in Pentecostal History," *Church History* 65 (1996): 405–24.

21. For a brief, biographical essay on Horn, along with a small selection of her sermons, see Collier-Thomas, *Daughters of Thunder*, 173–93. For Horn's place in the Harlem community and religious life including descriptions of her church building, see Cheryl Lynn Greenberg, *"Or Does It Explode?" Black Harlem in the Great Depression* (New York: Oxford University Press, 1991), 59, and James Campbell, *Talking at the Gates: A Life of James Baldwin* (New York: Viking, 1991), 36.

22. "Church of All Faiths Now Favorite of Air Waves," *Amsterdam News,* October 31, 1936, in the Sherry Sherrod DuPree African-American Pentecostal and Holiness collection, 1876–1989, Box 10, Folder 17, at the Schomburg Center for Research in Black Culture, New York Public Library, New York.

23. Quoted in Wallace Best, *Passionately Human, No Less Divine: Religion and Culture in Black Chicago, 1915–1952* (Princeton, N.J.: Princeton University Press, 2005), 160.

24. Ibid., 115, 180; see also Best, "The Spirit of the Holy Ghost is a Male Spirit," 121.

25. Fauset Collection, unnumbered page. The reference to being baptized in Jesus' name suggests that Mrs. W. was connected with Apostolic Oneness Pentecostalism, a minority expression within the Pentecostal movement that challenged traditional Trinitarian doctrine.

26. Mary Magdalena Tate, *The Constitution Government and General Decree Book of the Church of the Living God, the Pillar and Ground of the Truth* (Chattanooga, Tenn.: New and Living Way, 1924), 58–59.

27. Jill Watts, *God, Harlem U.S.A.: The Father Divine Story* (Berkeley: University of California Press, 1992), 25. For more on Azusa Street's role as the mythical origin of the Pentecostal movement, see Creech, "Visions of Glory."

28. See Robert Weisbrot, *Father Divine: The Utopian Evangelist of the Depression Era Who Became an American Legend* (Boston: Beacon Press, 1983), 100–102; See also Charles S. Braden, *These Also Believe: A Study of Modern American Cults and Minority Religious Movements* (New York: Macmillan, 1949), 25–26.

29. Quoted in Jill Watts, *God, Harlem U.S.A.,* 88.

30. Quoted from "Report on Foreign Inspired Agitation among American Negroes in Philadelphia Division," Federal Bureau of Investigation File 100-135-37-2, August 9, 1942, in Trulear, "Ida Robinson," 317; see also Sherry Sherrod Dupree, *African-American Holiness Pentecostal Movement* (New York: Garland Publishing, 1996), 418.

6

Rites of Lynching and Rights of Dance

Historic, Anthropological, and Afro-Pentecostal
Perspectives on Black Manhood after 1865

CRAIG SCANDRETT-LEATHERMAN

In traditional African societies, males became men not only by biological maturation but by social intervention. In other words, men were made by the community. Men were made through ritual process, through a communal rite of passage. This rite involved three stages. First, the boys-to-become-men were separated from the society of women and children. Second, the community of boys was subjected to an extended time of humiliation, ordeal, and instruction. Finally, the males were elevated to the status of men and reincorporated into the community with the rights and privileges of adult manhood.[1]

But the middle passage of African slaves severely disrupted and destroyed these rites of passage. In the Americas, African males were not socially elevated to the status of men but were kept in a perpetual state of boyhood and submission by ongoing ordeals, humiliation, and violence. From the end of the Civil War until the 1930s, the common form of violence was lynching. Violence against African Americans, from the lynchings of this earlier period through contemporary patterns of incarceration, have become the bases of segregation, suffering, economic oppression, and emasculation in many black communities.[2] Rituals of lynching were, and rituals of incarceration are, dehumanizing. Though concentrated on individuals, lynchings were performed against the whole black community and were concentrated against black men to reduce their options, squelch their energy, and threaten their lives.

But black people resisted dehumanization and reinvigorated their identity and lives through their own rituals. I submit that the Afro-Pentecostal tradition, as signaled and initiated by the Church of God in Christ (COGIC), developed, in part, as a black ritual system of liberation in response to the white ritual system of lynching. More particularly, I contend that Afro-Pentecostal dance was (and is) an expression of life that resists the dehumanizing effects of violence.

In this chapter we review the history and rituals of an Afro-Pentecostal leader (and his denomination) who was born at the peak of lynching and observe how these function as a response to violence, as a defense of the black community, and as a definition of black manhood. Charles Harrison Mason (1866–1961) was the founder of the largest Afro-Pentecostal church, the Church of God in Christ. Mason's practice and defense of dance is related to his resistance against military conscription. Afro-Pentecostal dance and conscientious objection were affirmations of life, which resisted the expected norms for black men: lifeless acquiescence comportment or life-taking participation in military violence. Black men in COGIC would not allow their masculinity to be made or unmade by violence. Dance and conscientious objection became the rites of black manhood performed as an alternative to practices of either acquiescence or violence.

More precisely, Afro-Pentecostal dance and spirituality were expressions of black male agency in a world that attempted to reduce their lives to passivity. If lynching was designed to exercise control over the fate of black men, dance and conscientious objection were intentional countercultural acts of resistance. Thus African American Pentecostal males in the American South in the early twentieth century refused to resign themselves to the dictates of others, but instead they created alternative ecclesial and public spaces within which they shaped their own lives and identities. Within the crucial historic and contemporary conversation about lynching, the rights of Afro-Pentecostal conscientious objection and dance both expand the conversation about the rites of lynching and the rights of black manhood.

Lynching: Story, Survey, Mythology

In April 1899 a black man, Sam Hose, was lynched in Newnan, Georgia. The day after Hose's alleged murder of his employer Alfred Cranford and rape of his wife Mattie, before any investigation had been initiated or a physician's examination had been made, the front page of the Atlanta *Constitution* announced: DETERMINED MOB AFTER HOSE: HE WILL BE LYNCHED IF CAUGHT. Six days later, still with no investigation, examination, or trial, the newspaper offered a $500 reward and informed readers of the method of Hose's death: "he will be either lynched and his body riddled with bullets or he will be burned at the stake . . . the mob which is in pursuit of him is composed of determined men . . . wrought up to an unusual degree."[3] Once Sam Hose was captured and his lynching announced, two special, unscheduled trains, ran from Atlanta to Newnan so spectators could participate in the festivities of violence.

The torture involved dismembering his body—starting with his ears, then fingers, one at a time, chopped off and then offered to the cheering crowd. The dismemberment concluded with a quick slash to the naked groin, after which his genitals were held aloft. Next the bloody body was covered with kerosene and lit with fire. Hose managed to snap the chains around his chest, but when he broke loose and his weakened body fell, several spectators grabbed heavy pieces of wood to hold Hose in the flames. Sam Hose sank his teeth into a log and eventually died. After investigating the case, detective Louis LeVinto concluded his report by writing, "I made my way home thoroughly convinced that a Negro's life is a very cheap thing in Georgia."[4]

Violence was used both before and after the Civil War to keep blacks submissive, but after emancipation the form of violence changed. Before the war, black bodies were valued as a means of service and production. Each purchased slave became the property of an owner, with male slaves' peak worth being more than one thousand dollars. But after the war, the slave was not owned and could not be sold, so black people had no bodily "value" except what could be extracted as labor. The extraction was accomplished through southern economics: rental of houses (former slave quarters), farm land, and tools; landlords required that ex-slaves make seed purchases on credit from plantation stores with inflated prices (and inflated loans rates), and that cotton and other produce be sold on the plantation (for deflated prices). Ex-slaves were almost never able to buy themselves out debt in the South. In short, slavery continued. Though the forms of slavery were altered, the actors and roles largely remained the same. The owners of the land, houses, tools, and all the means of production and distribution continued to run the South, no longer through bodily ownership but through economic control— and when black laborers resisted, through violence.

As a post–Civil War innovation, lynching resulted from three factors: (1) revaluing black bodies in response to postwar legal and economic arrangements; (2) reconfiguring violent control; (3) renegotiating roles and boundaries. First, since the black body was no longer purchased and owned, it was worth nothing to the economic "master" and could therefore be killed without loss of property. In *Festival of Violence*, Stewart Tolnay and E. M. Beck demonstrate a significant collation between low cotton prices and increased lynchings.[5] When cotton prices fell, lynching and the threat of lynching was a way to keep blacks from "complaining" about unjust economics, conditions, or wages of economic slavery. Lynching was a threat against resistance—a means to keep cheap labor cheap. Second, the former masters and "patty rollers" were used to executing their own justice by their own ways and means. After the war, using courts and legal processes would have unduly hindered the pace and pattern of their own particular form of "justice," so they took the law into their own hands, and the southern courts did not, generally, restrain that justice. Third, African Americans had greater mobility and public presence after emancipation; segregated boundaries were maintained no longer by a master's violent discipline but by public acts and threats of lynching. As slaves had been gathered so that owners could visually publicize the violent consequences of "misbehavior," now bodies were hung and displayed as a message to the whole "free" ex-slave community. Thus, land owners continued to use violence to maintain control of black bodies no longer owned. During slavery, whips, dog bites, shackles, and blood were used to maintain that submission; after the Civil War lynchings served the same purpose.

According to public records, 4,742 black persons were lynched in the United States between 1882 and 1968.[6] This number may represent half or less than half of the actual number.[7] These lynchings were festivals of violence, celebrated by white perpetuators, with children, food, and cameras; they were memorialized with photos and postcards.[8] Lynchings were also public events for black people because the bodies were left hanging near the roadways of black communities—a reminder of the cost of assertion. Always the bodies were limp, usually they were seared, often they were naked, and sometimes they were emasculated. In the rural South, few black children escaped the sight.

Ida B. Wells, in *Southern Horrors: Lynch Law in All Its Phrases*, exposed the racial and gendered injustice that undergirded lynching, and its violence.[9] Jacquelyn Dowd Hall, in *Revolt against Chivalry*, showed how lynching was a gendered reenactment of southern social order.[10] White land-owning men were the apex of southern social hierarchy; from that elevation, their sexual liberties (with black women) were preserved. Lynching reinforced the concept of white purity and betrayed the fact that most black-white sexual and romantic relationships were initiated by whites: when white men initiated romantic/sexual relationships with black women, no one was charged with rape; when white women initiated romantic/sexual relationships with black men, the black men were often charged with rape even when the woman refused to initiate legal charges. Though *alleged* rape made up only 25 percent of lynching cases, the idea of sexual relations between white women and black men seemed to be what united whites in the South and North in their support or tolerance of lynching. The dominating myth-metaphor of lynching was the black-beast-rapist male acting against the white-pure-passive female. The myth itself, however, was not a strong enough basis for the gross violence of lynching. This violence was founded on a broader religious perspective and a particular theology of atonement.[11]

The Religion of Lynching: Human Sacrifice

Donald Matthews's three-part historical/theological article provides a bridge between southern race-purity mythology and the practice of lynching.[12] First, his article applies an anthropologically informed definition of religion to southern mythology. Second, he reviews a theology of atonement, which lent itself to religion as ongoing sacrifice. Last, he uses this penal theology as a connection between the sacrifice of Christ and the lynching of black men. Drawing on Clifford Geertz's definition of religion and on the work of Mary Douglas,[13] Matthews states that "the bodies of white females symbolized the social body,"[14] which would be "polluted" by sexual contact with black bodies, so that "sin and sex and segregation" pervaded the lives of southerners:[15] "[White] Southerners had become fascinated with other people's evil rather than their own and had somehow been compelled to find personal salvation in the 'death of Christ' without carrying the cross" of Christ.[16]

Matthews identifies the specific theological foundations of lynching that he sees represented by Robert Lewis Dabney in *Christ our Penal Substitute.*[17] This theology seems to put the law above God, who, in the process of forgiving humans, needed to find a way to "satisfy" the law, or repay the "debt of sin." In focusing on St. Paul's legal and economic metaphors, Dabney identifies the cross as the culmination of God's saving action. In this view, the resurrection of Christ and its metaphors of victory and first fruit are downplayed. When the law and code of honor are so elevated, and when the resurrection victory is so diminished, then the possibility seems to exist that the law continues to demand ongoing sacrifice. The social corollary was that ongoing violence was justified against those who do not meet the standards of "the law." In the socio-theological development of the South, "the law" was the myth of white female purity and black male impurity. This law of race-based social and "moral" order took precedence over the law of the state. To restore right social and economic order, lynchers took the law into their own hands to purge southern society of its impurities. Maintaining the purity of white society required expurgating infectious social "elements" by assigning guilt to the black-beast-rapist—by sacrificing the black man.

The myths of white-woman-purity and black-beast-rapist became the basis of many white southern parables of sin, guilt, punishment, and salvation.[18] Mathews writes that "plunging all the meaning of community into one act of violence . . . resolves the potential collective conflict and therefore 'saves' the community."[19] Lynchings were rituals of human sacrifice that required the shedding blood for the purpose of restoring the "natural" social order, resolving conflict, and fulfilling the requirements of "justice."

From the perspective of land-owning white men, the icon of southern society was a graceful white woman leisurely serving her husband in his agrarian success. She was a pure woman at the center of a peaceful household. At the edge of this ideal was a black community happily fulfilling their subservient roles like children, or, when necessary, forced to fulfill their roles as subjected beasts.[20] The sexual "freedoms" of white landowning men were well known throughout the South. They were known among black women; they were known among the black men who were unable to protect their wives, sisters, daughters, and mothers; they were known by all who observed the births of many mulatto children.

Underneath the southern ideal was the actuality of white land-owning men who were served sexually by a pure white wife and also by a community of black women, but the whole system was served economically by black men whose sexual rights (minimally, the enjoyment of the rights of marriage) were denied.[21] The ideal was symbolized and the reality actualized by strict segregation of white women from black men. This ideal was threatened, however, by the notion or expression of a white woman's desire for a black man or by the black man's resistance to the controlling power of white men. In any case, the white woman was the icon of purity, the black man was the icon of pollution and danger; and lynching was a ritual of purification—a sacrifice of substitutionary atonement used to contain him.

The sins of society were laid on the black man. Yet, the white community did not call lynching a sacrifice, nor did they see the connection between the cross and the lynching tree—certainly no connection was made between Jesus and the black man. For them, lynching was a ritual of visceral response, for the "natural law" (the law of social order, i.e., segregation) had been violated. They could not wait for the "due process" of governmental law. Restoring order involved human sacrifice, the noose and the tree, violence and blood, oil and burning, the death of a black man—again and again, thousands of times.

Dabney wrote in the South, surrounded by lynching, but in *Christ Our Penal Substitute*, he made no connection between theology and the ritual of lynching. Six years later, however, Edwin Talliaferro Wellford turned this neglect on its head when he published *The Lynching of Jesus.*[22] Wellford argued that the cross and lynching demand empathy with the victim. He insisted that white southerners focused on the law and its fulfillment; they saw both the cross and the lynching tree as a sacrifice for the preservation and restoration of law and social purity, but because they ignored the victim they failed to see the suffering, and failed to make the connection between a lynched black man and a lynched Jewish man. Wellford made that connection, and he saw what the black community saw. They saw their brother suffering. They saw the southern culture conspiring to kill him. And they saw Jesus, of whom it was said, "they put him to death by hanging him on a tree" (Acts 10:39, NRSV).

A Theology of Lynching: Jesus and Black Men

In his Harvard Divinity School lecture, "Strange Fruit: The Cross and the Lynching Tree," James H. Cone continued Wellford's tradition by recalling the identification that black people feel with the crucified Christ through their common suffering.[23] They sing:

> Were you there when they crucified my Lord?
> Were you there when they crucified my Lord?
> Oh-Oh-Oh-Oh, sometimes it causes me to tremble, tremble, tremble.
> Were you there when they crucified my Lord?
>
> Were you there when they nailed him to a tree?
> Where you there when they nailed him to a tree?
> Were you there when they nailed him to a tree?
> Oh-Oh-Oh-Oh, sometimes it causes me to tremble, tremble, tremble.
> Were you there when they nailed him to a tree?

"Black people were there," says Cone.[24] Through the experience of being lynched and seeing their black men lynched by white mobs, blacks transcended their time and place and found themselves existentially and symbolically at the foot of Jesus' cross, experiencing his fate. According to Cone:

The gospel is God's message of liberation in an unredeemed and tortured world. On the one hand, the gospel is a transcendent reality that lifts our spirits to a world far removed from the hurts and pains of this one. . . . On the other, it is an immanent reality, that is, a powerful liberating presence among the poor right now. . . . The gospel is the suffering word of the cross, a lynched word hanging from a tree. The gospel is a tortured word, a black word in the world of white supremacy. The gospel and the cross cannot be separated. The cross stands at the center of the gospel. Take the cross away and the gospel is no longer the gospel of the God of Jesus. . . . The cross is the most empowering symbol of God's loving solidarity with the "least of these." . . . God's suffering solidarity with today's crucified people, which bestows on them the power to resist the daily crosses of injustice in their lives. . . . The cross and the lynching tree need each other: the lynching tree can liberate the cross from false pieties of well-meaning Christians. The crucifixion was a first-century lynching. The cross can redeem the lynching tree and thereby bestow upon lynched black bodies an eschatological meaning for their ultimate existence.[25]

As blacks identified with Jesus suffering on the cross, they found Jesus identifying with "hanging and burning black bodies on the lynching tree"—in the solidarity of suffering; paradoxically, Christ made "beautiful what white supremacy made ugly."[26] Cone notes that the gospel of Jesus is an ugly story, but the cross and the lynching tree become "windows for seeing the love and beauty of God."[27]

What makes the ugliness of Jesus' crucified body important is not that it was the greatest physical ugliness, but that we are asked to see through it to the unspeakable beauty of God. The crucifixion inverts our ordinary bodily aesthetic by claiming that the radiant source of all beauty was disclosed in a scourged, crucified dead body. . . . Paradoxical assertions about Jesus' beauty on the cross invite us to learn that bodies can be beautiful in ways we hadn't expected—or were afraid to think.[28]

The paradox of the cross and lynching tree is that suffering can become a "window for seeing the love and beauty of God . . . [and] that black bodies can be beautiful."[29] Black worshippers participated in this paradox when the preacher preached about the cross of Jesus:

People shouted, groaned, and moaned, clapped their hands, and stomped their feet as if a powerful, living reality of God's Spirit had touched them and lifted them out of the "muck and miry clay" of white supremacy and thus transformed them from nobodies in white society to somebodies in the black church.[30]

Here, Cone suggests that the theology of the cross is the foundation of black worship. It is a place where black people are released from the confining images, aesthetics, and imaginations of white society/supremacy.[31] The preaching of the cross and the communal response takes the suffering and ugly put-downs of white society and transforms them into a ritual experience that is victorious, beautiful, and uplifting—into a personal and communal life that is participatory, active, emotional, and dignified.

Cone reviews very ugly rituals: the cross and the lynching tree. And he suggests that the beauty of black worship does not deny but is rooted in this ugliness, in this violence. The lynchings of men were rituals of emasculation that violated the communities of poor first-century Jews and post–Civil War African Americans. But somehow these rituals restored the men, lives, and communities of these oppressed groups. Cone's theological observation serves as a foundation for my own observation as an anthropologist and ritual historian. We can shed light on the transforming ritual process of black worship by turning to a religious tradition of Afro-Pentecostalism, and specifically to a leader and a ritual in that tradition, who sought to reverse the pattern, theology, and effects of lynching.

Dancing Right against the Rite of Lynching: An Afro-Pentecostal Case

In 1890, Lucy Norman wrote an article whose title asked the question, "Can a Colored Man Be a Man in the South?" She concluded "that mob violence could never diminish black manhood,"[32] but her conclusion did not end the debate. The American Methodist Episcopal bishop Henry McNeal Turner argued that "there is no manhood future in the United States for the Negro. . . . He can never be a man—full symmetrical and undwarfed."[33] In a letter to a friend, James Dubose held out the possibility that there might be places in the United States for a black man to be a man, but definitely not in the South.[34] The state of Mississippi led the nation in attacking black manhood: 509 men were lynched between 1882 and 1930—more than any other southern state.[35] The attacks peaked between around 1891: in 1890 Mississippi severely limited black men's ability to vote; in 1892 there were more lynchings than in any other year.[36]

At the height of Mississippi's attacks on black men, Charles Harrison Mason sensed a call to ministry *and to manhood*. In 1891 Mason was ordained in Mississippi; in 1893 he entered Arkansas Baptist College.[37] He became the leader of one of the first Pentecostal denominations, the Church of God in Christ, which would become of the largest Pentecostal bodies in the United States. Lelia Mason Byas recalled her father's call to ministry: "The Lord seemed to deal with him strangely and told him that if he would let him make a man out of him, he would have his blessing throughout a lifetime"[38] For Mason, his entrance into manhood would include ministry aimed at renewing manhood—against masculinity defined by violence, against the lynching of black men, and against the fear of lynching.[39] We focus on Mason's story beginning in the middle of his life, with his conscientious objection, and then move backward to the basis of his boldness.

Following President Woodrow Wilson's entry of America into World War I in April 1917, Congress approved a massive national conscription campaign. Charles Mason encouraged men in the COGIC to avoid war-making by registering as "conscientious objectors." Because of this, the FBI began an investigation of Mason and began proceedings accusing him of draft obstruction. When the word got out among whites in Lexington, Mississippi, a lynch mob formed and Sheriff Palmer had to arrest Mason in order to prevent him from being lynched.[40] Palmer took Mason to Jackson, Mississippi. The Jackson *Daily News* reported: LEXINGTON NEGRO PASTOR HELD UNDER NEW U.S. ESPIONAGE LAW.[41] But when Palmer examined Mason's suit case for incriminating evidence of an enemy connection, he found several pieces of anointed cloth and a bottle of German cologne, but didn't consider this sufficient evidence.[42] "Arraigned on draft obstruction, Mason pleaded not guilty . . . and posted a $2,000 bond guaranteeing his appearance in federal court in November."[43]

While he was out on bond Mason went to Memphis to preach and oversee the large COGIC annual baptism. His sermon, given on June 23, 1918, was titled, "The Kaiser in the Light of the Scriptures":

They tell me that the Kaiser went into prayer and came out and lifted up his hands and prayed, and afterward declared war. . . . If he had been praying for peace he would not have declared war. . . . The German Kaiser . . . not satisfied with the rape of Belgium, has overthrown governments of Romania and Montenegro, and through hypocrisy and deceit he betrayed Russia into a disgraceful peace. . . . If anyone is building hopes on the victories of the Kaiser in the present war, their hopes are in vain. . . . The devilish spirit of the Kaiser that causes women to be ravished, infants to be dashed to pieces and prisoners of war to be tortured and put to death by methods is only equaled by the Spanish Inquisition and the persecution of the Christians under Nero. . . . When the disciples James and John saw [the inhospitality of the Samaritans toward them] they said, "Lord, will thou that we commend fire to come down from heaven and consume them—even as Elias did?" But Jesus turned and rebuked them, and said, "ye know not what manner of spirit ye are of. . . . The Son of Man is not come to destroy men's lives, but to save them." . . . [B]efore he would kill, he offered up himself, and by his death came peace, and if the Kaiser had been willing to die rather than shed the blood of his fellow men, we would now have peace.

[Mason's concluding prayer:] for the time when the German hordes should be driven back across the Rhine, the independence of Belgium restored and victory of the allied armies restoring peace to a war-torn world—especially for the coming of the Prince of Peace and the day when men would beat their swords into plowshares and learn to war no more.[44]

This sermon and prayer delivered at the large annual Memphis baptism indicates that Mason understood baptism as an immersion into the way of Jesus' nonviolence. Those baptized into Christ would not seek justice through violence but by speaking the truth and accepting suffering. By preaching this sermon at the annual and central rite of the church, Mason was making it clear that the way of the cross and nonviolence is central to Christian discipleship and to peacemaking in an unjust and violent world. Discipleship is an act of making instruments for life-taking into instruments for life-tending.

Mason's theology of nonviolence was based on his experience of violence against the black community, against black manhood in the South. His theology undoubtedly evolved first from visceral responses, probably as a lad, to the lynched black men that he had seen and knew about in Mississippi, so that after articulating his theology of nonviolence regarding the First World War, Mason returned to the topic of lynching. He wrote: "Lynchings are being carried out because the preachers are leading people away from the reproof of God and not to the glory of God. They are cowards until they are baptized with Jesus' baptism."[45] In an era of white "imperialism and hypermasculinity," Mason's use of the word "coward" questioned the masculinity of some preachers.[46] He challenged a form of masculinity that proved its manhood by violence, and suggested, instead, that "real men" would protest against violence rather than tolerate it. Only a coward preacher would keep silent.

Mason identified what the coward preachers lacked: "They are cowards until they are baptized with Jesus' baptism." Mason connected cowardice with ritual deficiency: they lack "Jesus' baptism." It is unlikely that Mason is suggesting that these preachers were not baptized by the church, but that they lacked a particular *kind* of baptism: a baptism that is into the way of the Jesus (whose way is the cross: nonviolence) and in the Holy Spirit.[47] The Holy Spirit baptism was given to the first disciples by the Spirit of the resurrected and victorious Jesus. When the apostles received this baptism at Pentecost, it transformed them from cowardly followers to bold witnesses. And this was also Mason's experience. It was, as Cone described, an out-of-the-South experience of black worship: "they were lifted out of the 'muck and miry clay' of white supremacy and [were] thus transformed."[48] It was *this baptism* that emboldened Mason to oppose the violence of war and lynching.

Mason's transformation occurred at the Azusa Street Revival in April 1907. This revival was not only the spiritual source of Mason's conscientious objection, it was also the foundation of the Pentecostal movement in the United States.[49] News of the revival spread to the South, and Mason, along with two other elders from St. Paul COGIC in Lexington, Mississippi, traveled more than 1,500 miles to Los Angeles in March 1907 to observe the revival. It was led by William J. Seymour, a black man, along with a multicultural leadership team of men and women.[50] This revival occurred during the peak of national machismo and racial segregation, but a reporter, Frank Bartleman, observed that "the color line was washed away by the blood."[51] At Azusa, the sermons were few and short, but the services were lively. Sometimes a dozen people might tremble "under the power of God"; the standard revival invitation was not needed because

> God himself would give the altar call. Men would fall all over the house like the slain in battle, or rush for the altar en masse, to seek God. The scene often resembled a forest of fallen trees. . . . [Then] in a burst of "glory," they would "come through" to salvation, or sanctification, or baptism in the Spirit with shouts and songs of praise, speaking in tongues, leaping, running, jumping, kissing, and embracing one another.[52]

One of the Azusa leaders estimated that there were more than twenty nationalities represented at the meetings. Those named included Ethiopians, Chinese, Indians, Mexicans, Portuguese, Spanish, Russians, Norwegians, French, Germans, and Jews. Another observer noted that the meetings were "noticeably free from all nationalistic feeling. . . . No instrument that God can use is rejected on account of color or dress or lack of education."[53] Twelve elders were appointed. Half of the elders were women, a fourth were African American, and one was a ten-year-old girl.[54]

During his five-week stay Mason felt a strong desire to seek the baptism of the Holy Spirit. When the baptism did not come he became discouraged. Then a sister came and said, "Satan will try to make you feel sad, but that is not the way to receive him—you must be glad and praise the Lord."[55] Shortly thereafter, someone requested a song during a service, and Mason rose and started singing "He Brought Me Out of the Miry Clay; He Sat My Feet on the Rock to Stay." Then the Spirit came upon the saints and upon Mason. His hands went up and he resolved not to take them down until the Lord baptized him. "The enemy" suggested that it might be painful to keep his hands up that long and that he might not be able, but again the voice said that "the Lord was able."[56]

> The sound of a mighty wind was in me and my soul cried, "Jesus, only, none like you." My soul cried and soon I began to die. It seemed that I heard the groaning of Christ on the Cross dying for me. All of the work in me until I died out of the old man . . . when He had gotten me straight on my feet there came a light which enveloped my entire being above the brightness of the sun. When I opened my mouth to say glory, a flame touched my tongue which ran down in me. My language changed and no word could I speak in my own tongue. O, I was then satisfied. I rejoiced in Jesus my Savior, whom I love so dearly. And from that day until now there has been and overflowing joy of the glory of the Lord in my heart.[57]

Mason's experience of dying, of knowing someone's suffering for him, and being raised straight on his feet is characteristic of both slave conversion narratives, and rites of passage into manhood.[58]

The process of a male being taken down, unto death, and then being brought up and back to life was bodily expressed not only in the tongue now loosed to speak freely, but also by the man standing to his feet and his whole body being freed to dance. In Afro-Pentecostal ritual Jesus' baptism of the Holy Spirit and the rite into manhood (the right of men) often involves dance. This can be understood as a celebration of the freedom to be a black man in the multicultural body of Jesus

One of a handful of Mason's widely distributed essays was titled, "Is it Right for the Saints of God to Dance?" The first word gives the answer: yes. For a male to become a man he must give up both his shame and his pride; he must participate in Spirit. Becoming a man is not only a strong thing, it is a sweet thing. According to Mason, "The children of God dance of God, for

God and to the praise and glory of His name. They have the joy of the Spirit of the Lord in them. They are joyful in their King. . . . How sweet it is to dance in Him and about Him, for he that dances in the Spirit of the Lord expresses joy *and victory*. Amen."[59] In the American South, where manhood was characterized by cool control and, when necessary, violence, dancing seemed a strange way to enter manhood. But if the liminal male was one shackled or hung, or in a state of perpetual boyhood, then the rite into manhood often involved being raised up to speak and to move freely. Afro-Pentecostals gave men the right to speak freely without uttering a word, and the right to move freely without serving a white master—the sweet rights of dancing in joy and victory.

Conclusion

In the United States, violence has often been concentrated against black men. Before slavery, African communities transformed black boys into men through rites of passage, but these rights were shattered by enslavement. After the Emancipation Proclamation, white society tried to keep black men in a perpetual state of servitude.

Lynchings were national and religious rituals against black men. As national rituals: common, widely dispersed, publicized and public—often attended by thousands in the South and politically tolerated in the north. As religious rituals: tied to beliefs about purity and danger, about atonement and sacrifice. They were southern rites against African American status elevation—attacks on black manhood.

Resistance to lynching occurred through political organizing and through theology. Ida B. Wells and others influenced and created women's campaigns against lynching. Wellford wrote *The Lynching of Jesus* as an alternative to Dabney's *Christ Our Penal Substitute*. In 1901 William G. Schell wrote a refutation of Charles Carroll's (1900) book, *The Negro a Beast*.[60] But what has often been overlooked is that black men also resisted lynching.

One of the important ways black men resisted the subjugation of their manhood was by becoming preachers—ritual leaders. Preachers retold biblical stories from black perspectives and moved with bodily freedom when they preached: strutting, sweating, shouting, and dramatizing. And individual preachers resisted violence. William Seymour resisted emasculation by getting out of the South, by migrating north and then west, by praying with other black folk in Los Angeles, by speaking in tongues, and by gathering a team of elders, which included a young white girl. Mason resisted by ordaining hundreds of white preachers, hugging while people in public, and speaking against violence and lynching. But Mason's most significant protest was in ritual. Before much Pentecostal theology was written, Mason was doing Pentecostal theology through rituals. Before Gustave Aulén wrote *Christus Victor*, Mason was dancing victoriously.[61]

Rituals are enacted cultural and religious systems applied to persons and communities. African rites of passage were meant to elevate black males into manhood; lynchings were meant to emasculate black men and keep the community of men as boys. Resistance to lynching could not be accomplished by words alone, or through retaliation, or even legislation. Resistance to the system reproducing rituals of emasculation required alternative rituals—rites of manhood. This was not "pulling yourself up by your own bootstraps," but participating in a community that redefined what was pure (clean) and beautiful. Before "black is beautiful" became a movement, Mason's worship involved a celebration of blackness; it involved black styles of dress, movement, and color; it included roots, guitars, drums, oil, testimonies, healings, and dance as a protest against white interpretations of black ugliness and as a celebration of black beauty—a celebration of black ritual aesthetics.

We have highlighted how black Pentecostal men developed alternative ritual practices in the Pentecostal church to counter the acts of violence that were threatened and inflicted upon them. At the same time, they also formulated public stances that reflected their own commitments to peace in a world of war. Dance and spirituality, particularly among black males, reflects countercultural strategies of resistance in the Afro-Pentecostal community. Moving forward to the present, we have seen James Cone's insistence that there will be no healing of the racial divide in the church or in U.S. society without a conversation about the cross and the lynching tree. If renewal of hope and lifting of black people occurs in the Black Church, then a healing connection between the cross and lynching tree will not be made by talk alone. African American healing involves rituals of political aesthetics: the community reenacting, participating in, and producing social, physical, and spiritual realities of beauty and abundance. For Afro-Pentecostals the cross was a violent lynching of an innocent man, but their shouts came from the knowledge that the death of innocent men is not their end. The Spirit that Afro-Pentecostals celebrated was victory over violence, life beyond lynching, truth against injustice, beauty against gore, dancing against death. These were the moods and movements, the religion and rites, by which Afro-Pentecostal males became men.

1. Arnold Van Gennep, *Rites of Passage*, trans. Monika B. Vizedom and Gabrielle L. Caffe (Chicago: University of Chicago Press, 1960). For the theory of ritual assumed in this essay, see Victor Turner, *The Ritual Process: Structure and Anti-Structure* (Ithaca, N.Y.: Cornell University Press, 1977).

2. Prisons are the current means of black emasculation: one out of nine young African American men is in prison, nearly one-third are under court supervision, and there are now more African American men in prison than in college. See Jennifer Warren, "One in 100: Behind Bars in America" (2008 Pew report), available at: http://www.pewtrusts.org/uploadedFiles/wwwpewtrustsorg/Reports/sentencing_and_corrections/one_in_100.pdf; Jan Chaiken, Director of United States Bureau of Justice Statistics, report in Paul Street, "Race, Prison, and Poverty," *Z Magazine,* May 2001, available at http://www.zmag.org/zmag/viewArticle/13291; and a Justice Policy Institute report, "Cellbocks or Classrooms: The Funding of Higher Education and Corrections and Its Impact on African American Men," available at http://www.justicepolicy.org/images/upload/02-09_REP_Cellblock-sClassrooms_BB-AC.pdf—each of these links last accessed November 19, 2008.

3. Philip Dray, *At the Hands of Persons Unknown: The Lynching of Black America* (New York: Random House, 2002), 5.

4. Ibid., 14–16. Detective Louis LeVinto's investigation produced a story that bore little resemblance to that circulated by the Georgia newspapers. Rather than being a murderer, Hose had acted in self-defense and the alleged rape was unlikely.

5. Stewart E. Tolnay and E. M. Beck, *A Festival of Violence: An Analysis of Southern Lynchings, 1882–1930* (Urbana: University of Illinois Press, 1995).

6. James Allen, Hilton Als, John Lewis, and Leon F. Litwack, eds., *Without Sanctuary: Lynching Photography in America* (Santa Fe, N. M.: Twin Palms Publishers, 2000), 12.

7. The Tuskegee Institute recorded 3,417 lynchings of blacks between 1882 and 1944; see Dray, *At the Hand of Persons Unknowns*, viii. Wells cited a *Chicago Tribune* article that reported eight hundred lynchings from 1882 to 1892 (cited in Dray, *At the Hand of Persons Unknowns*, 90). But, according to Dray, these estimates are based on newspapers, NAACP, and Tuskegee archives, which rely on publicly recorded lynchings. Though public acceptance and celebration of lynching after the Civil War might suggest that many lynchings would have been recorded during that period, private parties and later public controversy of the practice assure than many, if not a majority, of lynchings were not publicly recorded.

8. See especially James Allen et al., *Without Sanctuary*, which collected and reproduced dozens of these postcards.

9. Ida B. Wells, *Southern Horrors: Lynch Law in All Its Phrases* (New York: New York Age Printing, 1892). Wells risked her life to attack the lynching of black men. Wells, Hall (see n.10), and the public roles of black and white women's groups show that this "men's issue" was a concern by and for the whole (black, national, moral) community. For an excellent review of Wells's contribution, see Patricia Schechter, "Unsettled Business: Ida B. Wells against Lynching, or How Antilynching Got Its Gender," in W. Fitzhugh Brundage, ed., *Under Sentence of Death: Lynching in the South* (Chapel Hill: University of North Carolina Press, 2007), 292–317.

10. Jacquelyn Dowd Hall, *Revolt against Chivalry: Jessie Daniel Ames and the Women's Campaign Against Lynching* (New York: Columbia University Press, 1974).

11. In addition to the works cited in this chapter, the following two books have informed and influenced my thinking: W. Fitzhugh Brundage, *Lynching in the New South: Georgia and Virginia, 1880–1930* (Chicago: University of Illinois Press, 1993), and George C. Wright, *Racial Violence in Kentucky, 1865–1940: Lynchings, Mob Rule, and "Legal Lynchings"* (Baton Rouge: Louisiana State University Press, 1990). This chapter is also related to other works that describe the religious foundations of southern politics during Reconstruction. See Beth Barton Schweiger and Donald G. Matthews, eds., *Religion in the American South: Protestants and Others in History and Culture* (Chapel Hill: University of North Carolina Press, 2004), and Edward J. Blum, *Reforging the White Republic: Race, Religion, and American Nationalism, 1865–1898* (Baton Rouge: Louisiana State University Press, 2005).

12. Donald G. Matthews, "The Southern Rite of Human Sacrifice," *Journal of Southern Religion* 3 (2000), available at http://jsr.fsu.edu/jsrlink3.htm. Thanks to Cheryl Sanders for introducing me to Matthews's article at the Afro-Pentecostal Colloquium held at Regent University, February 23, 2008.

13. See Clifford Geertz, "Religion as a Cultural System," in *The Interpretation of Cultures: Selected Essays* (New York: Basic Books, 1973), 87–125, and Mary Douglas, *Purity and Danger: An Analysis of Concepts of Pollution and Taboo* (London: Routledge and Kegan Paul, 1966).

14. Matthews, "Southern Rite," 8; page numbers indicated for printed version from electronic journal with continuous pagination applied across three parts of the single article. Though Matthews does not reference this, the idea of the interrelationship between personal and social bodies was articulated in the field of medical anthropology by Nancy Scheper-Hughes and Margaret Lock, "The Mindful Body: A Prolegomenon to Future Work in Medical Anthropology," *Medical Anthropology Quarterly* 1 (1987): 6–41.

15. This particular phrase by Smith is in an editorial of the *Atlantic Constitution,* cited in Matthews, "Southern Rite," 8n51; see also "A report from Lillian Smith on Killers of the Dream," in Lillian Smith Papers 1283A in the University of Georgia Library, Box 30.

16. Summary of Smith, *Killers of the Dream* (1949; repr., New York: W. W. Norton, 1961), 224–52, in Matthews, "Southern Rite," 8.

17. Robert Lewis Dabney *Christ our Penal Substitute* (Richmond, Va.: Presbyterian Committee of Publication, 1898). Matthews, "Southern Rite," 15–16, indicates that Dabney's "substitutionary atonement" theology was based on the theology of Anselm of Canterbury (1033–1109) who explained that human salvation could be accomplished only if the law (and character of God) was "satisfied" by the payment of death.

18. Matthews, "Southern Rite," 18; see also Kimberly Kellison, "Parameters of Promiscuity: Sexuality, Violence, and Religion in Upcountry South Carolina," in Edward J. Blum and W. Scott Poole, eds., *Vale of Tears: New Essays on Religion and Reconstruction* (Macon, Ga.: Mercer University Press, 2005), 15–35. Both summarize two books by Rene Girard, *Violence and the Sacred* (Baltimore, Md.: The Johns Hopkins University Press, 1977), and *Things Hidden Since the Foundation of the World* (Palo Alto, Calif.: Stanford University Press, 1987).

19. Matthews, "Southern Rite," 19. Matthews explains that the scapegoat mechanism that emphasized Christ as taking on the sins of the world was an atonement reading, which Christians also occasionally used against Jews. For example, during the plagues in the fourteenth century, Christians murdered Jews in order to stop the fatal consequences of the Black Death. Similarly the 1915 lynching of Leo Frank in Georgia indicated that it was not only blacks but also Jews who could become victims of ethnic scapegoat lynching

in the South; see Nancy MacLean "Gender, Sexuality, and the Politics of Lynching: The Leo Frank Case Revisited," in W. Fitzhugh Brundage, ed., *Under Sentence of Death: Lynching in the South* (Chapel Hill: University of North Carolina Press, 1997), 158–88.

20. Charles Carroll, *"The Negro a Beast"; or, "In the image of God": The Reasoner of the Age, the Revealer of the Century! The Bible as It is! The Negro and His Relation to the Human Family!* (St. Louis, Mo.: American Book and Bible House, 1900).

21. Ownership of persons legally ended with the Civil War, but slavery continued in peonage agricultural systems that combined farming tenancy and economic exploitation; James Cobb, *The Most Southern Place on Earth: The Mississippi Delta and the Roots of Regional Identity* (New York: Oxford University Press, 1992). On a related matter, slavery also continued through construed convictions, imprisonment, and convict leasing. Using chains and shackles continuously from sleeping quarters to work sites, convict leasing was the direct descendant of slavery and represented a form of control between tenant farming and lynching. Convict leasing is another significant historic violence that demands further attention especially as a bridge of history and practice between slavery and contemporary patterns of black imprisonment. The practice of leasing prisoners for private and public projects has been documented by Matthew Mancini, *One Dies, Get Another: Convict Leasing in the American South, 1866–1928* (Columbia: University of South Carolina Press, 1996), and Douglas Blackmon, *Slavery by Another Name: The Re-enslavement of Black People in America from the Civil War to World War II* (New York: Doubleday, 2008).

22. Edwin Talliaferro Wellford, *The Lynching of Jesus: A Review of the Legal Aspects of the Trial of Christ* (Newport News, Va.: The Franklin Publishing Company, 1905). Note that the hanging of Jesus on a Roman cross was not unique in its day. Not only were two crucified beside Jesus, but thousands of Jewish "rebels" were crucified by Romans during and around the life of Jesus; on a single occasion two thousand Jews were crucified. See Marcus Borg, *Conflict, Holiness and Politics in the Teachings of Jesus* (Lewiston, N.Y.: Edwin Mellen Press, 1984), 40.

23. James H. Cone, "Strange Fruit: The Cross and the Lynching Tree," *Harvard Divinity Bulletin* 35.1 (2007): 46–55.

24. Ibid., 54.

25. Ibid., 51–53. Cone indicates that a conversation about the cross and lynching tree is crucial for healing America's racial divide. "The cross can also redeem white lynchers, and their descendants too, but not without profound cost, not without the revelation of the wrath and justice of God, which executes divine judgment, with the demand for repentance and reparation, as a presupposition of divine mercy and forgiveness. Most whites want mercy and forgiveness but not justices and reparations; they want reconciliation without liberation, the resurrection without the cross" (53). "The church's most vexing problem today is how to define itself by the gospel of Jesus' cross as revealed through the lynched black bodies in American history" (55). "I want to start a conversation about the cross and the lynching tree and thereby to break our silence on race and Christianity in American history" (49). The need for such conversation was illustrated in an interview with Bill Moyers in which Cone said that his mother and father talked about lynching all the time. but Moyers, who was raised only about one hundred miles away, never heard anything—and didn't know anything—about lynching until his father died and he found a newspaper article among his father's effects. The article and accompanying photo was of a lynching in Paris, Texas, where five thousand people had come to watch. See Bill

Moyers "Interview with James Cone," *Bill Moyers Journal* (November 23, 2007): 1–15, esp. 4, available at http://www.pbs.org/moyers/journal/11232007/transcript1.html. Cone argues that silence about suffering since slavery needs to be broken. "Unless the cross and the lynching tree are seen together, there can be no genuine understanding of Christian identity in America and no healing of the racial divide in churches and seminaries as well as in the society as a whole" ("Strange Fruit," 48).

26. Ibid., 54. Cone recalls Reinhold Niebuhr's article, "The Terrible Beauty of the Cross," *Christian Century* (March 21, 1929): 386–88, in which he suggests that only "a tragic and terrible love" is an adequate symbol of reality, and that "Life is too brutal and the cosmic facts too indifferent to our moral ventures to make faith in any but a suffering God tenable."

27. Ibid., 54.

28. Mark D. Jordan, *Telling Truths in Church: Scandal, Flesh and Christian Speech* (Boston: Beacon Press, 2003), n.p., cited in Cone, "Strange Fruit," 54.

29. Cone, "Strange Fruit," 54.

30. Ibid., 50.

31. In Cone's interview with Bill Moyers, "Interview with James Cone," 5, he says that the black church is the "one place where you have an imagination that no one can control."

32. Lucy V. Norman, "Can a Colored Man Be a Man in the South," *Christian Recorder* (July 3, 1890): 2.

33. Henry McNeal Turner, "The American Negro and the Fatherland," in J. W. E. Bowen, ed., *Africa and the American Negro: Addresses and Proceedings on the Congress of Africa* (Atlanta, Ga.: Gammon Theological Seminary, 1896), 195–98, cited in Michele Mitchell, *Righteous Propagation: African Americans and the Politics of Racial Destiny after Reconstruction* (Chapel Hill: University of North Carolina Press, 2004), 58.

34. Mitchell, *Righteous Propagation*, 59.

35. Tolnay and Beck, *Festival of Violence*, 273.

36. Ibid., 271.

37. Ithiel Clemmons, *Bishop C. H. Mason and the Roots of the Church of God in Christ* (Bakersfield, Calif.: Pneuma Life, 1996), 5.

38. Lelia Mason Byas, interview by Brother Percy Jordan, transcribed by Raynard D. Smith, 2001.

39. I make the connection between Mason's call and lynching based on the following: the "coincidence" of chronology (call to ministry and manhood at the peak of Mississippi lynching); Cone's theology already reviewed (transformation out of suffering) ; the interpretations of Afro-Pentecostal member-scholars—see Leonard Lovett, "Aspects of the Spiritual Legacy of the Church of God in Christ: Ecumenical Implications," *Midstream* 24 (1985): 389–97, and Clemmons, *Bishop C. H. Mason*; the contrasting purposes of rituals of lynching and Afro-Pentecostal worship (black man labeled "evil," dismembered his body, pouring oil to burn him, death; verses, anointing black man with holy oil, remembering his body/connecting him to the powers of community, Spirit and resurrection life); metaphorical connections (lynched man vertical and dead; Afro-Pentecostal man diagonal and dancing); and, finally, my contemporary experience of ritual and testimony that continues to relate, not explicitly but implicitly, to "legal lynching." Thus, the connections I suggest between lynching and Afro-Pentecostal (COGIC) history are made by plausibility and persuasion rather than by proofs and texts. African history has been advanced by anthropologists who proceed not only by explicit connections of records and written histories (people's

history precedes their literacy) but also by the distribution of language cognates, artifacts, perspectives, and ritual patterns. Historians of African American culture benefit from a similar confluence of methods. See John Janzen, *Ngoma: Discourses of Healing in Central and Southern Africa* (Berkeley: University of California Press, 1995), and "Self-Presentation and Common Cultural Structures in *Ngoma* Rituals of Southern Africa," *Journal of Religion in Africa* 25 (1995): 141–62; and Jan Vansina, *Paths in the Rainforest: Toward a History of Political Tradition in Equatorial Africa* (Madison: University of Wisconsin Press, 1990).

40. Theodore, Jr. Kornweibel, *"Investigate Everything": Federal Efforts to Compel Black Loyalty During World War I* (Bloomington: Indiana University Press, 2002), 156–57.

41. *Jackson Daily News* (June 19, 1918), in Kornweibel, *"Investigate Everything"*, 296n25.

42. Kornweibel, *"Investigate Everything"*, 157; cf. 296n25.

43. Ibid., 156. Holt's bond was $5,000, and he stayed in jail while Mason raised money for his bond.

44. Sermon by Mason, in James Oglethorpe Patterson, German R. Ross, and Julia Mason, eds., *History and Formative Years of the Church of God in Christ with Excerpts from the Life and Works of Its Founder—Bishop C. H. Mason* (Memphis, Tenn.: Church of God in Christ Publishing House, 1969), 26–29.

45. This is from a sermon Mason preached on Sunday at Convocation, December 7, 1919. See Charles H. Mason, *The History and Life Work of Elder C. H. Mason, Chief Apostle, and His Co-Laborers*, ed. Mary Mason (n.p.: 1924), 49. The statement raises a question of what cowardly preachers Mason was talking about: white or black, present or absent preachers? Given the lack of political voice of black men, and their constant life-risk in the South, it seems unlikely (though possible) that Mason would have been making this evaluation of them. The vast majority of the nation's preachers were white men, and the voices of white men (including preachers who had been abolitionists) were all but silent against lynching. It seems likely that he was directing it to whomever "the shoe fit," and however it fit.

46. Mitchell, *Righteous Propagation*, 75.

47. The theology of baptism in Jesus and with the Holy Spirit is based on scriptures such as Acts 2:1–4 and 19:1–6. There Paul came to Ephesus and found believers who had been baptized into repentance and were disciples of Jesus, but they had not heard of the Holy Spirit. When they heard about the Holy Spirit, they were baptized in the name of Jesus and received the Holy Spirit.

48. Cone, "Strange Fruit," 50. One observer of the Azusa Street Revival characterized Azusa as black religion: "There was a beautiful outpouring of the Holy Spirit in Los Angeles. . . . Then they pulled off all the stunts common in old camp meetings among colored folks. . . . That is the way they worship God, but what makes my soul sick, and make[s] me sick at my stomach is to see white people imitating unintelligent, crude negroisms of the Southland, and laying it on the Holy Ghost"; See Charles Parham, "Editorial," in *Apostolic Faith* (Baxter Springs, Kans.) (April 3, 1925): 9–10, cited in Robert Mapes Anderson, *Vision of the Disinherited: The Making of American Pentecostalism* (New York: Oxford University Press, 1979), 190. With a less pejorative tone Joseph Murphy, *Working the Spirit: Ceremonies of the African Diaspora* (Boston: Beacon Press, 1994), also observes Afro-Pentecostalism as an African diaspora religion along with Cuban Santería, Brazilian Candomblé, Haitian Vodoum and Jamaican Revival Zion.

49. The Pentecostal movement spread around the world and became the fastest growing religious movement of the twentieth century.

50. In a 1906 photograph of the Azusa Street Revival Committee, William Seymour is in the middle of the group, immediately on his left is a woman who looks his age; they don't appear to be touching but are sitting comfortably close. The most dramatic aspect of the photo is the twelve-year-old girl immediately to the right of Seymour. She is sitting on the lap or leaning against an older man with a white beard. Seymour's right hand, on the girl's side, is slightly inside his right knee and is holding a Bible. This photo of Azusa Street Revival Committee is the aesthetic antithesis of photos of southern lynchings. It protests the myth of black bestiality against young white women. Photo in Rufus G. W. Sanders, *William Joseph Seymour: Black Father of the Twentieth-Century Pentecostal/Charismatic Movement* (Sandusky, Ohio: Alexandria Publications, 2001), 50.

51. Frank Bartleman, *Azusa Street: The Roots of Modern-day Pentecost* (1925; repr., Plainfield, N.J.: Logos International, 1980), 54. Mason appeared to have caught the multiracial vision of Azusa Street. In an age of strict segregation, Mason hugged a white man (William B. Holt) in public and appointed him to the second highest position in the church; he also ordained hundreds of white ministers, alongside of thousands of black ministers. Mason promoted the rhythms of drums (African *ngoma*) and the wonders of roots (African *min'kisi*) in an age of Eurocentric modernity. He became a minister and man in the peak of lynching; see Craig Scandrett-Leatherman, "'Can't Nobody Do Me Like Jesus': The Politics of Embodied Aesthetics in Afro-Pentecostal Rituals" (PhD diss., University of Kansas, 2005).

52. Anderson, *Vision of the Disinherited*, 69.

53. Ibid.

54. Ibid., 70. Sanders, *William Joseph Seymour*, 105, identifies the girl as twelve years old and reproduces the same photo that includes the young girl and elderly man, seven females and five males, three blacks and nine whites (50).

55. Mason, *History and Life Work*, 28.

56. Ibid., 29.

57. Ibid., 29–30.

58. These phases and much of the process here is also characteristic of conversions as revealed in ex-slave narratives; see R. Earl Riggins Jr., *Dark Symbols, Obscure Signs: God, Self, and Community in the Slave Mind* (Maryknoll, N.Y.: Orbis Books, 1993).

59. Charles H. Mason "Is it Right for the Saints of God to Dance?" in Patterson, Ross, and Mason, *History and Formative Years of the Church of God*, 36, emphasis added.

60. William G. Schell, *Is the Negro a Beast? A Reply to Charles Carrol's Book Entitled: "The Negro a Beast"* (Moundsville, W.Va.: Gospel Trumpet Publishing, 1901).

61. Gustave Aulén's *Christus Victor: An Historic Study of the Three Main Types of the Idea of Atonement*, trans. A. G. Herbert (1931; repr., Eugene, Ore.: Wipf and Stock, 2003), was a theology of the cross that emphasized not the substitutionary sacrifice of Jesus but the victory of Jesus. Similar atonement interpretations have been written by Mark Heim, *Saved from Sacrifice: A Theology of the Cross* (Grand Rapids, Mich.: Eerdmans, 2006), and J. Denny Weaver, *The Nonviolent Atonement* (Grand Rapids, Mich.: Eerdmans, 2001).

7

Crossing Over Jordan

*Navigating the Music of Heavenly Bliss and
Earthly Desire in the Lives and Careers of
Three Twentieth-Century African American
Holiness-Pentecostal "Crossover" Artists*

LOUIS B. GALLIEN JR.

Introduction

This chapter centers on the lives and relatively brief careers of three African American male "crossover" artists whose religious and musical roots were in the Holiness-Pentecostal church. The lives of Sam Cooke, Donny Hathaway, and Marvin Gaye are well chronicled in popular rock and roll, R&B, and soul musical literature. All three were versatile singers and songwriters, but perhaps their greatest gift was their ability to write and sing with conviction and spirit the songs they learned in church for secular audiences. Unlike their Pentecostal contemporaries, the iconic legends Jerry Lee Lewis and Lil' Richard Penniman, neither of whom attempted to justify their long secular recording careers,[1] at different phases of their careers, Cooke, Hathaway, and Gaye were clearly "tormented" by the dualistic appeal that gospel and secular music maintained over their lives. While their musical talents were crafted in Holiness-Pentecostal churches, all three struggled to reconcile their religious backgrounds and gospel music genesis with their desires to maintain successful secular careers.

We explore how their secular and spiritual conflicts complicated and resurrected the depths of their pathos and ambivalence in singing for two cultures. Marvin Gaye, in particular, is viewed by scholars and ministers such as Rev. Michael Eric Dyson, as a transitional figure in both the black church and contemporary soul music.[2] Dyson contends that Gaye was able to effectively influence both audiences without denying his faith—that he was, in reality, a true "soul" singer.[3] In examining the life of Donny Hathaway, we find a man who was both psychologically and spiritually disturbed. The ambivalence that he felt toward his career and music is palpable and even more complicated as he found even greater financial success in his recordings with the R&B legend Roberta Flack. In the 1970s their albums represented one of the more lucrative duo recording partnerships of that era. Finally, the soul, R&B, and contemporary music legend Sam Cooke exemplifies in many ways the complex nature of attempting to honor one's roots in the church while delivering secular songs which have attracted the admiration and loyalty of people around the world. Cooke's life and music, much like Lil' Richard's, held enormous attraction for white audiences that neither Gaye nor Hathaway would match. Their combined musical compositions, however, have been imitated (and even stolen) by more white artists (such as Pat Boone, the Beatles, Simon and Garfunkel) than any other musical scores of black artists in the past century.[4]

When we investigate the aggregate lives and impact of all three musicians on the shifting discourse between sacred and secular music, we can see more clearly how the discourse regarding the chasm between these two disparate musical genres began to close, especially as African Americans understood and experienced the marketability and commercial success of their musical heritages. All three were able to financially capitalize on their extensive gospel backgrounds and, in the mean time, gain approval from their local church communities based on a very pragmatic argument: they were able to shape a lucrative career that could positively impact both their immediate families and local congregations. While this argument did not assuage most sanctified folk, it made the men's transition from gospel music to secular success a bit more palatable to the larger community.

Before examining the lives of Cooke, Hathaway, and Gaye, we need to place their lives within the context of a Pentecostal cultural framework.

The Crossover Appeal of Black Holiness-Pentecostal Church Culture

Scholars have outlined at least four aspects of black Holiness-Pentecostal culture that have been identified as containing a broad crossover appeal into secular music: (1) integration of body and soul; (2) forms of worship that appeal to the head, heart, and hands; (3) songs based on freedom and hope; and (4) performance orientation.

First, with regard to the aspect of body and soul, as Teresa Reed and other scholars have suggested, one of the roots of black Pentecostal music is the pre-Christian rites utilized among many African tribes.[5] Most distinctly, worship styles that are centered on musical genres oriented toward drum beats, rhythms, shouts, clapping, and dancing—all integrated within the service—have a direct kinetic impact that few other church practices in the United States can replicate. The result is the integration of the body (dancing and shouting), mind (singing), and spirit (moaning) with the music—which taken as whole, makes the Pentecostal experience unique and facilitates the appeal of "crossing over" into secular entertainment where these performative aspects of worship are equally appreciated.

Significantly, there has historically been no formal distinction between the sacred and the secular in African religious worldview.[6] There is no word for religion among African tribes because the idea of "religion" was integrated into all aspects of life, and all of life is considered religious. As a result, in most African cultures spiritual beliefs never became dogmas. But for Holiness-Pentecostal churches the idea of crossing-over from the sacred to the secular makes no theological sense. Either a person is saved and on her way toward sanctification or she is living in a "back-slidden" condition. There is only one sanctified movement for the believer and that is following the teachings of Jesus Christ. Even though Gaye (and others) believed that the dual language of the profane and secular found in Western thought was irrelevant to the cultural and spiritual condition, it would never be acceptable in their church circles.

Second, in relationship to the head, heart, and hands, the distinct forms of worship found in these churches also have ties to the continent of Africa. As the musicologist Eileen Southern notes:

The Spirit possession, holy dancing, speaking in tongues, improvisational singing and the use of drums and other percussive instruments were common practice among the Holiness Church members. Obviously, the Pentecostal church fell direct heir to the shouts, hand-clapping, and foot-stomping jubilee songs, and the ecstatic seizures of the plantation "praise houses.[7]

It is also important to note that these forms of worship were highly influential in the lives of white Pentecostal crossover artists as well. It is well documented that both Elvis Presley and Jerry Lee Lewis regularly sneaked out of their houses on Sunday nights to attend Holiness-Pentecostal churches in black neighborhoods in order to delight in and learn about the singing of black gospel performers and choirs. The eventual crossover *racial* appeal of both men (like Sam Cooke and Lil' Richard Penniman) was a result of the vast appeal of their duplication of the kinetic and musical forms of worship that they experienced in the black church.[8]

The appeal of these services was in direct contrast to most white main-line denominational churches and a few assimilated black churches. The asynchronous environment led to a feeling of unexpected blessing; the kinetic nature of the music loosened the body; the call and response of the preacher invited group participation and fellowship; the gestures, moans, shouts, foreign tongues, and divine healings all pointed to the mystery and awe found only in the power of the Holy Spirit.

Third, the songs that have appealed to both sacred and secular audiences have always contained messages of hope and freedom that were central to the early slave spirituals. By the mid-1950s, Sam Cooke and others were composing songs whose messages appealed to all audiences, and these were among the first to be considered as songs that could be "legitimately" sung in all churches. In 1957 Cooke and the Soul Stirrers released the song "That's Heaven to Me," which Reed considered an integrative song between the secular and the sacred. She notes that "The lyrics of 'That's Heaven to Me' teeter on the threshold between traditional black Christian theology and the social awareness that characterizes the progressive black church of the 1950s."[9]

By the late sixties, songs that began in the church became popular with a secular audience such as the Edwin Hawkins Singers hit "Oh Happy Day." During this same period, white singers like Judy Collins and Joan Baez performed traditional church hymns like "Amazing Grace" and other black spirituals that had been heard previously only in church. The famous Concert for Bangladesh that Beatle George Harrison engineered in the seventies featured a variety of international "hit makers," including Billy Preston's electrifying rendition of "That's the way God planned it." And, of course, by the eighties black artists were regularly recording tunes that could be heard on the radio and in the church.[10] Although not a product of the Pentecostal church, Aretha Franklin is one of a few gospel singers who seemed to effortlessly (and without widespread criticism) produce albums of both secular and sacred music that resulted in platinum recordings. And, presently, Kirk Franklin and Yolanda Adams's gospel songs are regularly played alongside their inspirational recordings on popular radio stations across the United States.[11]

Finally, the nature of performing before large audiences attracts many crossover gospel singers. The thrill and exhilaration that many singers feel after their performances is addictive. For some singers like Patti LaBelle and Shirley Caesar, interaction with the crowd is central to their performances. Others testified to an unusual amount of stress and strife before concerts, but afterward, they would bask in the glow of roaring audiences and overwhelming reviews from both musical critics and peers. As many preachers can relate, the call to preach includes with it the mandate to reach a crowd for Christ. Many musical artists feel equally called to perform or minister to their audiences through verbal dexterity, physical appeal, and gifted voices. Indeed, many of their fans attend their concerts as much to hear them "testify" as well as to listen to them sing.[12] If restricted to the studio, we would hear much less of their music. (Again, considering the unusual case of Aretha Franklin, her pathological fear of flying has not unduly restricted her performing career, except to places overseas where she cannot take her enormous van and entourage.)

When all four parts of the typical Holiness-Pentecostal culture are considered as a whole—the integration of body and soul, the ways that the service connects to the heart, head, and hands, together with songs of freedom and hope in a performative, and at times electrifying atmosphere—it is little wonder that musical artists can so seamlessly "crossover" from the church to the secular stage and studio, and do it so effortlessly and well.[13]

Sam Cooke (January 22, 1931–December 11, 1964)

There was a deep sense of goodness about Sam. His father was a minister, and he obviously had spent a lot of time in church. His first success came at an early age as a gospel singer, and he expanded into R&B and pop. It looked like he was making the right choices in life until he got shot by the night messenger of a motel. You wonder who he had fallen in with.[14]

Sam Cooke's all-too-brief career spanned a breadth of musical genres that few musicians could match—from gospel to R&B, soul, and pop. Cooke's musical career was known not just for his "crossover" appeal but also for the cross-racial appeal his music had on white singers and audiences. Few black song writers (with the possible exception of Richard Penniman) have been imitated as much or as long as Cooke. From singers as diverse as Art Garfunkel to Kanye West, Cooke's songs remain of international scope and acclaim.

Sam was born in segregated Mississippi in 1931 to Reverend Charles Cook and his wife, Annie Mae. (Cook later added an "e" to his name for some originality.) He was one of seven children initially raised in the Deep South, but like many other black families in the World War II era, the family migrated North for greater economic opportunity. Chicago was one of those economic epicenters for both black and white itinerant workers. His father moved from the Baptist church in Mississippi to pastor a Holiness church called Christ

Temple in Chicago Heights. The depth of Rev. Cook's preaching and appeal soon "filled the church up."[15] Young Sam's life was firmly rooted in the church with services that spread from Sunday morning and night to midweek prayer service, calling rounds, and youth fellowship.

To financially support for his family of nine, Cooke's father took a job at Reynolds Metal Plant. As one church member summed up, "They lived in a slum neighborhood, but, Reverend soon held a union position at the plant. The children had clothes, food and a roof over their heads. He could have done better if he had been a crook. But he just wasn't."[16]

Cooke was unusually attractive and retained his southern manners and charms. He always used the honorifics "sir" and "ma'am" when talking to his elders—a habit that would endear him to his father's church members and neighbors. Both his father and mother doted on Sam, and he clearly had a special place in his mother's heart. At one point, she later recounted, "he was sweet and thoughtful, always doing things for me. Whenever he made any money, he would come and offer it to me before spending a penny."[17]

By 1942 Sam was baptized, began to sing in church, and started piano lessons so that he could assist his father in church. During this time in Chicago, the Holiness movement was taking hold in both white and black neighborhoods of the city. In the African American section of Chicago, C. H. Mason's Church of God in Christ was growing even faster than Moody Memorial Church led by the immensely popular holiness preacher and author Alan Redpath.

During the summers, Rev. Cook's popularity included a short stint as a traveling evangelist. His children—all of whom could provide for the requisite singing that warmed up each congregation—traveled with him. His wife brought along their food and cooked for her own family as well as the families with whom they stayed. It was a lucrative, part-time itinerant career, and these revivals marked the start of Sam Cooke's gospel career.[18]

At the age of nineteen, Sam joined the Soul Stirrers, one of the more popular male gospel groups in Chicago. For Sam, some of the memorable events were trips to Detroit at the burgeoning New Bethel Church, led by an ambitious and charismatic Baptist minister, C. L. Franklin. It was at this church that the pastor's young daughter, Aretha Franklin, heard Cooke and his group sing, and that church became one of the major "stops" on the gospel music circuit. Though heavily influenced by the piano chording style of James Cleveland and the throaty swoops of Clara Ward, it was Cooke who, Franklin claimed, would eventually inspire her to crossover into secular music and sign with Columbia Records by 1961.[19]

The critical key to Sam and Aretha's crossover success was the wholehearted support of their fathers. This was no small feat as both men were well-known preachers in the Midwest African American community, and C. L. Franklin's reputation eventually spread nationwide among African Americans. When their children (who had obediently performed in their churches for years), signed recording contracts, both Rev. Cook and Rev. Franklin felt that Sam and Aretha could sing professionally and be rewarded financially. Rev. Cook's reaction to his son's recording contract is rather apt: "Man, anytime you got to move up higher, move up. . . . The man's making a living. He ain't singing to save souls!"[20] While Aretha's father's thoughts were more muted, he kept a tight hold on his daughter's career until she switched labels in the 1960s.

For some Holiness folks, Rev. Cook's quotes seem rather cynical. In the 1950s, the idea that a Holiness gospel singer could crossover and remain sanctified was tough to defend to the faithful. But the compelling rationale behind that statement got to the heart of the economic dilemma facing black men since slavery. After working two jobs, Rev. Cook knew more than most that a black man needed to have an extraordinary "break" to earn an upper- or even middle-class lifestyle *legally*. The financial possibilities for his son's future appear to have given way to his concerns over his sanctification. Since the Franklins were Baptists, the idea of Aretha crossing over and remaining true to her gospel calling, while difficult for some Baptists, was influenced by the prejudicial lenses of her legendary father. In addition, Aretha has continued to make gospel recordings during her long and storied career. Indeed, her gospel album, *One Lord, One Faith, One Baptism* (recorded in her father's church and with one of his sermons included) is one of her best-loved recordings.[21]

Some within the gospel industry were hurt by Cooke's crossover. Marion Williams recalled, "it hurt my heart when Sam crossed-over," and Albertina Walker added, "for him to walk off and go with the rhythm and blues, rock and roll and whatever you want to call it, it really showed a bad reflection on the gospel singer."[22] In many ways, Cooke paved the way for Franklin and others in the ensuing decades to cross over with less criticism from folks in the gospel circuit. However, both Williams and Walker admitted that he remained "beloved" in the gospel community until his death.

In 1957 Cooke signed with Keen Records and released one of his biggest hits, "You Send Me," which spent six weeks at number one on the Billboard R&B charts. The song also had mainstream appeal, spending three weeks on the pop charts as well. Before his death in 1964, Cooke had focused on singles and had twenty-nine Top 40 hits on the pop charts and even more on the R&B charts. His most critically acclaimed album, *Ain't That Good News*, was released shortly before his death.[23]

Cooke's personal life, however, was stormy. Married twice, and with several children in and out of wedlock, he could not remain faithful to either wife during their marriages. His attraction to the opposite sex was magnetic, lustful, and addictive. By the time he began touring for a majority of the year, Cooke no longer performed in churches nor did he attend church very much while on the road. However, the pull of his roots was never far from his thoughts even when performing secular music. His biographer, Daniel Wolff, describes the dualism in his voice while performing both gospel and R&B:

> The R&B form is straight gospel: the little bits of advice between numbers, the handkerchiefs, the chorded segues from tune to tune so the mood continues to build. But the content is secular: that "good loving" which, years later, Marvin Gaye would call "something like sanctified." Raw-voiced, interspersing his gospel laugh, repeating and bending phrases, Cooke does a version of "Somebody Have Mercy" that calls up the healing power of sex, maybe even love.[24]

Michael Eric Dyson's evaluation of the dualism is just as stark when he asserts that the church failed to resolve Cooke's sexual complexities:

> Cooke's gladness and grief gained a hearing that no secular arena could provide. There the passionate and paradoxical mixture of protest and praise in "Any Day Now" and "A Change is Gonna Come" was immediately understood. There Cooke's valiant attempt to confront the evils of the world might have generated a theology worthy of his struggle. But the gospel world failed him by telling him that leaving gospel music meant leaving God. Bumps Blackwell, who helped Cooke with his first secular hits, captures the moral contradictions of the anti-pop sentiment in gospel when he declared that preachers "say if you sing a pop song . . . you can't be religious. Preachers can be homosexuals; they can drink whiskey; they can do all kind of sinful things, but they can't sing a pop song." The gospel world's confusion on this point drove Cooke away, and denied him spiritual succor.[25]

While it is clear that Cooke's gospel roots were never far from him in his performances, he never reconciled his "backslidden" state with what he knew about Holiness doctrine. Because Cooke gave few interviews on his spiritual life and left nothing written on the subject, scholars can only conjecture about his spiritual state. He left only a tragic footnote when he was found dead in a Los Angeles motel in December 1964. The exact circumstances surrounding his death are still uncertain, but it is clear that he was visiting a prostitute and was found with few clothes on in a pool of blood. The motel manager, Bertha Franklin, claimed she shot him in self defense after he lunged for her.

In her book, *Rage to Survive*, Etta James claimed she viewed Cooke's body in the funeral home and saw he had been beaten so badly that his head was nearly separated from his shoulders. The saddest racial commentary on his postmortem was that even though he was an international musical figure, the Los Angeles police force clearly botched the investigation because of their apparent blatant disinterest in solving the case.[26]

Donny Hathaway (October 1, 1945–January 13, 1979)

It has taken me so many years to accept the fact that somebody who was so much a part of my breath in terms of music, somebody who was that close to me, could be gone. It seems that the music should have saved him. Could have saved him. Probably would have saved him if he had been able to be as involved with it as he wanted to be. . . . Donny wasn't able to because he lost contact with himself, with his own spirit.[27]

Donny Hathaway was the son of Drusella Huntley. He was born in Chicago in 1945 near the end of World War II. When it was clear that his mother could not raise him, Donny was sent to live with his grandmother, Martha Crumwell, a well-known paraplegic gospel singer in St. Louis. Hathaway began singing in his grandmother's Holiness church, and at the young age of three he was labeled the "Nation's Youngest Gospel Singer."[28] Not only did he have a gifted voice but was also a prodigy at the piano. Eventually, his talent at the piano earned him a fine arts scholarship to Howard University in 1964.

Religious music was my first influence and we played around a lot, with some of the very popular gospel groups. But eventually my grandmother stopped traveling and she just stayed around the church. I was at high school in St. Louis, Missouri, and from there I got a scholarship to Howard University in Washington, D.C. But it was my grandmother who got me started and I guess you could say I've been in music all my life.[29]

Educated in the rich gospel traditions by his grandmother, Hathaway combined jazz, classical, gospel, and blues into his arrangements to engineer a complex and intricate sound that has stood the test of time. But it is clear from the few interviews and recordings that he never left his gospel roots; almost every album included at least one classic gospel recording.

While still at Howard, he distinguished himself as an outstanding pianist and arranger on recording sessions with Phil Upchurch, Jerry Butler, and Curtis Mayfield, the one who assisted in moving his career forward with his contacts at Atlantic Records. Mayfield recalls:

> This fella you could just talk to him over the phone and play him a piece of music and he could call out every chord and every movement and where the fifth was and them augmented and tell you what key it was in. . . . He had a lot of learning in him, but, he was instilled with a lot of depth of the religious feeling of black music.[30]

It was at Howard University that Donny had to come to terms with the idea of crossing over from his roots in gospel to jazz, soul, and pop. His college roommate, Leroy Hutson, described Hathaway as being "overwhelmed" at the choices his talent afforded him: "He eventually found himself living at so fast a pace, he couldn't really handle it. The contrast between his religious upbringing and what he found in DC and the record business was something he never came to terms with."[31]

Another factor that led to Hathaway's instability was his growing mental illness. Depression was never far from his door, and he also began showing signs of a much more serious mental illness—schizophrenia—which would manifest itself later in the studio and on the road.

Roberta Flack, his college friend and later recording partner, reflected on his fusion of gospel music with his new found penchant for the secular. After his first big hit, "Everything is Everything," Hathaway began recording with her, and together they performed some of the major hits of the early seventies including "Where is the Love," "The Closer I Get To You," and "You Are My Heaven." But it was the integration of his gospel background that amazed his colleagues. Flack comments:

> One of my favorite tracks is "Come Little Children." It's basically a call 'n' holler song, like the slaves in the fields would sing, and yet Donny made it 5/4—not a rhythm you'd associate with Afro-Americans at all. He would combine the church and the secular like nobody else. I was just glad the record company didn't make him sit on top of some "rose garden" strings; like they did to Sam Cooke. . . . There was no end to what he would try. We had learned about writing a tone poem as the opening to a piece of

music at college—but black people was [sic] not supposed to do that in their own music. So, in "I Love the Lord (He Heard my Cry)," he put it right there at the opening of the album, as the first track. He couldn't be contained.[32]

In many ways, Flack's observation that "he could not be contained," became the quixotic and complex theme of Hathaway's personal life. Hathaway met and married his college sweetheart, Eulaulah Donyll, and had two daughters, Lalah and Kenya. It was Eulaulah who discovered the depths of Hathaway's mental illness and had him hospitalized in 1973, when he was diagnosed as being paranoid schizophrenic. He was subsequently hospitalized several more times before his death in 1979. Toward the end, he stopped taking his medication. Flack noted: "he would be talking to us in one voice and then answering himself in another."[33] Tragically, he either jumped or fell out of a high-rise window and was killed at the Essex Hotel in New York on January 13, 1979. The coroner ruled it a suicide; his family believed he fell off the ledge accidentally.

Many of Hathaway's recordings, like those of other popular black musicians, dealt with the daily realities of ghetto life. It was in his recordings about this life that he wove in the historic spiritual resilience of black people's faith in a God who could enable them to look beyond the miseries of life. For example, in "Thank you Master for My Soul," which features one of the most brilliant jazz piano solos in R&B history, Hathaway wails: "Oh you didn't have to hear my groanin', but you kept me. . . ." "Thank you Master" is a testament to Hathaway's ultimate faith in an interventionist God.[34]

While it was evident that Hathaway did not find much solace from his mental illness in the church, it was equally clear that his faith in God permeated his music. During this same time period, Marvin Gaye was another emerging artist whose struggles with mental illness and holiness background mirrored Hathaway's.

Marvin Gaye (April 2, 1939–April 1, 1984)

I still remember when I would go by Marvin's house and he was working on it [*What's Going On*], he would say, "Smoke, this album is being written by God, and I'm just the instrument that he is writing it through."[35]

Marvin Gaye was born in 1939 to Marvin Gay Sr., and Alberta Cooper in Washington, D.C., where his father was a minister at a Pentecostal church called the House of God.[36] Marvin Gay Sr., belonged to a very small sect of black Pentecostals who believed in a combination of Orthodox Judaism with Pentecostalism. They worshipped on Saturdays, held to certain Old Testament dietary laws, advocated strict separation from the world, and celebrated the Passover but not Christmas. But they also believed in speaking in tongues and divine healing—much like other Pentecostal churches. However, the House of God also believed in teaching both the Old and New Testament covenants as an avenue toward sanctification. Gaye related to a journalist in 1974 that the combination of the rituals made the congregation and himself "feel special."[37]

By adolescence, Marvin had honed his skills on the piano and drums well enough to enter talent shows in junior high school. By high school he formed a band called the DC Tones that sang what was then called *doo-wop* and *boogie woogie* music. Rev. Gay was especially displeased over his son's early crossover into secular music and never approved of his early career. He was particularly harsh on Marvin, as he realized that he not only had a free spirit on his hands, but that his son was a more charismatic and talented man than himself.

Besides the frequent beatings from his father (who was a cross-dresser with very effeminate manners), his father's brother (Uncle Howard) raped Marvin when the boy was fifteen years old. Between the beatings of his father and the forced rape by his uncle, Marvin's self-image was at continual low ebb for some very valid psychological reasons. Later on in his life, due to these early horrific encounters, Marvin suffered from depression, bipolar disorder and paranoia—though the paranoia could have been possibly due to his addiction to cocaine and long-term sexual fears. These horrific acts can be viewed as possessing a stronger impact on their fears and insecurities than their struggle over their religious upbringings.[38] By the time Marvin Jr. dropped out of high school at the age of seventeen to join the Air Force, he had accumulated some very deep psychological and emotional scars, and witnessed firsthand the hypocrisy of the church in the form of his own father.

Gaye's military career lasted about a year since he had as much trouble with male authority as he had had at home and, after faking mental illness, was honorably discharged. Not too long after his arrival back in D.C., Gaye reorganized the DC Tones. They were unable to produce a hit, so Marvin moved to Chicago and joined a group called the Moonglows. Here Marvin experienced his first taste of freedom—without the supervisory capacities of his father or the military.

Like Sam Cooke, with his tall, sensual good looks Marvin was especially attractive to the opposite sex. Although both men married relatively young, neither man was able to remain faithful to any woman over an extended period of time. The irony in Marvin's case is that his first wife was also the sister of his manager, the Motown mogul, Barry Gordy. Even within this tight family sphere tied together by matrimony and career, it had no permanent hold on Marvin's life.[39]

Gaye scored his first single hit, "Stubborn Kind of Fella," in September 1962. In 1963 he followed up with several others including "Hitch Hike," "Pride and Joy," "Can I Get a Witness" (an obvious play on the "call and response" of his church upbringing), "You are a Wonderful One," and "How Sweet it is to be Loved by You." Then, in the sixties, several collaborations with Martha and the Vandellas, Smokey Robinson, the Supremes, and the best of Motown led to a particularly successful partnering duet with Tammi Terrell, much like the Hathaway/Flack duo that would come later. After several big hits like "Ain't No Mountain High Enough" and "Your Precious Love," Gaye and Terrell became the most successful duet in Motown history. Tragically, while playing at Hampton University in Virginia, Terrell collapsed in Gaye's arms and was later diagnosed with a terminal brain tumor. She died three years later, sending Gaye into a clinical depression.

After dealing with the loss, Gaye returned to the studio and produced one of his greatest and most controversial albums: *What's Going On*. Many music critics point to the release of this album as the signal event of Gaye's great interracial and crossover appeal that placed him directly in league with many of the white popular musical artists of his era. The songs on this album centered on the rawness of urban life in lyrics such as "Makes Me Wanna Holler" and concern for the ecology in "Mercy, Mercy, Me," placed him at the apex with other performers with a social and political conscience. Ironically, while Gaye initially fought Barry Gordy over the release of this album because of Gordy's concern over the lack of record sales, it earned Gaye the title of "Prince of Soul."

With the release of his 1973 album, *Let's Get It On*, Gaye began an open dialogue with his friends and musical critics over the dual and conflicting nature of his gospel background and his libidinous sexuality. By this time, Gaye was seeing other women and eventually divorced Anna for a woman seventeen years younger, Janis Hunter. Although he loved both women until his death, he could not remain faithful to either one of them for any extended period of time.

Martha Reeves, lead singer of the Vandellas, noted a very *quixotic* spirituality about Marvin:

Marvin was very spiritual. You knew when you heard him sing, that his father or somebody had been a minister, or that he would soon be one. Because he always had the Lord in the forefront of everything he delivered or anything he sang. I'm not sure a lot of people realized how sensual and how sensitive Marvin Gaye was as a person. But I recognized his spirituality and always respected him as a child of God on a mission. Some of his songs indicate that. I'm not just talking from what I don't know. He always had Jesus or God in his lyrics. And he said "Lord have mercy" so beautifully he had girls screaming.[40]

Gaye's abilities to improvise music, play the piano by ear, and his mastery over several instruments were traditionally nurtured by other gifted performers in the church. He also admitted to having sensitivity to the Spirit since he was a youngster and attempted to utilize it in all of his music. And by his own admittance, his early church experiences were never far from his mind, his recordings, or his performances.[41]

Even Gaye's father admitted that "he had a quicker grasp of Scripture" and at times "sounded like a grown man, a minister."[42] Although Gaye never attended church regularly after he joined the Air Force, he did not neglect his spiritual roots through his musical writings and performances. It was these roots that also tormented him as he attempted to find a via media or an avenue toward crossing over into the erotic that would allow him his earthly "right" to the sexual freedom and expression that he sang with such spiritual gusto.

Gaye was caught up in two problematic dimensions of his background: his church and his father. Regarding his church background, Gaye was constantly looking for either a détente with or an avenue toward a sanctified sexuality. As he struggled between his legalistic background and his hedonistic lifestyle on the road, Gaye sought to find a way to integrate his almost insatiable need for sex with his equally emotional need for God. In essence, he was looking for an honest and transparent spiritual life that acknowledged the lust of the flesh with the need for forgiveness. What Gaye sought was not possible in a sanctified Pentecostal church. In addition, Gaye, like many sons of preachers, felt both an attraction for and displeasure in his father's ministry and career over the lack of a genuine sanctification in his father. Gaye knew that ultimately his life would be judged not just by the church members and his father but also his fan base and the musical critics and producers. His unresolved spiritual problem was with (what he viewed as) hypocritical attitudes in both the church and his father toward himself and his music.

Gaye sought to make the church sanctuary and the dance floor one and the same in his song, "Praise," an up-tempo song based on percussions and bass. On "Life is for Learning," he commented that the "Devil has his special place to make songs for sinners while God will turn it around and makes songs for winners." Later on Gaye would wax eloquent on his war with "the flesh, this stupid flesh." No one black male singer, outside of the contemporary singer R. Kelly, has so openly and honestly dealt with both his sexuality and his spirituality in such raw terms. In fact, Dyson calls upon the black church to come to terms with a spirituality or theology, which encompasses the erotic for tortured souls like Gaye and Kelly.[43]

Another of Gaye's biographers, David Ritz, believed like Dyson, that in *What's Going On*, Gaye was openly wrestling with his Pentecostal roots:

> The album may be viewed as the positive public expression of Marvin's religious beliefs: that God is love, that justice should prevail, and that human beings should treat each other with respect. Marvin's Pentecostal church roots and Christian ethics fueled his loving critique of the world. But Marvin's learning in the world allowed him to return the favor: his experience beyond the church doors allowed him to reshape his religious beliefs. *What's Going On* was outward looking: it cast a searching spiritual eye on social relations. *Let's Get it On* was inward looking; it gathered data from the erotic sensibility that had been repressed in his religious life. If Marvin delivered perceptive analyses of social injustice and political failure on *What's Going On*, he was equally prophetic in rejecting the punitive aspects of his Pentecostal bearing. But he vividly brought to life its insistence on the spiritual character of sexual union…his art elicited a powerful desire to wed feeling and flesh.[44]

Here again, we see Gaye wrestling both with the teachings of his church background that eschewed any acknowledgement of the "flesh" (which would lead to a back-slidden condition) and with his desire to "feed the flesh" as he blatantly maintained in the lyrics of "Sexual Healing." Ritz concludes:

> Part of Marvin was too sophisticated to subscribe to the tenets of his father's Pentecostal church, but another part—was never able to shake off those notions. Spiritually, *In Our Life Time* represents the best of his old-time religion, the part of Pentecostal preaching that insists on unrelenting praise, on the expression of gratitude as a way of coping with a worrisome world.[45]

Gaye sought a merger of the "lust of the flesh" with the pure desire of the heart in an unfettered and nondogmatic search for complete love.

By the late seventies, Gaye's two failed marriages, combined with his continuing drug use and signs of growing mental illness, led to an impotent career.[46] He crossed the globe from Hawaii, London, and then back to the States, only to believe even more deeply that he had no one that loved him for himself. When asked if he ever thought of going into therapy, Gaye offered a classic refrain among many men:

> "Are you kidding?" he answered with a laugh. "What am I going to tell a stranger? And what's a stranger going to tell me? Never! Besides, the cure is already inside us. All we have to do is bring it out. All answers are contained within. God is within each of us. If we stop long enough to listen to the rhythm of our heartbeat, that's the rhythm of God's voice. After leaving Washington, I've never regularly attended church, but neither did I ever leave the church. The church never left my heart. I had religion, so why did I need head doctors? No, I didn't need to go to cocktail parties and talk about psychoanalysis; I didn't need no shrink. It was a matter of changing styles."[47]

By 1984 Gaye was living in the same house he had bought for his parents in California a few years previously. In the morning of April 1, one day before his forty-fifth birthday, Gaye had a violent argument with his father (both men had been consuming intoxicating substances, vodka for Marvin Sr., and cocaine for Marvin Jr.), and under the influence of these lethal combinations, Gay Sr. shot and killed his son. The courts found Gay Sr. guilty of manslaughter, and he served six years in prison before his death in 1998. Later, Gaye's brother, Frankie, who held the dying Marvin in his arms, revealed that as he was dying, his brother admitted that he wanted his father to kill him because he could not do it himself.[48]

The extent of his true musical genius is still being mined from the frequent writings about Gaye. His contributions to both Motown and soul music—from the sixties to the present, are still appreciated and lauded by fans of all ages and races. While his spiritual cry for wholeness in his personal life was elusive, Gaye's ability to reach an audience on a deep emotional level is unparalleled in the immediate past or present musical history.

Conclusion

> That's what the great men like the Marvin Gayes, and the Donny Hathaways, the Michael Jacksons [have in common] . . . we believe in letting people know about our struggle.[49]

Considering the role that the black Holiness-Pentecostal church had on each of these men is an enormous task, but there are some similarities that are inescapable. It is clear that their musical abilities, talents, and gifting were honed and crafted by their early church experiences—their families considered that their main purpose for singing and playing music was to perform and contribute to the worship services of their respective churches. Two men, Cooke and Gaye, had fathers who were ministers and, therefore, both sons had a familial responsibility to the church. However, Hathaway's dedication was also animated by the fact that his grandmother was a well-known and dedicated gospel singer whose influence in Hathaway's life was immeasurable.

While none of these men attended church on a regular basis after their teenage years, neither did they use their church backgrounds as a scapegoat for their moral failures. Each one wrote and recorded his own inspirational songs and would perform with great relish all the gospel standards of their day—much to the delight of their audiences. Their clear reverence for gospel music remained unfettered and fiercely personal.

The act of crossing over, in many ways, occurred before any record contract. All three men had abandoned the formal hold the church held on them before they turned professional and thus were prepared to make a way for themselves in the secular world. None had any illusions their ambitions and career goals could be fulfilled in the church. Also, being members of Holiness-Pentecostal churches made it almost impossible to simultaneously integrate secular and gospel careers. In some ways, this makes inspirational singers who currently and effortlessly cross back and forth between Saturday nightclub performances and Sunday morning services possible.

In terms of musical artistry, all three were brilliant at improvisation and played more than one instrument by ear. Hathaway stands as perhaps the most truly gifted overall musician due to his formal training. But it is clearly evident that the church nurtured all their gifts and paved the way for their future secular success.

Still, it is difficult to accurately assess the full measure of the impact of black Pentecostalism on the lives of these three troubled men. Hathaway's mental illness showed every sign of being genetic. He had been under psychiatric care long before his apparent suicide. In Cooke, we see evidence of a pathological egoism that isolated him from others and contributed to his habitual drinking, philandering, and violent temper. He was clearly unstable before his death. Gaye's psychological condition was inflamed by a physically and emotionally abusive father along with a familial rape in his adolescent years. These factors were certainly a major dynamic behind his drug and sexual addictions. Consequently, one can only surmise the total impact the church might have had on their lives (if they had chosen to remain active), given these collective challenges to their mental health.[50]

Finally, in examining their careers through the previously framed Pentecostal lenses of the integration of body and soul; heart, hands, head; songs based on freedom and hope; and performative orientation, we find that all three artists combined music that was based on black liberation and hope within a very particularistic performance orientation. All three men were basically introverted and had to learn to become freer in their physical expressions on stage. However, once they shaped and honed their stage performances, all three were unique in their individual performances.

Clearly these three men wrote and performed songs that were based on hope and freedom. In that vein, Cooke and Gaye were musical prophets with their respective renditions of Cooke's "A Change is Going to Come" and Gaye's "What's Goin' On?"—both songs represented the long struggle for civil rights and black liberation that was manifestly evident in their lyrics. From the early sixties to the eighties, these men represented a community that held equally longed-for idealized hopes of full emancipation with long realized civil rights.

Marvin Gaye perhaps best represents the ideal of body and soul with a very popular form of physical performance, dramatically highlighted by the genesis of music videos. Videos were not as widely used or as sophisticated during the eighties when Gaye took full advantage of that particular medium, and thus he gained a wider fan base than either his predecessors. Gaye's music videos are popular even today while one sees little footage of either Cooke's or Hathaway's performances.

However, it was the musical adaptability and natural talent of Donny Hathaway that appealed to the head, heart, and hands. Within the context of musical critics and knowledgeable audiences, Hathaway was the most versatile musician and arranger in contrast to either Cooke or Gaye. Hathaway was also able to sing gospel with more passion and depth of experience than the other two as well. Neither Gaye nor Cooke was musically mentored in the church by a relative and neither had the gospel reputation at such a young age as Hathaway.

What all three men had in *fateful* commonality was the struggle they took on with the world, the flesh, and the Devil by signing professional secular musical contracts within a church background, which promised ultimate victory over all three if they refused to compromise. In the end, by accepting this compromise, they forfeited their spiritual peace of mind.

With regard to the shifting discourse on "crossing over" from their rather deep gospel roots to the secular stage, these men, in many ways, can be viewed as pioneers of this ever-increasing phenomenon across the twentieth century. This phenomenon was not relegated only to the black community: White entertainers such as Jerry Lee Lewis and Dolly Parton had deep roots in country Pentecostal churches where the men and women in their families held pastoral positions. And by the turn of the century, most producers assumed that many of their potentially successful artists honed and crafted their musical skills in the church. While the debate between the sanctified branches of the Holiness-Pentecostal churches and scholars such as Michael Eric Dyson over the theological legitimacy of such musical transference continues to this day, the number of musicians from sanctified backgrounds who continue to cross over from the music of heavenly bliss to earthly desire shows no signs of abating.

NOTES TO CHAPTER 7

1. While both men attempted to return to gospel music for very brief periods, neither men believed that a fully sanctified Pentecostal member could "successfully" cross over and remain either sanctified or saved. Jerry Lee Lewis commented to a *Rolling Stone* reporter when asked: "Why would playing rock and roll damn you to hell?" Lewis replied, "I can't picture Jesus Christ doin' a lotta shakin'" (Robert Palmer, "The Devil and Jerry Lee Lewis," *Rolling Stone* [December 13, 1979]: 57–61). Penniman's definitive biography includes a similar question about the dual career of Pat Boone with the following quote from Lil' Richard: "I like Pat Boone as a friend, but he's trying to serve two masters. Pat believes you can go to Las Vegas and do your thing, then preach on Sunday. I don't believe we can do that. I can never see myself going back to rock and roll" (Charles White, *The Life and Times of Little Richard: The Authorized Biography* [London: Omnibus Press, 2003], 221.

2. The Reverend Dr. Michael Eric Dyson is both an ordained Baptist minister and professor of sociology at Georgetown University.

3. Michael Eric Dyson, *Mercy, Mercy, Me: The Art, Loves and Demons of Marvin Gaye* (New York: Civitas Books, 2004). Dyson and others have challenged "the black church" to find ways to develop a theology of black sexuality that "freely embraces our God-given sexual gifts" (228). As Dyson points out, the attraction of black Holiness-Pentecostal services are the degree to which they differ from the more staid forms of worship in non-Pentecostal churches since so much of their services are dedicated toward integrating the physical with the spirit that results in their whole bodies and souls belonging to the Lord. While Dyson views such services through erotic and sexually charged lenses, the Holiness-Pentecostal churches eschew any idea that their services are deliberately erotic or can or should be evaluated from that perspective. As a result, Dyson's call for a theology of the erotic in these churches has received little response.

4. Dyson, "Soul Stirrer: The Gospel Sounds of Sam Cooke" (a review of Daniel Wolff's *You Send Me: The Life and Times of Sam Cooke* [New York: Morrow, 1995]), in *Christian Century* 112.18 (May 24, 1995): 18. Dyson believes that the confluence of the ethos of black

Pentecostalism, the great migration of southern blacks to urban areas, and the civil rights movement combined to explain the unusual popularity of Sam Cooke.

5. See Teresa Reed, *The Holy Profane: Religion in Black Popular Music* (Lexington: University of Kentucky Press, 2003), 104–6.

6. Alphonso Simpson Jr., "A Thin Line between Saturday Night and Sunday Morning: The Secularization of Sacred Song in the African American Religious Culture" (unpublished paper, 2006), 4.

7. Eileen Southern, *The Music of Black Americans: A History* (New York: Norton, 1997), 263.

8. Stephen Tucker, "Pentecostalism and Popular Culture in the South: A Study of Four Musicians," *Journal of Popular Culture* 16.3 (March 2004): 68–80.

9. Reed, *Holy Profane*, 106.

10. However, this relatively new phenomenon and détente between black secular and sacred music was not easily negotiated, particularly with "sanctified" black Holiness and Pentecostal churches that maintained a much stricter standard in the choice of music in their church services and the music they approved for their members on secular radio stations. Shirley Caesar's quip is often quoted in such circles: "The only rock and roll I could sing is rocking for Jesus and rolling with Christ." *The Story of Gospel Music*, produced and directed by Wyatt Tee Walker, 1 hour and 30 minutes. BBC, 2005. Digital video disk.

11. Portia Maultsby, "The Impact of Gospel Music on the Secular Music Industry," in Gena Caponi-Tabery, ed., *Signifyin(g), Sanctifyin', and Slam Dunking: A Reader in African-American Expressive Culture* (Amherst: University of Massachusetts Press, 1999), 174.

12. Indeed, one of the more moving funerals of this decade was the memorial service of R&B legend Luther Van Dross at the Riverside Church in New York a few years ago where singers Patti LaBelle, Aretha Franklin, and others gave stirring testimonies along with their musical tributes to this extraordinary singer. In many ways the formal eulogy was anticlimactic. See: www.youtube.com for scenes from the Van Dross service that was taped in New York.

13. Dyson, *Mercy, Mercy, Me*, 18. Again, Dyson believes that Cooke's career was fundamentally about "crossing over" from gospel to secular, from segregation to integration, and to making it on equal terms with other white entertainers who played at the Copa or in Las Vegas. In a sense, this extensive crossing over separates Cooke from Hathaway or Gaye since neither artist attempted to cross over racially as much as Cooke had in his career. Gaye has found more interracial appeal since his death in 1984.

14. Art Garfunkel, "Rolling Stone Interview: The Immortals: The Greatest Artists of All Time: Sam Cooke," *Rolling Stone* 946, April 14, 2004. 16.

15. Wolff, *You Send Me*, 27.

16. Ibid., 29.

17. Annie Mae Cook, cited in Wolff, *You Send Me*, 29.

18. Anthony Appiah and Henry Louis Gates Jr., eds., *Arts and Letters: An A–Z Reference of Writers, Musicians, and Artists of the African American Experience* (London: Running Press, 2005), 146.

19. In a later interview, Aretha Franklin intimated that it was more than merely his music that inspired her: "[H]e wore down a whole lot of ladies when he got married. He wore me down. I loved him. I just loved him. That man could mess up a whole roomful of women" (Wolff, *You Send Me*, 233).

20. Wolff, *You Send Me*, 66.

21. It should be noted that most Baptist groups do not believe in *entire* sanctification like many Holiness denominations. Also, Baptists believe strongly in soul competency and that anyone of their members must clear their conscience with God before they give an account to their church.

22. Cited in Wolff, *You Send Me*, 179.

23. See the Sam Cooke discography at www.wikipedia.org/wiki/Sam_Cooke.

24. Wolff, *You Send Me*, 263.

25. Dyson, "The Soul Stirrer," 573.

26. Etta James, with David Ritz, *Rage to Survive: The Etta James Story* (New York: DaCapo Press, 2003), 151.

27. Susan Taylor, "An Intimate Talk with Roberta," *Essence* 19.10, February 1989, 4.

28. C. N. Harold, "Donny Hathaway: Celebrating the Spirit and the Soul," *All About Jazz,* January 28, 2007, 3.

29. Richard Williams, "Donny—One of the New Breed," *Melody Maker,* August 7, 1971, 15.

30. Harold, "Donny Hathaway," 2.

31. Leroy Hutson, as commented in Chris Wells, "Pop: His Soul Goes Groovin On," *Independent* (London), February 26, 1999, 12.

32. Roberta Flack, cited in Wells, "Pop: His Soul Goes Groovin' On," 12.

33. Wells, "Pop: His Soul Goes Groovin' On," 12.

34. Harold, "Donny Hathaway," 3.

35. Smokey Robinson, "Marvin Gaye: The Greatest Artists of All Time," *Rolling Stone Special Issue*, April 15, 2004, 18.

36. Gay added the "e" ending to his name after he turned legal age in order to quell jokes about his sexuality, to separate himself from his father, and to imitate Sam Cooke; see Dyson, *Mercy, Mercy, Me*, 6.

37. Tim Cahill, "The Spirit, the Flesh and Marvin Gaye," *Rolling Stone*, April 11, 1974, 41.

38. Gerald Posner, *Motown: Music, Money, Sex and Power* (New York: Random House, 2002).

39. Barry Gordy, *To Be Loved: The Music, the Magic and the Memories of Motown* (New York: Warner Books, 1994).

40. Martha Reeves, cited in Dyson, *Mercy, Mercy Me*, 104.

41. Dyson, *Mercy, Mercy Me*, 125.

42. Rev. Gay, cited in Dyson, *Mercy, Mercy Me*, 106. It is safe to conclude that Marvin believed there was a difference between his religious roots in Pentecostalism and his newfound spirituality, which was tentative. He was hesitant to make dogmatic statements regarding one's religious behaviors.

43. Graham Cray, "Through Popular Music: Wholly Holy!" in Jeremy Begbie, ed., *Beholding The Glory: Incarnation through the Arts* (Grand Rapids, Mich.: Baker Books, 2000), 123–24.

44. David Ritz, *Divided Soul: The life of Marvin Gaye* (New York: Capo Press, 1991), 137–38.

45. Ibid., 283.

46. Ironically, it was in 1983 that Gaye delivered his most controversial and last hit before his death, *Sexual Healing*, which secured his status as a sexual icon.

47. Dyson, *Mercy, Mercy, Me*, 221.

48. Ibid., 226.

49. R. Kelly, cited in Dyson, *Mercy, Mercy, Me*, 248.

50. The African American psychologist Alexandra Jackson writes that Gaye's mental condition was a classic case of a "dysphoric life"—characterized by depression, anxiety, and restlessness rising from the physical abuse of his father. She summarizes: "God was always in one of Marvin's corners and the Devil was on the other." Alexandra Jackson, review of the DVD, *What's Going On: The Life and Death of Marvin Gaye* (May 14, 2008), available at http://blogcritics.org/video/article/dvd-review-whats-going-on-the/ (last accessed November 30, 2009).

III

Prophetic Ethics

The ongoing struggle for black Pentecostals to find a prophetic, public voice has been largely ignored by most scholars of the movement. Indeed, the reductionist assumption that black Pentecostalism is largely an ecstatic, other worldly escape from social reality has precluded serious consideration of the wealth of ethical discourse found among black Pentecostal scholars and even church leaders. Indeed, discussions of the prophetic and social witness of Afro-Pentecostalism are often obscured by presuming that such is either absent or can be easily subsumed (although often marginalized) within categories of the black church tradition. The two essays in this section provide a glimpse into the thought of two ethicists formed both by the experience of blackness within American society and involvement in the African American Holiness-Pentecostal community. Both essays provide sharp self-critique of ethical shortcomings of some factions of Pentecostal-Charismatic culture both within and outside the black church while suggesting a way forward to a more holistic Pentecostal ethic. While in various respects the prophetic stream within Afro-Pentecostalism can be understood as part of the larger black church response to racism, the essays in this section not only unveil common concerns within the black Christianity (Sanders's focus on the prosperity gospel) but also the need for a prophetic Afro-Pentecostal stance vis-à-vis the dominant white Pentecostal traditions (Lovett's autobiographical reflections).

8

Pentecostal Ethics and the Prosperity Gospel

Is There a Prophet in the House?

CHERYL J. SANDERS

Introduction

A dominant theme of modern Pentecostal preaching has been the promotion of the prosperity gospel, which emphasizes God's will for the believer to become wealthy. But how many pastors who nurture their flocks with this message also embrace the social ethical role of the biblical prophets as advocates for the rights of the poor? Many Pentecostal preachers are abandoning the African American struggle against white racism, accepting faith-based government funding for their community development programs with all the strings attached, and buying into the divisive family values discourse crafted by political conservatives to attract the votes of white evangelicals. Are there any signs of a resurgence of prophetic activism among those who are willing to call forth the fires of Pentecost as the struggle for the souls of black folk rages on?

To be sure, there are Pentecostal preachers who do not buy into the prosperity perspective. Instead, they offer prophetic ministries with an emphasis upon activism informed by a keen awareness of social concerns beyond the acquisition and accumulation of wealth. In *Streets of Glory*, a study of black Pentecostal pastors and congregations in Boston, Massachusetts, Omar McRoberts labels as "activist" those churches with food pantries and shelters for survivors of domestic abuse, those that build homes and run welfare-to-work programs, or whose leaders organize marches and protests:

> This understanding of religious activism is partly the legacy of the civil rights movement, during which African-American churches transmitted a powerful normative message about the ability and necessity of religious institutions to work in some way for social change.[1]

McRoberts's book examines the thought of activist Christians who see themselves as called to fight against sin in all its forms, especially social injustice and inequality. Among these Christians are Pentecostals, Charismatics, and Evangelicals, whose religious ethos relies heavily upon the Holy Spirit and the Bible. This ethos fuels liberatory struggle and community development work as well as the priestly and personal functions of congregational ministries.[2]

In his article "Preaching the Spirit: the Liberation of Preaching," William Turner offers a general critique of the theological and ethical shortcomings of Pentecostalism in this regard. He notes that Pentecostals have historically taken a definite posture against elements of culture involving destructive personal morality, but "stopped short of showing the procession of the Spirit in liberative praxis and prophetic witness against structures of oppression."[3] This chapter addresses the ethical, political, and ecclesiological significance of Pentecostal preaching with particular attention to two perceived polarities among Pentecostal preachers: the social gospel and the prosperity gospel.

The Pentecostal Social Gospel

Reflecting on the Holiness roots and precedents of Pentecostal social activism in his recent book *Thy Kingdom Come*, the historian Randall Balmer offers this observation:

> The most effective and vigorous religious movements in American history have identified with the downtrodden and have positioned themselves on the fringes of society rather than at the centers of power. The Methodists of the nineteenth century come to mind, as do the Mormons. In the twentieth century, Pentecostalism, which initially appealed to the lower classes and made room for women and people of color, became perhaps the most significant religious movement of the century. A counterculture identifies with those on the margins.[4]

In my own work, I have devoted considerable attention to the role played by marginalized populations such as the black urban poor in the emergence and formation of the countercultural dimensions of Pentecostal religion.[5] An important but ambiguous expression of this ethos of marginalized counterculturalism is the testimony of being "in the world, but not of it." In "An Introduction to Pentecostalisms," the dean of Pentecostal studies, Walter Hollenweger, laments the loss and denial of the initial revolutionary, pacifist, and political drive of early evangelicalism, including the antislavery movement, female pastors, and noncapitalistic forms of production. Citing Donald Dayton's reprint series "The Higher Christian Life," with a characteristic note of sarcasm, Hollenweger asserts that although "the Holiness and early Pentecostal movement stood at the cradle of all modern pacifist, emancipatory, and feminist movements, Pentecostals and their antagonists, the Evangelicals, are united in forgetting their past."[6] According to Hollenweger, political and social texts were actually purged from the first editions of the works of pioneers of the Holiness movement in order to create the impression in subsequent editions that sanctification is purely a religious and personal experience.

Notwithstanding these desperate efforts to eliminate evidence of the political and social content of the Evangelical, Holiness, and Pentecostal traditions, it remains a matter of record that men and women of great faith and courage took a stand against sin in all its forms, both personal and social. David Daniels includes Holiness preachers in his survey of the political witness of twentieth-century African American Pentecostals.[7] Daniels's list of Pentecostal social activism begins appropriately with the pacifist campaign of Charles Harrison Mason, founding bishop of the Church of God in Christ, during World War I, which Daniels identifies as the first major political activity of Pentecostal African Americans. Lillian Brooks Coffey, the head of the International Women's Department of the Church of God in Christ, spearheaded the passing of a racial justice resolution at the denomination's Women's Convention in 1953. Also in the 1950s, Smallwood Williams of the Bible Way Church, Worldwide, led a legal battle against segregated public schools in Washington, D.C. During the 1960s, Arthur Brazier and Louis Henry Ford were active in the civil rights efforts in Chicago, Ithiel Clemmons was involved in civil rights campaigns in New York, J. O. Patterson Sr. participated in the local civil rights campaign in Memphis, and Charles E. Blake participated in the march from Selma to Montgomery. Herbert Daughtry was one of the founders of black nationalist political groups such as the Black United Front and the African Christian People's Organization. He and Al Sharpton were the main fixtures of protest politics in New York during the post–civil rights era, pursuing a progressive political agenda with a justice emphasis as a means of empowerment and liberation. Another major voice among Pentecostals in New York is James Forbes, a preacher, scholar, and activist who served for many years as pastor of the bellwether of liberal mainline Protestantism, the historic Riverside Church in New York. Forbes has argued for "the theological liberation of the Holy Spirit from the ecclesial arena and the theological acknowledgment of the Holy Spirit within political and economic sectors."[8]

Daniels credits not just my scholarly contributions but those of Robert Franklin as well as significant representations of Pentecostal and Holiness social thought. Franklin, the president of Morehouse College in Atlanta, advocates a prophetic radicalism that embraces the liberation framework and keeps social justice in view as the goal of Christian political activism.[9] In my own work, I substitute an ethics of empowerment for the liberation/ oppression framework, with the aim of fortifying the "sacrificial struggle of empowered individuals who maintain creative partnerships with the oppressed and who identify unambiguously with the best interests of the oppressed group."[10] I helped compile a collection of sermon manuscripts by Holiness and Pentecostal preachers for publication in a recent anthology of African American sermons which offers introductory essays outlining their historical context, homiletical content, and relevance to the broader tradition of African American preaching.[11]

Last, but not least, Clarence Taylor's *Black Religious Intellectuals* includes two essays detailing the contributions of Smallwood Williams and Al Sharpton. Taylor acknowledges that a strong political message advocating racial and social justice was central to Williams's brand of Pentecostalism, as "he urged his fellow clergy to fulfill their 'Christian duty' by becoming advocates for the poor, the racially oppressed, and the downtrodden."[12] He notes that Sharpton "has defiantly confronted the system by using words as his major weapon."[13]

The Prosperity Gospel, Televangelism, and the Impact of Pentecostalism

In 1978 James Tinney, editor of *Spirit*, a journal devoted to African American Pentecostalism, published his own critical analysis of the prosperity gospel in the article "The Prosperity Doctrine: Perverted Economics."[14] Tinney complained that "more money turns over in the Pentecostal churches on any given Sunday than circulates through all the other black businesses during an entire week," but "these churches have little to show for their millions, except devotion to the American ethos of materialism."[15] Some thirty years later a new generation of scholars of African American religion and society are advancing this line of critical inquiry, including Milmon Harrison, Shayne Lee, and Marla Frederick. Their work interrogates the materialistic leanings of Pentecostalism and assesses its impact on the exilic, countercultural identity of the marginalized inhabitants of the urban underbelly of American capitalism, especially African American women. Of particular concern is the seductive, hypnotic influence the televised propagation of the prosperity gospel brings to bear upon African American prophets, preachers, and congregations, effectively threatening to dismantle the biblical mandate to observe and oppose the ongoing systemic manifestations of poverty and disenfranchisement within African American communities. Which gospel, then, do African American Pentecostals preach to the poor? Is the good news that the kingdom of God offers an open invitation for everyone to experience and promote an ever-increasing realm of divine justice, healing, and peace without regard to race, sex, or class? Or is the good news the exhortation for the poor to use the word of faith as a private password to personal affluence that compels endorsement of the dominant culture's disregard of the causes of poverty, exempts the hearers from acknowledging their own history, and transforms their political sensibilities into a mess of conservative pottage?

Milmon Harrison's book, *Righteous Riches: The Word of Faith Movement in Contemporary African American Religion*, describes some of the key organizations and structures associated with this movement, which consists of approximately 2,500 churches, ministries, fellowships and television networks in the United States and in more than sixty nations abroad.[16] He defines this contemporary American religious subculture as one of several new forms of Evangelical, Charismatic Christianity that emerged in the United States after World War II. His overview of the origins of the movement is centered on the contributions of Kenneth Hagin Sr., founder of the Rhema Bible Training Center in Oklahoma, and mentor to Frederick K. Price, Kenneth Copeland, and other popular prosperity televangelists. Harrison employs the sociological methodology of participant observation of "the people in the pews" at the pseudonymous Faith Christian Center in Sacramento, California, to demonstrate how African American believers construct meaning out of the religious doctrine of the prosperity gospel as articulated by the Word of Faith Movement. Without being overtly critical of this movement and its doctrine, Harrison aptly illustrates the creativity and energy believers bring to the task of translating the prosperity message they receive in church into the vernacular of everyday living.

Shayne Lee provides a critical analytical overview of the prosperity gospel preached by T. D. Jakes and others in his refreshingly readable text, *T. D. Jakes: America's New Preacher*.[17] He carefully traces Jakes's ascendancy from poverty and obscurity in West Virginia to prominence and prosperity as pastor of the Potter's House, the prototypical African American Pentecostal megachurch, located in suburban Dallas, Texas. Lee compares Jakes's affinity for fine fashions, immense mansions, luxury automobiles, and private jets, with the black Pentecostals of the early and middle twentieth century "who shunned lavish living as worldliness that brought enmity from God.

Even when Pentecostal pastors began to prosper beyond the socioeconomic echelons of their congregants, their avarice was rarely flaunted or swanked behind the pulpit."[18] He observes that the prosperity gospel has a particular resonance in our culture of materialism, as African American prosperity preachers continue to live like CEOs of Fortune 500 companies while encouraging their members to confess and possess the same financial prosperity. Lee concludes that Jakes offers an American gospel that supports the status quo and sits well with bourgeois democratic American sensibilities.[19]

Marla F. Frederick's text *Between Sundays* is a detailed cultural anthropological study of the lives of black women of faith in rural Halifax County, North Carolina.[20] She takes care to illustrate the impact of televangelism on these women, especially the preaching of Jakes, Juanita Bynum, and Creflo Dollar. Frederick argues persuasively that the black church is "caught" between two distinctive traditions:

> The first tradition . . . reflects the church's more radical history of critiquing political and economic institutions and systems that repress social and economic progress. The second tradition, represented by television ministries, reflects the more conservative integrationist approach to social problems, as it encourages radical changes solely in the individual desiring to advance swiftly in the American mainstream. Between these two polarities resides a black church pulled in different directions by its calling to be both prophetic and priestly in its ministry.[21]

Frederick offers the important insight that the black church is called to be both priestly and prophetic in its ministry because of the history of racism in the United States. In full view of the social and historical complexity of the challenges presented by televangelism, she warns that its totalizing and reductionist tendencies "allow for an easy and immediate articulation and appropriation of individualism, materialism, and a simplistic multiculturalism."[22] Importantly, she identifies a crucial blind spot of American televangelism, namely, the emphasis upon multiculturalism without a systematic critique of racism, creating an illusion of racial progress that precludes discussion of the social forces that perpetuate race-based discrimination.[23]

An enduring conundrum of African American religious discourse has been the prevalence of a vantage point which is both theologically conservative and politically progressive. The theological conservatism of African Americans derives largely from their reliance upon the Bible as a source of comfort, inspiration, empowerment, and insight that has rendered divine affirmation of the quest for liberation, justice, and equality from the slave era to the present. However, because these biblically based affirmations of African American existence are most often set forth in prophetic opposition to the enduring evils of racism, poverty, and injustice, it is illogical to expect persons who have been made aware of the sources and consequences of these evils to adopt a conservative political position, which favors preservation of the status quo in the social order. On the contrary, a realistic acknowledgment of the legacy of oppression suggests that a progressive social analysis is more likely to concur with the best interests and highest aspirations of African Americans than any appeal to conservative social values and principles. However, despite the apparent contradictions and for whatever reasons, politically conservative black Christians may rise to greater prominence in the future. For example, it appears that a small but not insignificant cadre of black voters may have given George W. Bush the margin of victory in the 2004 presidential election because they were persuaded to join the majority of white evangelical voters in the selective adoption of conservative moral positions related to sexuality while rejecting or disregarding biblical teachings on poverty, materialism, and war.[24] Meanwhile, some of these politically conservative pastors and congregations were rewarded with the allocation of faith-based government funding for community outreach programs.

In her later study of African American women and television preachers, Marla Frederick approaches this question of the political leanings of theologically conservative Christians with specific reference to poor black women in the rural South.[25] She discovered that the political messages of televangelists did not resonate with the experience of African Americans living in a poor community: "it appears that African American women's alternative contextualized readings of religious television allow them to dissent from the politically conservative messages of televangelists while adopting the more biblically conservative tenets of evangelical Christianity."[26]

Stephen Hunt also addresses the question of the political views and involvement of African American Pentecostals in his extensive studies of the link between Pentecostalism in the United States and the theme of deprivation. He draws attention to the fact that the political awakening of black Pentecostals transcended the political inactivity exhibited in the great bulk of white Pentecostal churches: "These churches regard political involvement and picketing as a gift of the Holy Spirit. In practical terms they have organized job training centers and lower income housing, not only for their own members but for those who need it."[27] It is to this practical dimension we now turn in search of signs of a resurgent Pentecostal prophetic activism in the twenty-first century.

Signs of a Resurgent Pentecostal Prophetic Activism

Omar McRoberts has devoted considerable scholarly attention to understanding the "new" black Pentecostal activism, the title and subject of his 1999 article published in *Sociology of Religion*.[28] There and in *Streets of Glory* he offers a detailed account of the activism and community involvement of African American pastors and congregations in Boston, Massachusetts, with a particular focus on the work of Rev. Eugene Rivers, pastor and founder of the Azusa Christian Community in the Four Corners neighborhood of Dorchester. In McRoberts's view, activism entails a broad range of activities and programs designed to address the needs of whole persons and to transform entire communities, including community organizing, youth outreach, mentoring programs, low-income housing, and ecumenical networking to extend the influence of individual pastors and congregations beyond the immediate neighborhood to the city, state, nation, and the world. McRoberts further defines this activism in terms of three considerations: vocation, pastoral care, and church growth:

> The Boston pastors see community activism as a personal vocation, an extension of pastoral care, and as a way to attract and retain members by projecting a more worldly variety of Pentecostalism. . . . An activist calling . . . can be used as a strategy for congregational growth and enrichment.[29]

Some of the pastors in McRoberts's study were personally influenced by the social activism and intellectual ferment of the 1960s and '70s. However, they also feel that their distinct mission is to attract a growing subset of younger Pentecostals who are yearning for a more socially relevant, worldly spirituality that speaks to the believer's entire life experience.[30] In typical fashion, (i.e., like other black Christians in general and black Pentecostals in particular) these pastors are liberal on most political issues, yet theologically conservative:

> On one hand the pastors believe in affirmative action, welfare and state involvement in economic and social matters. They are politically conservative only in regards to issues of sexual and reproductive freedom. On the other hand, they take the Bible literally and as the Word of God and are otherwise conservative on doctrinal issues. . . . They feel that they are *called* to integrate community activism with Pentecostal spirituality, thereby releasing a powerful new force into the world.[31]

While all of the pastors agreed that both structural and personal transfor-
mations were necessary to improve life in inner-city neighborhoods, most
of them also face indifference and objection to their community outreach
efforts from their own congregants.[32]

This problem of sustainability is related to the priestly/prophetic dichot-
omy that challenges activist pastors to attend to the incessant priestly
demands of the worshipping congregation while also allocating significant
time, energy, and resources to the prophetic task of managing projects of
community transformation. The black liberation theologian Gayraud Wilmore implicates Pentecostals in his negative characterization of the "climate"
of charismatic showmanship, biblical literalism, and historical and cultural
ignorance in which modern black pastors must operate.[33] At the same time,
however, he laments his own failure as a theological educator to equip his
students to negotiate the demands of prophetic activism:

> I weep for the men and women I have taught who are out there strug-
> gling but who have little to show for what they presumably learned from
> me and scholars of my generation. There are . . . some prominent excep-
> tions . . . but they are an unheralded minority in today's climate of char-
> ismatic showmanship, biblical literalism, and historical and cultural
> "know-nothingism."[34]

Undaunted by his own challenge to theological education to do better to
equip pastors to promote black liberation and community transformation,
Wilmore sets forth an extensive list of the "burning" issues needing to be
addressed by activist pastors and congregations:

> The burning issues of the twenty-first century—preventive war, terror-
> ism, gay rights, human sexuality, family structures and values, the hip-
> hop culture, prison construction and reform, abortion, stem-cell research,
> genocide and ethnic cleansing, Afrocentrism and the explosion of African
> Christianity, globalism, HIV/AIDS and the desperate needs of the Two-
> Thirds World—are scarcely touched by our Sunday sermons, conference
> addresses, church governing bodies, or literature.[35]

Aside from Wilmore, so many other black liberation theologians seem
unavailable to assist pastors and congregations in addressing these social
ethical issues or in the development of their activist projects because these
theologians have shifted their focus from the prophetic critique of the

oppression and impoverishment of African Americans to the promotion of marriage equality and the acceptance of homosexuals in the black churches. This state of affairs strikes me as an oblique and ironic reflection of the manner in which political conservatives oppose homosexuality and abortion with much greater energy than they seem able to devote to such concerns such as war, poverty, and health care.

Conclusion

The most important task of black preaching and activism is to build prophetic community, that is, to exercise one's individual gifts of ministry and leadership toward the end of empowering congregations to hear the voice of God and speak the word of God in conversation with the deepest concerns of the people and communities one is called to serve. William Willimon and Walter Brueggemann have both commented on the role of preaching in the formation of prophetic community. In Willimon's view, prophetic preaching should help the church to discover its social responsibility. Its purpose is "the production and equipment of a community of prophets. Therefore, our . . . preaching has as its goal the evocation of prophetic schoolteachers, shopkeepers, nursing home residents and sixteen-year-olds who can speak the truth to power."[36]

Brueggemann's idea is that the main task of prophetic ministry is the struggle to "evoke, form, and reform an alternative or counter-community with a counter-consciousness."[37] This speaks directly to the prophetic agenda of African American Pentecostals as they understand it in the twenty-first century, namely, to reorient themselves to a biblically based social justice advocacy for the poor and to resist being conformed to the worldly consumerism, simplistic multiculturalism, and political conservatism implicit in the prosperity gospel.

It would be good for more Pentecostal preachers and congregations to heed the warning issued by Cornel West in his 2004 book, *Democracy Matters*: as the black church succumbs to the seductions of free-market fundamentalism and loses its prophetic fervor in the age of the American empire, the future of American democracy is imperiled.[38] Instead, West calls for the black prophetic churches to "fight their way back into prominence in our public discourse."[39]

In classic Pentecostal perspective, Walter Hollenweger sees prophecy as a gift of the Spirit, whose purpose is not to distinguish Pentecostals from other Christians but rather to facilitate an ecumenical ministry of reconciliation, recalling the influence and intent of the founder of Pentecostalism, William

Joseph Seymour.[40] While Hollenweger may be correct in his observation that this reconciling ministry has been relegated to Pentecostal churches for the poor,[41] both poor and affluent African American Pentecostals will have a unique opportunity in the twenty-first century to foster genuine reconciliation among themselves and within the broader ecumenical community. To undertake this task of reconciliation, however, African American Pentecostal leaders must be willing to acknowledge the negative impact of race, sex, and class distinctions upon the past history, present condition, and future credibility of the message and ministry of the gospel. The authenticity and effectiveness of this effort will require serious prophetic engagement of consumerism, conservatism, and TV studio multiculturalism by men and women who truly understand what it means to be "in the world but not of it."

NOTES TO CHAPTER 8

1. Omar McRoberts, *Streets of Glory: Church and Community in a Black Urban Neighborhood* (Chicago: University of Chicago Press, 2003), 100.

2. Ibid., 109.

3. William C. Turner Jr., "Preaching the Spirit: the Liberation of Preaching," *Journal of Pentecostal Theology* 14.1 (2005): 12.

4. Randall Balmer, *Thy Kingdom Come* (New York: Basic Books, 2006), 190.

5. Most notably in my books *Saints in Exile: The Holiness Pentecostal Experience in African American Religion and Culture* (New York: Oxford University Press, 1996), *Ministry at the Margins: The Prophetic Mission of Women, Youth, and the Poor* (Downers Grove, Ill.: InterVarsity Press, 1997), and *Empowerment Ethics for a Liberated People: A Path to African American Social Transformation* (Minneapolis, Minn.: Fortress Press, 1995).

6. Walter J. Hollenweger, "An Introduction to Pentecostalisms," *Journal of Beliefs and Values* 25.2 (August 2004): 128–29.

7. David D. Daniels III, "'Doing All the Good We Can': The Political Witness of African American Holiness and Pentecostal Churches in the Post-Civil Rights Era," in R. Drew Smith, ed., *New Day Begun: African American Churches and Civic Culture in Post-civil Rights America* (Durham, N.C.: Duke University Press, 2003), 164–82.

8. Ibid., 178.

9. Robert Franklin has written three books addressing liberation and social justice as prophetic ministry: *Liberating Visions: Human Fulfillment and Social Justice in African-American Thought* (Minneapolis, Minn.: Fortress Press, 1990); *Another Day's Journey: Black Churches Confronting The American Crisis* (Minneapolis, Minn.: Fortress Press, 1997); and *Crisis in the Village: Restoring Hope in African American Communities* (Minneapolis, Minn.: Fortress Press, 2007).

10. Daniels, "Doing All the Good We Can," 179.

11. See Martha Simmons and Frank A. Thomas, eds., *Preaching with Sacred Fire: An Anthology of African American Sermons, 1750 to the Present* (New York: W.W. Norton, 2010).

12. Clarence Taylor, *Black Religious Intellectuals: The Fight for Equality from Jim Crow to the Twenty-first Century* (New York: Routledge, 2002), 48–49.

13. Taylor, *Black Religious Intellectuals*, 126.

14. James S. Tinney, "The Prosperity Doctrine: Perverted Economics," *Spirit* 2.1 (1978): 44–53.

15. Ibid., 45.

16. Milmon Harrison, *Righteous Riches: The Word of Faith Movement in Contemporary African American Religion* (New York: Oxford University Press, 2005).

17. Shayne Lee, *T. D. Jakes: America's New Preacher* (New York: New York University Press, 2005).

18. Ibid., 98.

19. Ibid., 121.

20. Marla F. Frederick, *Between Sundays: Black Women and Everyday Struggles of Faith* (Berkeley: University of California Press, 2003).

21. Ibid., 142.

22. Ibid., 159.

23. Ibid., 142.

24. For statistics regarding support for President Bush by black Protestant voters in 2004 see John C. Green, Corwin E. Smidt, James L. Guth, and Lyman A. Kellstedt, "Religion and the 2004 Election: A Post-Election Analysis," a survey published by the Pew Forum on Religion and Public Life, February 3, 2005, 1.

25. Marla Frederick-McGlathery, "'But, It's Bible': African American Women and Television Preachers," in R. Marie Griffith and Barbara Dianne Savage, eds., *Women and Religion in the African Diaspora* (Baltimore, Md.: Johns Hopkins University Press, 2006), 266–91.

26. Ibid., 287.

27. Stephen J. Hunt, "Deprivation and Western Pentecostalism Revisited: The Case of 'Classical' Pentecostalism," *PentecoStudies* 1.1 (2002): 21.

28. Omar McRoberts, "Understanding the 'New' Black Pentecostal Activism," *Sociology of Religion* 60.1 (1999): 47–70.

29. Ibid., 65–66.

30. Ibid., 57.

31. Ibid., 54.

32. Ibid., 60.

33. Gayraud Wilmore, "The Black Church in the Age of False Prophets: An Interview with Gayraud Wilmore," in Iva E. Carruthers, Frederick D. Haynes III, and Jeremiah A. Wright, eds., *Blow the Trumpet in Zion: Global Vision and Action for the 21st-century Black Church* (Minneapolis, Minn.: Fortress Press, 2005), 167–76.

34. Ibid., 176.

35. Ibid., 167–68.

36. William Willimon, quoted by Chang-Hoon Kim, "Prophetic Preaching as Social Preaching," *Evangelical Review of Theology* 30.2 (2006): 150.

37. See also Ibid., 149.

38. Cornel West, *Democracy Matters: Winning the Fight against Imperialism* (New York: Penguin Press, 2004), 164.

39. Ibid., 164.

40. Hollenweger, "An Introduction to Pentecostalisms," 125.

41. Ibid., 128.

9

Ethics in a Prophetic Mode

Reflections of an Afro-Pentecostal Radical

LEONARD LOVETT

Between (Auto)Biography and Ethics: Prophetic Ethics "on the Way"

The ancient prophets were sent not only to foretell and predict events but to challenge the status quo in the name of YHWH. Any theology that does not seek to radically probe the nature and meaning of reality for our present moment is truncated and invalid. Ethics deals with the realm of "oughtness." Its primary task at its best is to radically critique "what is" in light of "what ought to be." To begin with, "what is" must be reality-based rather than a figment of one's imagination before it can authentically move on to "what ought to be." Sound ethics utilizes good theology to examine and make claims for the good of the larger community. Heretofore I have defied labels—sometimes being called a theologian, other times an ethicist—but always radically both in some respect. However, my radicality has been tempered not by age but by loving concern for others. Since I am too busy to hate I have become more discerning and am now driven by two things: a deep, passionate, intuitive sense of the truth that reinforces discernment, and an insatiable intellectual curiosity that preoccupies most of my waking moments.

Reflecting on the dilemmas and challenges I have experienced as an Afrocentric Pentecostal theologian-ethicist, my journey has at times brought me in conflict with colleagues who embrace other perspectives. I rehearse these episodes here not to dig up the past but to liberate the past for the future. In highlighting elements of my own story, I make no apologies for deploying the narrative mode of autobiography since the telling of stories—the giving of testimonies—is central both to the tradition of black theology on the one hand and to Pentecostalism on the other.[1] My hope is that polemic and testimony will combine in a way that attests to the power of grace, healing, and transformation in the midst of adversity.[2] Ultimately for Pentecostals, human motives must always be informed by an ethic of love. As the German theologian Helmut Thielicke put it, "the specifically 'Christian' element in ethics is rather to be sought explicitly and exclusively in the motivation of the action."[3]

Like my educational mentor, Benjamin Mays, president of Morehouse College, I honestly believe that I too was "born to rebel."[4] My paternal grandfather was a third-generation slave. I was informed at a family reunion that whatever he did to his oppressor in his bid for freedom, they are still looking for him. The danger in reflection is balancing the task of self-disclosure with certain limitations. But if theology and ethics can indeed be gleaned from autobiography—and I believe they not only can, but must—then let the narrative begin.

The Civil Rights Background of Afro-Pentecostal Radicalism: The Beginnings of My Journey

My interest in religion with a bent toward justice can be dated from my early childhood days in the segregated elementary school on Florida's east coast where I grew up. At an early age I witnessed the trivialization and demeaning of black life. I saw good people physically brutalized and intimidated by racists. But, we were fortunate to have teachers who had for the most part graduated from black colleges and who cared enough to educate us about prominent African Americans who had influenced the course of history in North America. Because my teachers taught with clarity and purpose, learning was never a chore. I was introduced to our "sheroes" and heroes at an early age, so that by the time I graduated from high school, I had engaged in the process of fusion within a segregated society that created—both intentionally and otherwise—an identity crisis for people of color.

I then spent two years at Saints Junior College, in Lexington, Mississippi, the only school owned by the Church of God in Christ (COGIC) at that time. I journeyed to Mississippi, the "magnolia state," two years after the brutal slaying of Emmett Till by white laborers. This incident sparked nationwide concern among many black Americans. At Saints, I was personally mentored by the school's president, Dr. Arenia C. Mallory, personal protégé of Mary McLeod Bethune, an early twentieth-century educator and civil rights leader who was instrumental in founding Bethune-Cookman College. I owe a debt of gratitude to Dr. Mallory for instilling in me a strong desire for knowledge. She once challenged me to memorize an essay by Howard Thurman, titled "Good News for the Underprivileged," for an oratorical contest, and I won first place.[5] I also served as one of Dr. Mallory's part-time chauffeurs. During those times, I heard many stories about Pentecostal leaders and the challenges of life in a segregated society. I recall personally driving Dr. Mallory and Lillian Brook Coffey, the second national supervisor of women in the Church of God in Christ. Both knew Bishop C. H Mason, COGIC founder. I am indebted to these mentors for modeling a life of disciplined study.

I transferred to Morehouse College as a junior, matriculating in January 1960, the same month in which Martin Luther King Jr. arrived from Montgomery, Alabama. As a junior at Morehouse, I recall Dr. King and Malcolm X frequenting the campus. Morehouse was a site of intense debate during the radical activist sixties. As students, we frequently had sidewalk discussions with Malcolm X and other prominent civil rights leaders in which Eurocentric myths about African Americans came under severe and intense scrutiny, while the struggle for black identity became the norm.

It is astonishing how certain myths can pervade an entire society. Myths are inescapable, and I began to discover their real power, slowly coming to understand how they tend to replicate and authenticate themselves. As I learned about the function of myth philosophically and theologically, I also came to see how the mere use of language could become a powerful tool toward a deeper understanding of truth. The mythic narratives of the creation in Genesis provide examples of the power of myth. The writers of the Genesis narrative are not out to prove the creation, but rather to witness and attest to the presence of a Divine Being in the activity of creation. The language of myth becomes the vehicle that conveys a depth of reality that would otherwise be incomprehensible.[6] My time at Morehouse introduced me to the power of myth to which I would later return during my doctoral studies.

During my years at Morehouse, the commitment of Dr. Mays to educating through not only the written, but also the spoken, word made a profound impact on me and became a deep source of intellectual stimulation. As students we looked forward with eager anticipation to Tuesday morning chapel. Not only did we hear Vernon Johns, prominent minister and civil rights leader, Mordecai Johnson, former president of Howard University, or Kyle Haselden, former editor of the *Christian Century* but also Lucius Tobin, a professor of religion at Morehouse, who in the words of Immanuel Kant concerning David Hume, "awoke me from my dogmatic slumber." Under the tutelage of Dr. Tobin, I was immersed in the relationship of faith to social realities via the thought of Reinhold and Richard Niebuhr, Paul Tillich, and other social theorists. I graduated from Morehouse with a major in history and a double minor in social science and religion.

At Morehouse, I had been introduced to a critical approach to religion within our prevailing social and political situation. This exposure motivated me to pursue ethics as a lifelong vocation. My journey continued at Crozer Theological Seminary, in Chester, Pennsylvania. I took every course taught by Kenneth Smith, an ethicist and personal friend of Reinhold Niebuhr, who also taught Martin Luther King Jr. and Samuel Dewitt Proctor. Dr. Smith also led by example—as when he directed a protest march against the segregated town of Folcroft, Pennsylvania, in Delaware County, even amidst the intimidation of the John J. McClure political machine that challenged anyone who dared to promote creative social change during that era.[7] At graduation I was the recipient of the Rebecca Gore Cohen award in Christian ethics as the outstanding student in my field.

After graduation, I began a pastorate at Memorial Church of God in Christ in Haverford, Pennsylvania, in suburban Philadelphia near Bryn Mawr and Haverford College. I was successor to my mentor, Bishop O. T. Jones Jr., who left Memorial to become senior pastor of Holy Temple Church of God in Christ, Philadelphia, as successor to his father. It was during his mature years that he became a general board member within his denomination. Under careful guidance of my pastor, mentor, and close friend, I was able to integrate my graduate studies in theology with a live parish experience. This was a new experience for me, having previously spent all of my life in the South. It instilled in me a bi-vocational love for church and academy that provided a pragmatic focus for my life journey. I vividly recall my first attempt at teaching a course in Black History at Haverford Township evening adult class. Our text was John Hope Franklin's classic, *From Slavery to Freedom*.[8] Reading Franklin with that adult class proved to be challenging and rewarding.

O. T. Jones had completed his doctoral studies on Søren Kierkegaard under the guidance of Richard Kroner (at one time a colleague of Paul Tillich at Union Theological Seminary),[9] and it was Dr. Jones who motivated me to continue in my theological studies. Two years after my seminary degree, I enrolled at Bryn Mawr Graduate School of Social Research as a fellow in community organization. There I encountered the radical historicism of Herbert Aptheker, a renowned historian who articulated a provocative analysis of the African slave trade.[10] Simultaneously, I was the recipient of a significant portion of the library of the late Dr. Ira Reid, sociologist and friend of W. E. B. Dubois. My serious encounter and engagement with the thought of Dubois changed my entire perspective on American history, particularly as it pertains to the plight of African Americans. In my social theory class at Bryn Mawr, I argued vehemently for the rightful place in the curriculum of the Dubois classic, *The Philadelphia Negro*, one of the first significant studies of community in America, predating the highly influential Chicago Warner studies on community.[11] Dubois's book was rediscovered by Digsby Baltzell, a sociologist at the University of Pennsylvania, and republished in the late 1960s.[12] It was Dubois's writing that assisted me in exploding the Eurocentric lies about peoples of African descent.

Pentecostal Origins and the Afro-Pentecostal Contribution: Bearing our Personal and Collective Pain

It was at this time, about four decades ago, that I embarked upon an intellectual quest prompted by a cultural suspicion that black Holiness-Pentecostalism was far more African than Western at its core, a claim I continue to embrace. I recently recovered the 1970 edition of *Black Pentecostal Concept*, in which the Swiss theologian and scholar of Pentecostalism, Walter Hollenweger, urged scholars to examine the blackness of Pentecostalism.[13] As pioneering dean of the first fully accredited Pentecostal seminary in North America, the Charles Harrison Mason Seminary, an affiliate of the Interdenominational Theological Center in Atlanta, Georgia, I contended for the truth about black origins, history, and development. Was I right then? Time has a fugitive quality about it that either validates or renders judgment upon us.

My views continued to develop in this direction after I entered Emory University during the winter of 1971. This was a time of adversity in several ways. It was at Emory that I returned to reflect on the sacralization of myths. It was Dubois who convinced me, contrary to E. Franklin Frazier's argument for discontinuity with the African past,[14] that the Black Church was the only institution among blacks that started in Africa and survived slavery.[15] Such thinking when contextualized is in concert with the views of the homiletician Henry Mitchell, who argued in *Black Belief* that African American religion is a continuation of African traditional religion, much of which existed long before the European colonial invaders set foot on African soil.[16] What Europeans introduced in the form of religion was simply affixed to an already existing theological and social structure.

These views crystallized, during my doctoral studies, when I had the rare privilege of studying for a year with Dr. H. W. Turner, a renowned British authority on traditional religion in West Africa. Initially I could not make the connection with religion in the New World. It was later that I began to see the implications of African religion for the origins of black Holiness-Pentecostalism. It is primarily in form and phenomenology that West African indigenous religion compares to black Holiness-Pentecostalism. My studies with Turner were focused primarily on the Church of the Lord Aladura, found largely in Nigeria, West Africa. The use of water in the ritual of baptism and oil for anointing in certain West African indigenous movements is similar to Western Pentecostalism ritual, especially among peoples of African descent. It gradually became clear to me that Pentecostal origins in the United States were linked just as much, if not more, to William J. Seymour, son of third-generation slaves, than to Charles Fox Parham, generally recognized as the leader by Pentecostal white historians. The issues involved here vis-à-vis the origins of Pentecostalism in America were similar in many ways to the Franklin Frazier/Melville Herskovits exchange on discontinuity/continuity in the New World: here Frazier argues that most of African culture was lost during the harshness of the middle passage and the period of slavery, but Herskovits argues that there were a number of cultural elements—"survivals"—which continued to exist either in the memories of slaves or simply in their psyches and later reappeared within the colonies.

Simultaneously, and throughout my graduate studies at Emory, I was in dialogue with James Cones, progenitor of black theology, and members of the newly founded Society for the Study of Black Religion. (Cecil Cone, older brother of James, completed his doctoral studies in systematic theology at Emory during my academic sojourn.[17]) My radicality grew intensely as my thinking began to mature.

The first push-backs occurred as I began to reinterpret the origins of black Holiness-Pentecostalism in the United States according to the emerging Afrocentric lens that I was developing. My doctoral studies had commenced during the formative years of the Society for Pentecostal Studies (SPS), and it was with my first formal presentation at an SPS meeting in Cleveland, Tennessee (1973), titled "Perspectives on the Black Origins of the Pentecostal Movement,"[18] that I entered almost unknowingly into a debate on the origins of the contemporary classical Pentecostal Movement. Dr. Vinson Synan, one of the co-founders of the SPS, had not too long before that published his provocative and groundbreaking work, *The Holiness Pentecostal Movement in the United States*.[19] He invited me to publish my SPS paper in a book he was editing. I pleaded with Synan's publisher not to assign the title "Black Origins of the Pentecostal Movement" to my article because one of my collaborators, James Tinney, a political scientist at Howard University, had published an earlier essay under the same title.[20] I was concerned that using the same title as Tinney's earlier article would create confusion. However, even after a telephone conversation with the publisher, my request was disregarded, and my article appeared as assigned.[21] I am still at a loss as to why my wishes were ignored in this matter; perhaps it had something to do with my challenging the dominant view highlighting the significance of Charles Fox Parham for the origins of modern Pentecostalism.

Invitations became fewer while the persons I had introduced to the debate forum became the new stars on stage. In 1974 at the Pittsburgh Charismatic Conference I was cited and marked as a liberal for lecturing for three days on "Liberation and the Holy Spirit." Later, I recalled being literally booed during an entire presentation of an SPS meeting in Vancouver in 1979 after announcing my eponymously titled paper.[22]

This marginalization of Afrocentric perspectives has continued to the present in many ways. A review of the recently published *Encyclopedia of Pentecostal and Charismatic Christianity* by Roswith Gerloff highlights many of the issues in the ongoing debate.[23] Dr. Gerloff, a former student of Hollenweger and recently retired professor at the University of Leeds, is a Christian of German-Jewish extraction who, like Hollenweger, has taken particular interest in black Pentecostalism. She notes that while the editor of the *Encyclopedia* warns against "American historiographic assumptions . . . many entries are limited to perspectives drawn from white classical Pentecostal concepts. . . . Metaphorically, the encyclopedia can be likened to a house which has opened many windows but keeps the front door shut so not to let the winds of Pentecost enter and disturb the order, contents, and perspectives within."[24] As Pentecostals on other continents outnumber those in North America, we should be on guard against too conveniently pressing Pentecostal experience into the systematic language of abstract (even if not fundamentalist) categories. A more "carefully crafted renewal historiography" would have acknowledged and been informed by the major shift initiated by Hollenweger who affirmed the African roots of the movement as most significant for America's white-dominated society.[25] Oral theologies are thus just as influential and meaningful as abstract formulations of the Christian faith. Instead, not only is the *Encyclopedia* dominated by the propositional language of classical Pentecostalism, but Gerloff notes that the bibliographies are largely dominated by white American scholars and regrets that more serious attention had not been given to scholars such as Tinney, Lovett, Richardson, Sanders et al., for America; to Oosthuizen, Daneel, Kalu, Larbi et al., for Africa; to Campos, Ramirez, Sepulveda et al., for Latin America; and to the "Birmingham school" of Nelson, Gaxiola, Gerloff, Gill, McRoberts, Beckford, and others.[26]

More important was the *Encyclopedia*'s failure to observe and analyze institutional racism. It should also be said that racism is not merely an issue in white-dominated societies such as North America, Britain, and Europe as a whole, but deeply intertwined with Eurocentrism and Amerocentrism in general. In my own work, I have tried to call attention not only to the theoretical issues of the debate but also to the ways that matters of theory have practical consequences.[27] Racism is not just an ideological bias but a structural, systemic, and ethical matter.

While at Emory, I learned to articulate the connection between theology and ethics from the late Dr. Clinton Gardner, my major professor and professor of ethics at the university. Gardner wrote of social ethics as a "study of what is, in light of what ought to be."[28] This contributed to inspiring my dissertation on "Black Holiness-Pentecostalism: Implications for Ethics and Social Transformation."[29] Upon submitting my proposal, I was admonished by a professor that I would "never" complete a study of this magnitude. He wanted me to write on some German or American theologian with whom he was familiar. His use of the word "never" motivated me to delve into this study with all of my energy. I selected Theodore Runyon, professor of systematic theology, to chair my dissertation committee. It was through the knowledge, wisdom, and expertise of Dr. Runyon that I was able to weather the storm of the doctoral challenge. I defended my dissertation by telephone conference during the spring semester of 1979.

The Quest for Authenticity and Afro-Pentecostalism: Signs of Hope and Promise

Several decades ago Reinhold Niebuhr, the renowned neo-orthodox theologian-ethicist, wrote his autobiography, *Leaves from the Notebook of a Tamed Cynic*, in which he talks about his early years as a pastor in Detroit, Michigan: "I make no apology for being critical of what I love. No one wants a love which is based upon illusions, and there is no reason why we should not love a profession and yet be critical of it."[30] Yet Niebuhr's well-known pessimistic view of human nature was balanced by an optimism that also recognized the good in humankind. It was he who, commenting on justice, stated: "love as a substitute for justice is odious, but love as a supplement to justice is an absolute necessity."[31]

From Niebuhr I came to see the importance of connecting love and justice. This lesson has been honed throughout a bi-vocational career, during which I put into practice what Gardner taught me at the level of theory. In retrospect, I am not sure which experience impacted my social consciousness the most, whether it was simultaneously working in the private sector as a Neighborhood Youth Corp Coordinator under the auspices of the U.S. Labor Department and as pastor in Memorial Church of God in Christ, or interfacing with young gang members while studying social theory at Bryn Mawr or, later, serving as pastor of the COGIC Church at the Crossroads, Peniel, in South Central Los Angeles and teaching at Fuller Theological Seminary. In each case it was the interface between the "hood" and the academy that helped me to integrate urban ministry with my scholarship.[32] Such integration is essential for the future of Afro-Pentecostal radicalism.

It was in my first teaching post, at Fuller Theological Seminary in 1978, where I also served as associate director of Black Ministries, that I recruited pastors, primarily from an urban environment, for a specialized Master of Arts program. Because of these efforts, that program increased from ten to fifty-five students in a short span. It was satisfying to observe men and women who otherwise would not have had a chance of excelling in theological studies. These students brought insights from the inner city that enriched and changed the way courses were taught at this mainline institution of higher education. Debates were constant and fruitful. My favorite course was titled Theology of Politics. In it, I attempted to integrate three disciplines—theology, ethics, and politics—engaging each in such a way to enable students to begin to think both theologically and ethically about political problems. I followed a similar pattern later at Oral Roberts University where I taught the same course under the title Christianity and Political Thought. My experiences with these students suggested to me that there was indeed hope for the future of not only for black Holiness-Pentecostalism in America but also for global Pentecostalism.

From the Azusa Street Revival of 1906, the fountainhead of modern Pentecostalism under the leadership of William J. Seymour, Pentecostalism has spread around the world and flourished even in underdeveloped nations. The spiritual cloud of divine effusion that hovered over North America during Azusa Street Revival appears now to be hovering over Africa, Asia, and Latin America. America in our time will be evangelized by those who have been despised for centuries as the "wretched of the earth,"[33] and who have never ceased their struggle against the Pharaohs of this world that have sought to keep them under the iron fist of oppression.

Some of the greatest revivals in contemporary history are taking place on these continents. Worship is charged with special meaning among new and old converts, and there is a new understanding of prayer as an essential element of the spiritual life. Christians, Pentecostal and otherwise, have dispensed with traditional formalisms and time-bound rituals. Yet from out of their deep spirituality, the churches on these continents have begun to address the reality of personal and social salvation without politics becoming a euphemism for evangelism. Amidst a new and deep spiritual hunger for the living God, there is an increasing recognition of the Holy Spirit's presence and activity in daily life. Spirituality and social awareness now go hand in hand, so that Spirit-filled believers realize their lives are no longer defined by oppressive circumstances.[34] Their chains of oppression are being challenged with a new freshness and vigor, which they attribute to the presence and power of the Spirit.

My appointment as ecumenical officer for the Church of God in Christ has presented an unparalleled opportunity to seek unity within the faith community. Within a five-year span my travels have taken me to Geneva, Switzerland, to visit the headquarters of the World Council of Churches (WCC), to Brazil as a delegate to the Ninth Assembly of the WCC in Porto Alegre, and to Accra, Ghana, as a participant in Destiny Summit, a conference sponsored by the International Central Gospel Church under the leadership of its overseer, Mensa Otabil. This is the greatest time in history for the faith community to live out the desire of our Lord in word and deed, "that they all may be one" (John 17).

New converts from Third World nations have watched oppressive regimes come and go. Being touched by the Holy Spirit they are in quest of that which is authentic. They have come full circle, and having come full circle they appreciate what it means to be civil. The lack of civility combined with loss of respect in our time is fertile ground for learning. If Pentecostals in North America are truly open to what the Spirit is saying and doing in our time, there may be much to learn from Pentecostalism in the Southern Hemisphere and throughout the global village. Whether it is among the West Indians in the Caribbean, South Americans in Chile, European Pentecostals, or members of the House Church Movement in China, we can be assured that the cloud of spiritual effusion is globally present and active.

Black Holiness-Pentecostals also have a perspective to contribute into this mix. We know what it means to be encountered at the deepest levels of personal existence. Religious experience is given primacy within the ethos of the movement. One does not receive the Holy Spirit as a "show piece" but rather as a gift for empowerment and personal transformation. *Metanoia* (repentance) must precede authentic faith, and "woe is me" must be uttered before authentic liberation can take place. In the presence of God one does not possess the Holy, and any attempt to do so leads inevitably to egocentrism and idolatry. To be possessed by the Holy, the "Numinous," to borrow a word from Rudolf Otto, is to encounter a presence where one's awareness and sensitivity is increased.

Pentecostals would insist that it is time to reconnect with our true humanity. Within the Afro-Pentecostal sphere of the movement such reconnection involves the affirmation of our cultural and spiritual roots simultaneously, for separation of either from the other leaves us unbalanced. Afro-Pentecostals have always given testimony about the Holy Spirit as exposing and destroying the false myths and misleading stereotypes of our lives. Afro-Pentecostals also believe that authentic liberation is a product of divine creation and is not restricted by social, political, and ideological constraints. It is not less than freedom from the bondage of sin, oppressive structures, and all the powers of enslavement. Such freedom is often expressed through the medium of the "testimony." Last, but not least, Afro-Pentecostals experience a sense of wholeness and healing through the vehicle of testimony. It is that portion of worship where converts are encouraged to share with the body of believers what "the Lord has done for me." It is a time when believers "thank God" for what God has done and "praise God" for who God is.

In this chapter, I hope to have reflected on the emergence and development of the young tradition of Afro-Pentecostal scholarship through the telling of part of my story. May these thoughts reflect in some way the workings of the Holy Spirit, for "where the Spirit of the Lord is, there is liberty" (2 Cor. 3:17, NIV).

NOTES TO CHAPTER 9

1. See Will Coleman, *Tribal Talk: Black Theology, Hermeneutics, and African/American Ways of "Telling the Story"* (University Park: Pennsylvania State University Press, 2000), and Jean-Daniel Plüss, *Therapeutic and Prophetic Narratives in Worship: A Hermeneutic Study of Testimonies and Visions* (New York: Peter Lang, 1988).

2. Here, I would go farther than James McClendon to argue that the mode of autobiography is not only fruitful for theology but also for ethics—more specifically, for what I am calling prophetic ethics; see James William McClendon, *Biography as Theology: How Life Stories Can Remake Today's Theology* (Nashville, Tenn.: Abingdon, 1974).

3. Helmut Thielicke, *Theological Ethics*, vol. 1: *Foundations*, ed. William H. Lazareth, trans. John W. Doberstein (Philadelphia, Pa.: Fortress Press, 1966), 20.

4. See Benjamin E. Mays, *Born to Rebel: An Autobiography* (New York: Scribner, 1971).

5. See Howard Thurman, "Good News for the Underprivileged," *Religion in Life* 4.3 (1935): 403–9.

6. E.g., Rudolph Bultmann et al., *Kerygma and Myth: A Theological Debate*, ed. and trans. Reginald H. Fuller (New York: Harper and Row, 1961).

7. For details, see the little known work of John Morrison McLarnon III, *Ruling Suburbia: John J. McClure and the Republican Machine in Delaware County, Pennsylvania* (Newark: University of Delaware Press, 2003).

8. John Hope Franklin, *From Slavery to Freedom: A History of African Americans* (New York: A. A. Knopf, 1947), with many editions since.

9. See Ozro T. Jones, "The Meaning of the 'Moment' in Existential Encounter according to Kierkegaard" (STD [Doctor of Sacred Theology] diss., Temple University; Ann Arbor, Mich.: University Microfilms, 1962).

10. Aptheker was a prolific author. His texts that made the biggest impression on me were *American Negro Slave Revolts* (New York: Columbia University Press, 1943), and *A Documentary History of the Negro People in the United States* (New York: Citadel Press, 1951)—both of which have been reprinted many times.

11. See the research agenda as sketched by Lloyd W. Warner, "Social Anthropology and the Modern Community," *American Journal of Sociology* 46.6 (May 1941): 785–96.

12. W. E. B. DuBois, *The Philadelphia Negro: A Social Study* (Philadelphia: University of Pennsylvania Press, 1899), repr, ed. E. Digby Baltzell and Isabel Eaton (New York: Schocken Books, 1969).

13. See Walter J. Hollenweger, *Black Pentecostal Concept: Interpretations and Variations* (Geneva: World Council of Churches, 1970).

14. Frazier made this argument in various places, including Edward Franklin Frazier, *The Negro Church in America* (New York: Schocken Books, 1963).

15. W. E. B. DuBois, *The Crisis Writings,* ed. Daniel Walden (Greenwich, Conn.: Fawcett Publications, 1972), especially the section "The Negro Church," 331ff.

16. Henry Mitchell, *Black Belief: Folk Beliefs of Blacks in America and West Africa* (New York: Harper and Row, 1975).

17. Cecil Wayne Cone, "The Identity Crisis in Black Theology: An Investigation of the Tensions Created by Efforts to Provide a Theological Interpretation of Black Religion in the Works of Joseph Washington, James Cone, and J. Deotis Roberts" (PhD diss., Emory University, 1975).

18. This was originally published as "Perspectives on the Black Origins of the Pentecostal Movement," *Journal of the Interdenominational Theological Center* 1.1 (Fall 1973): 36–49.

19. Vinson Synan, *The Holiness Pentecostal Movement in the United States* (Grand Rapids, Mich.: Eerdmans, 1971).

20. James S. Tinney, "Black Origins of the Pentecostal Movement," *Christianity Today* 16 (8 October 1971): 4-6.

21. Leonard Lovett, "Black Origins of the Pentecostal Movement," in Vinson Synan, ed., *Aspects of Pentecostal-Charismatic Origins* (Plainfield, N.J.: Logos International, 1975), 123–41.

22. A revised version of this presentation was eventually published as Lovett, "Liberation: A Dual-Edged Sword," *Pneuma: Journal of the Society for Pentecostal Studies* 9.2 (1987): 155–71.

23. Stanley M. Burgess, ed., *Encyclopedia of Pentecostal and Charismatic Christianity* (New York: Routledge, 2006).

24. See Roswith Gerloff, review of Stanley M. Burgess, *Encyclopedia of Pentecostal and Charismatic Christianity*, in *Pneuma: Journal of the Society for Pentecostal Studies* 29.2 (2007): 317–20, quotation from 317–18.

25. Gerloff review, 318, citing from Burgess, ed., *Encyclopedia*, 242; see also Walter J. Hollenweger, *The Pentecostals: The Charismatic Movement in the Churches* (Minneapolis, Minn.: Augsburg, 1972).

26. I had previously called attention to many of these matters in my essays, "The Spiritual Legacy and Role of Black Holiness-Pentecostalism in the Development of American Culture," *One in Christ* 23.1/2 (1987): 144–45, and "Black Holiness Pentecostalism," in Stanley M. Burgess and Eduard M. Van Der Maas, eds., *The New International Dictionary of Pentecostal and Charismatic Movements*, rev. ed. (Grand Rapids, Mich.: Zondervan, 2002), 419–28.

27. See Lovett, "The Present: The Problem of Racism in the Contemporary Pentecostal Movement," *Cyberjournal for Pentecostal-Charismatic Research* 14 (2005) [http://pctii.org/cyberj/cyber14.html].

28. E. Clinton Gardner, *Biblical Faith and Social Ethics* (New York: Harper, 1960), 9.

29. Leonard Lovett, "Black Holiness-Pentecostalism: Implications for Ethics and Social Transformation" (PhD diss., Emory University, 1979); see also my *Kingdom Beyond Color: Re-Examining the Phenomenon of Racism*, rev. ed. (Cleveland, Tenn.: Derek Press, 2009).

30. Reinhold Niebuhr, *Leaves from the Notebook of a Tamed Cynic* (1929; repr., San Francisco: Harper and Row, 1980), viii.

31. See Reinhold Niebuhr, "The Gospel in Future America," *Christian Century* 75 (June 18, 1958): 714.

32. Leonard Lovett, "'The African-American Pentecostal Experience and Urban Ministry: Contributions and Challenges," *Transformation* 12 (January–March 1995): 15–16, 27.

33. See the work of an important Afrocentrist author, Frantz Fanon, *The Wretched of the Earth* (New York: Grove Press, 1963).

34. See Donald E. Miller and Tetsunao Yamamori, *Global Pentecostalism: The New Face of Christian Social Engagement* (Berkeley: University of California Press, 2007).

IV

Pneumatology

Until recently the idea of a "Pentecostal theology" would have been considered an oxymoron, given the Pentecostal emphasis on the emotions, affections, and ecstatic worship. However, over the last generation there has emerged a growing consideration of how Pentecostal spirituality and piety harbors within itself a unique set of theological intuitions and sensibilities, and Pentecostal theologians have been working to articulate these in their own tongues. The result has been, at least in part, a distinctive Pentecostal contribution to the recent renaissance of interest in the doctrine of the Holy Spirit in the wider academy. Building on the fact that one of the most salient aspects of Pentecostal spirituality is its openness to a vibrant engagement with the Holy Spirit in the life and worship of adherents, the essays in this section speak to two arenas—preaching (Turner) and eschatology (Ware)—in which a more vigorous intellectual engagement with pneumatology might prove fruitful. They suggest that as a religion of the Spirit, Pentecostalism has possible implications for reversing dominant conceptions of power and providing a vehicle to introduce more just ways of conceiving pneumatic empowerment for a greater, more liberative future for the black Christians in particular and for the church ecumenical as well. These essays provide insight into how serious theological reflection on and re-working of major themes within Afro-Pentecostal Christianity can not only enrich the Pentecostal tradition but also allow those within the movement to make contributions, which can benefit the broader church.

10

Pneumatology

Contributions from African American Christian
Thought to the Pentecostal Theological Task

WILLIAM C. TURNER JR.

Introduction: Pentecostalism and Pneumatology

The maturity of Pentecostal theology demands development of a more robust theology of the Holy Spirit because of the centrality of the Spirit in Pentecostal spirituality and because the immanent and economic history of the Spirit is marked by movement toward liberty. A critical pneumatological discourse is essential for carrying Pentecostal theology beyond the apologetics that have come to be prominent in the tradition. What is needed is a pneumatology that moves the locus of discussion from narrow sectarian interests to those of the worldwide Christian communion.

An important clarification is in order here: Pneumatology as a contribution of African American Pentecostal theologians is not to be confused with "valorized history" or the torturing of texts to yield or reiterate the Pentecostal litmus test.[1] Neither does it devalue the positive contributions and pioneering work done as black theology. Rather, it attempts to fasten on an early critique raised among the first interlocutors of black theology, and to respond to a direct plea to African American Pentecostal theologians. Further, it gestures toward making explicit the pneumatological hermeneutic implicit in its prophetic version of Christian faith. In short, this essay is meant to contribute to the ongoing quest for an African American Pentecostal theology, and to do so by way of articulating a more ecumenical pneumatology forged in dialogue with the broader black theological tradition.

This chapter does not argue for "pneumatomonism" as a remedy for the "Christomonism" with which Christianity in the West has been charged.[2] Rather, it attempts to expand the company of interlocutors to include disciplined reflection by those who have been baptized both in the Spirit (as understood by Pentecostals) and in the fires of racist oppression. And it is precisely this emerging tradition of critical black Pentecostal theologians who do not settle for an experience without critical reflection. Instead, they embody the truths that learning does not interfere with burning; fire is not quenched by focus; education intensifies sanctification; the clean life enhances the keen mind; emotion and intellect do not run on a collision course. The hope is for a seminal contribution to pneumatology as a critical and systematic discourse to assist in guiding a church in search of and open to the Spirit, whose mission is transfiguring the world as the home of God.

African American Experience as a Source for Pneumatology

Where Christianity grows in the postmodern world, people tend to be at home with traditional (pre-Enlightenment) ways of knowing that world. In this culture, the testimony of Scripture resonates with the world people experience. Barriers to preaching and believing the gospel's "pre-scientific claims" are lower than in a world where science and history are the sole arbiters of truth. Even those who are trained in theology under Western tutors have learned to "indigenize their faith" by coming to know God for themselves. Where they cannot remove the impress of Western thought, there is the prospect for achieving a "second naïveté," which amounts to a critical appropriation of historical and scientific knowledges within bounded domains. Their worldview is more akin to that found in Christian scriptures in which the spirits are known and tried, and in which the Spirit of God possesses greater power.[3]

Because theology is reasoning about God, in the strictest sense there is no divine encounter that escapes pneumatology, even if implicitly. For Africans in America, theology was rooted in the struggle to make sense of capture and the ordeal of slavery. This included the sense of abandonment by the gods known to them from their lands. But it also meant coming to terms with the God of their captors, especially when enslavement was said to be sanctioned in his service. Theology had fruitful extension in the preaching moments during which slaves were participants, and in their experiences of conversion, visions, and other forms of rapture. The immediate issues of concern in these new communities were soteriology and doxology—salvation and the worship of God. Testimonies gave consistent witness to the encounters wherein their lives were transformed. Indeed, the testimony of conversion was the very staple of these early communities. Such conversion was often the content of preaching, and it formed the core of the songs they sang.[4] Closely related to these productions—indeed their purpose in many cases—was the interest of persuading others to believe: worship was for the praise of God and for bringing others to faith.

Pneumatology was implicit, but understated, in that little distinction was made between the work of Jesus and the work of the Spirit. Jesus was not a dead or ancient person, and surely he was not just an idea. Often there was a bias in these emerging Christian slave communities to the theology/Christology of Acts. Jesus was present, near, alive, one like them. He suffered with them. They called on him. Or, one might say Jesus was the Jesus of the gospels—anointed with the Holy Ghost and power. He went about doing good and healing those possessed by the devil (Acts 10:38). Calling the name of Jesus amounted to an invocation of the Spirit. The sense was that Jesus is the pneumatic Christ. But scarcely was this stated emphatically.

Closely linked with salvation and worship was a third accent on sin and evil. Enslaved Christians were taught sternly concerning sin. Salvation was from sin. Sins were named for the slaves. They were taken from the lists given in the Ten Commandments, the *Haustafeln* (household codes) of the epistles, and the slave codes of the colonies and plantations. However, from the slave's own knowledge of the Scriptures arose a sense of sin that extended to their masters. Not only did they know the masters who were particularly wicked; they came to know the sinfulness of slavery itself.

They made a deep connection between deliverance and experience of the Spirit, making the manacles of slavery inconsistent with the testimonies of God's saving work. Worse was the inconsistency between the testimonies of Christians and their practice of enslavement. The hint was of a healthy tension, which acknowledged that the Spirit who convicts of personal and inward sin is the same Spirit who prosecutes the world for the sake of righteousness and justice (John 16:8–11). This tension was taken up in the spirituals—songs inspired by the Spirit—to protest abuse and mistreatment of God's children. Trouble "don't last" always, and the slaves expected that those who oppressed the little ones would give an account at the judgment.

The prophetic sense was that God was going forth into the world to establish justice and to cause the faithful believer to know the vindication that has been promised. The wickedness of slavery was a challenge to the very integrity of the gospel of God. The defeat of Satan included breaking the manacles and repudiating those "who 'talkin' about heaven but ain't going there." Sin as all that is opposed to God is "antichrist" (see 1 John 4:1–3).

Thus enslaved black believers, who received the Spirit of the Risen Christ, believed that liberty was their inheritance in the Lord. It was magnified in those whose dungeons shook, whose hearts were set on hallowed fire, and who spread the gospel to brothers and sisters whom they saw as lost in the world without God. Some like Jarena Lee made explicit reference to the Spirit in naming the experience of sanctification.[5]

Though generally understated in systematic pneumatological reflection, the Black Church testified to "finding Jesus." He was the One to whom the gospels bear witness and was anointed for ministry with the Holy Ghost and power. As Risen Christ, the Spirit was breathed out upon those whom he blessed with his presence. The Second Adam is none other than the pneumatic Christ, the life-giving Spirit. In his name, devils were cast out, wonders performed, and signs followed. The very speaking of his name was an "epiclesis"—an invocation and release of the Spirit. This understatement, present in the early versions of black theology, did not go unnoticed by all of the first framers. It can be seen in the efforts of several contributors in that generation. It is important to acknowledge the neglect and the plea for remedy, and more significantly, to make the explicit plea to African American Pentecostal theologians to make further thrusts in that direction.

The Emergence of Pneumatology in Black Theology

As an academic discipline, the first moment of black theology recorded and codified the extant theology of the African American churches. Early texts in that regard are found in the Statement of the National Committee of Negro Churchmen (later Black Churchmen). Significantly, what is seen in them is a reaction to Joseph Washington and other social scientists who regarded Negro churches as sects, cults, or feeble copies of white Protestantism, without agency.[6] This early movement was spearheaded by pastors and professional theologians.[7]

The salvo comes with the publication of James Cone's *Black Theology and Black Power*, in which he forces the term "Black Theology" into the lexicon of the theological academy.[8] Cone's work catalyzed dialogue taking place then among African American theologians and compelled discussion among white theologians. Although pneumatology is underdeveloped in these early statements, there is consistent emphasis on Jesus as liberator, and Cone's work set the trajectory for the first generation of black theologians, many of whom sought to think within the tradition of Black Church experience.

The homiletician Henry Mitchell saw a synthesis, which he called the African base beneath black Christianity. For Mitchell this synthesis was accompanied in the American colonies where a sound and lasting metamorphosis took place: "Those who had once been healingly possessed by a variety of deities were now overshadowed by the one but triune God, in His person as Holy Ghost or the Holy Spirit."[9] More specifically, Mitchell attempted to account for the worship tradition that maintained a strong appreciation for and an orientation to spirit possession in some form as its zenith. As such, this thesis is diametrically opposed to that of the sociologist E. Franklin Frazier's contention that the blacks passively received their religion from the European evangelicals.[10] On the contrary, Mitchell contended "that the Blacks adapted their African tradition toward Christianity; not that Blacks took European patterns and changed them toward their own needs."[11]

According to Mitchell, the Holy Spirit possessed people ecstatically and gave them the inner strength and self-affirmation to survive. The Spirit also was known to "backstop" the cures of African indigenous traditions and, on occasion, to heal outright. Above all, the Holy Spirit made people "happy," a term which came to be synonymous with possession, from the slightest beginnings of the experience to the outright shout.[12] To be sure, the dynamics of conversion and other work of the Spirit were far more complex than Mitchell indicates. Yet, "getting happy" was a crucial manifestation that closely corresponded with familiar cultural forms. Mitchell's grasp of this epicletic sense moves a pace beyond mere testimony toward reflection on the inner motions of life inspired in the presence of God.

The pastor and liberation theologian Albert Cleage took a different view.[13] His pneumatology was not only critical of emotional impulses that had no connection to practices that moved toward political liberation but also was circumscribed by his hermeneutic of liberation, which was to be accompanied by revolution. For Cleage, Jesus was the "Black Messiah" who came to the oppressed Jewish Nation to lead them to their freedom. Following his failure, his disciples completely distorted his message, thereby giving rise to the church. Chiefly responsible for this confusion was Paul who, although being a Jew, conspired with the enemies of the Jewish people. It is within this context that Cleage says, "The Holy Spirit is the revolutionary power which comes to an exploited people as they struggle to escape from powerlessness and to end the institutional oppression forced upon them by an enemy" (249).

Cleage correlated a function of the nation-community's revolutionary struggle—which may well be one that the Spirit inspires—with the very essence of the Spirit. One might rightly question whether this is a Christian understanding of the Spirit, in that the Spirit is defined apart from any integral (much less ontological) relationship with God the Father or the Son. The Spirit was defined only with respect to the oppressed and their struggle for liberation.

Cleage questioned the necessity of elements in the episode that appear to be quite crucial to Luke. The mighty rushing wind and the tongues of fire, which for Luke capture crucial Old Testament symbolism, were regarded as arbitrary in Cleage's interpretation. For him, "There need not necessarily have been tongues of fire and the rush of a mighty wind. . . . Whether they were speaking strange languages in a literal sense we do not know" (250). What was important is that oppressed non-white people understood a very simple message to them, as is the case today throughout the world. In *Black Christian Nationalism* Cleage explored the possibility of the Spirit being "harnessed" in a manner such that a restructured black church "could raise enough money on a single Sunday to save black southern farmers" (258). Cleage saw clearly how the Spirit moves upon the creation to bring about social transformation, remedying the conditions of suffering and misery. For him, the church was relevant only as an instrument of this transformation. Yet it was exactly such "harnessing" of the Spirit that undermined the Spirit's sovereignty. Consequently, Cleage's pneumatology was not rooted in the Trinity as the source of the Spirit's movement and power. There was no perichoretic unity (referring to what the Patristic fathers understood as the interpenetrating and interrelational character of the Father, Son, and Holy Spirit), which determines the Spirit's character.[14] Within Cleage's framework, we see a type of historicism in which judgments cannot be made concerning legitimate and illegitimate claims to the Spirit's presence. Historical outcome alone supplies verification. If everything done in the name of rebellion and liberation is due to the Spirit's influence, however, we have an utter contradiction of the Messiah to whom the gospels bear witness.

In his article "Sanctification and Liberation," Cone, like Mitchell, moved in the direction of pneumatological reflection starting with the experience of worship in the black church, focused mainly on its pneumatological dimension.[15] In such worship, sanctification was to be understood in light of liberation—the historical struggle for freedom—but the primary focus was worship. While it cannot be viewed as disjointed from the larger political struggle for liberation, worship can also be viewed for itself—in its own right. Even though Cone contended that black theologians needed to show the liberating character of black Christianity in their struggle for social and political justice, they were "sometimes in danger of reducing black religion to politics and black worship to a political strategy session, distorting the essence of black religion."[16] This point was also made by his brother, Cecil Cone, in his work, *Identity Crisis in Black Theology.*[17]

But James Cone gave only sparing attention to who the Spirit was. Scarcely anything noteworthy was said concerning the Spirit's person or the Spirit's relation to the other Trinitarian persons. What was important for Cone was that the Spirit was the divine presence without which there could be no worship. But this divine presence, the author of all the worshipping acts, was none other than the one who also authored, empowered, and sustained the struggle for liberation in its manifold expressions. Indeed, it was the Spirit who drew black people together so that the worship event could take place. Cone came closest to addressing the person of the Spirit when he said:

> There is no understanding of black worship apart from the presence of the Spirit who descends upon the gathered community, lighting a spiritual fire in their hearts. The divine Spirit is not a metaphysical entity but the power of Jesus breaking into the lives of the people, giving them a new song to sing as confirmation of God's presence with them in historical struggle. It is the presence of the divine Spirit that accounts for the intensity with which black people engage in worship. There is no understanding of black worship apart from the rhythm of song and sermon, the passion of prayer and testimony, the ecstasy of shout and conversion, as the people project their humanity in the togetherness of the Spirit.[18]

In preaching, the Spirit was present to transform the preacher's words into prophetic utterance—a word from the Lord. The Spirit's work here was inseparable from the calling of the preacher that made him or her authentic. Neither was it separable from the appropriate rhythm and passion with which the story was told, or the gestures that become pictorial extensions of the Word. An indispensable sign that the human words had been transformed was the response of the people with their "Hallelujahs," "Amens," and other verbal and physical ejaculations of praise. Singing opens the hearts of the people for the coming of the Spirit and constitutes a barometer by which to determine whether the worshippers have the proper disposition for the Spirit. It is the congregation's singing that constitutes a gracious welcome to the Spirit. Although the Spirit's descent could not be manipulated, there were discourteous infractions (such as speaking or dancing out of turn) that regularly "killed the Spirit."

The work of the Spirit in the several components of worship contributed to the "sanctification" of the people. For Cone, sanctification was not equated with inward piety, and warm inner feelings could not be substituted for social justice. Indeed, for him, the essential difference between black and white Methodism turned on the insistence of African Methodists that it is impossible "to be sanctified and a racist at the same time."[19] The meaning of sanctification inhered within the social context of an "oppressed community struggling for liberation," and this meaning was hardly separable from the Spirit's empowerment for that struggle. Accordingly, Cone contended that "Sanctification in black religion cannot be correctly understood apart from black people's historical struggle for liberation. Liberation is not simply a consequence of the experience of sanctification—sanctification is liberation—to be politically engaged in the historical struggle for freedom."[20] The sanctifying work of the Spirit brought about true Christian liberty and freedom. This liberty covered every dimension of life, and allowed for the transcendence of history, granting knowledge that the struggle for justice is God's fight. Hence, the sanctifying Spirit signified the presence of God and was an installment of the victory that had been promised.

Although the personal and inward working of the Spirit in sanctification was not denied, this dimension received no prominent treatment in Cone's account. Yet the Spirit's empowerment is not tied directly to the personal, moral, and ethical responses to the divine presence that were by no means negligible in the Black Church tradition. It is not enough to say merely, as Cone does, that this emphasis is imported from white evangelicals, for this ethical dimension of sanctification and the corresponding work of the Spirit has received authentic appropriation within the Black Church. This unity of the outward thrust for liberation with inward holiness and spiritual empowerment bound with the person of the Spirit is glaringly absent in Cone's treatment. It is the person of the Spirit that holds the key to this unity.

A consequence of this lack of a clear pneumatology appeared in Cone's treatment of the blackness of God in *A Black Theology of Liberation*. Where Cone was discussing the Trinitarian implications of the Godhead for black theology, he said, "As Father God identified with oppressed Israel participating in the bringing into being of this people; as Son, he became the Oppressed One in order that all may be free from oppression; as Holy Spirit, he continues his work of liberation."[21] Up to this point Cone made a fairly rigorous Trinitarian application. The trouble came with the relationship between the Spirit and the oppressed community seeking liberation, where their identities are blurred. Cone continued: "The Holy Spirit is the Spirit of the Father and the Son at work in the forces of human liberation in our society today. In America, the Holy Spirit is black people making decisions about their togetherness, which means making preparation for an encounter with white people."[22]

Here we see the identity of the divine person, the Holy Spirit, blurred with the identity of the community in which the Spirit is said to be working. Even where the Spirit is present with the people to lead, guide, and empower them, such a blurring is not valid. The Spirit, who strengthens, reserves the prerogative to challenge, chastise, and resist. As divine person, the Spirit is the subject of personal acts, not the alter ego or even the superego of the community.

Rueben L. Speaks, a bishop in the African Methodist Episcopal Zion Church, offered a pneumatology that attempted to balance piety and devotion with social analysis.[23] Although there are some problems with technical matters regarding Trinitarian doctrine, Speaks's effort to hold in tension the inward and outward dimensions of the Spirit's work is noteworthy. He clearly acknowledged that the Spirit moves both within the believer and the community of faith. Moreover, the Spirit is not limited to those who possess faith; the Spirit moves throughout creation. But he maintained another crucial balance for the black theological project: showing how the Spirit is involved in the struggle for social justice while working in personal salvation and the work of the church. Thus, the same Spirit who provided insight into the ills of society and gave strength to correct them now empowers the believer for evangelism and witnessing. The Spirit was also present as the power who led the believer into a life of personal holiness and consecration.

Speaks's distinctive contribution was to root his theology of the Holy Spirit in a Trinitarian understanding of God that takes the dogmatic tradition seriously. Indeed, his thought suggests a great difficulty (if not impossibility) of conceiving the Holy Spirit apart from the Trinity. For while the Spirit "is of the same essence, substance, and nature of God," the Spirit "is not another person independent of God."[24] This paradox of the Spirit's unity with distinction from the Father and the Son is confessed through the doctrine of the Trinity.

Questions of rank, like those of nature and person, are tedious ones that require an enormous measure of precision. But such questions are just as practical as they are theoretical. Orthodox Christian theology has long insisted on the importance of knowing that the one who is experienced in regeneration, sanctification, healing, or any other spiritual experience is not less than the creator and sustainer who judges people and nations. The Father has not set the world on its course, leaving the powerbrokers in charge and relegating the little and suffering ones to the care of lesser deities—the Son and the Spirit.

Christian pneumatology is fundamentally different from conceptions of spiritual beings in African traditional religion. The Son who accomplishes salvation is Lord. But so is the Spirit who testifies to and comforts a sorrowing heart. The firm and careful insertion of Trinitarian thought into black theology fundamentally opposes the notion that the Father is the god of the strong, prosperous, and mighty, while the Spirit is the god of the weak and helpless. The Father defends the weak; the Son casts down the rich from their thrones of power; the Spirit convicts the mighty of sin and prosecutes them for a guilty verdict and proper judgment. The Spirit anoints that the yoke upon the oppressed might be broken.

One of the most perceptive calls for serious engagement with pneumatology under the rubric of black theology is found in the liberation theologian Major Jones's *The Color of God*.[25] His concluding chapter dealt with the Spirit as God's continuing personal presence in the world. Jones identified and labeled the problem of the "neglect" of the Holy Spirit in the theological tradition of Western Christianity, which he contended had to do largely with its Christocentric emphasis. Consequently, the Holy Spirit has "remained fuzzy" (106). Feeble attempts to uphold the mystery of the Spirit have remained underdeveloped and abstract, with little if any attention being given to the Spirit as person. Jones saw a rich possibility of correcting this deficiency in exploring the Afro-American Christian tradition, derived from African roots and spirituality. Without solving the problem of neglect, Jones pointed to a serious gap present in both the black theology project as well as in Western Christianity, particularly Protestantism, as a "systematic and logical deficiency," the correction of which was not merely academic but existential for black people (110). Pneumatology as an undernourished theme in black theology was especially crucial since parallel struggles for identity, freedom, and liberation are totally dependent upon the Spirit. Without the guidance of theological reflection that takes seriously the dogmatic tradition of the church, those who lay claim to experiences of the Spirit are left to chart their own way. This perpetuates the risk that impulses will be improperly credited to the Spirit, while at the same time those that properly come from the Spirit will not be identified as such. Jones insisted that "to know God fully can mean no less than to know God in the fullness of God's personhood as it is revealed to us now and from now on in the Holy Spirit" (110).

The liberation theologian J. Deotis Roberts has given one of the strongest possible calls for closing the glaring gap in black theology left by undeveloped pneumatology.[26] He did not see himself as the one to do the work, but he made it clear how crucial this challenge is. More importantly, he addressed his appeal directly to Pentecostal scholars, saying the work probably needs to come from one with strong pastoral sensitivities.[27] Roberts asserted emphatically that pneumatology is crucial to any Christology that takes seriously the incarnation of the Son. Admitting his reliance on Western tutors leaves him little to say, because of their notorious neglect of the Spirit. Roberts, nevertheless, sensed the urgent need for a pneumatology. His plea rose to a near mandate for Pentecostal scholars, given the growth and spread of these churches and their enormous influence on the larger church. The challenge is to be both constructive and critical, requiring reflection that is in dialogue with the rest of the church. For Pentecostals are being called "out of the corner," and there is an opportunity in the phenomenal growth of the black Pentecostal movement for theologians to "take up the doctrine of sanctification and give it a more balanced interpretation in the future."[28]

Pentecostalism and the Spirit: Pneumatology as Critical Discourse

As Pentecostalism comes of age, one of its enduring contributions to ecumenical dialogue may be in matters of pneumatology. Born in the crucible of a quest for the renewing of the Spirit, it refined methods inherited from its evangelical predecessors in the fires of revival that have since spread throughout the world. Scarcely was there a concern among these pioneer mothers and fathers that superseded immediate, fresh, and powerful experiences of the Spirit. In their view, God had blessed the nations with a Second Pentecost, and it was their glad duty to spread the tidings to the uttermost parts of the earth.

This revival traced to the earliest days of the twentieth century was, among other things, an experiment in crossing boundaries and passing through barriers. Like the first Pentecost, it blazed with fervent zeal. Embers were derived from the praying grounds where believers of African descent retreated from the watchful eyes of overseers and masters, as well as from camp meetings where the majority of seekers and worshippers were descendants of Europeans. A "tongue of fire" was lit in Topeka, Kansas, where Charles Parham operated a school. The flames were fanned under the leadership of William Seymour in Los Angeles.

But alas, Parham's teaching concerning tongues was laced with racist hermeneutics and heterodox views that threatened to erase the marks of the revival that identified it most with Pentecost. For Parham, tongues supplied the evidence of Spirit baptism and languages for spreading the gospel without the requirement of formally learning them. The revival was preparation for a new cleansing, including the annihilation of the wicked, to accomplish more fully the cleansing from the days of Noah, who was perfect in his generation.[29]

Seymour, on the other hand, understood the outpouring to be approbation of the new experiment of communion with the Spirit that had been poured out on all flesh. It was an instance of the new creation in Christ: "There is neither Jew nor Greek, there is neither slave nor free, there is neither male nor female; for you are all one in Christ Jesus" (Gal. 3:27–28, NKJV). Signs and wonders were divine approbation that, as one observer put it, "The colorline was washed away in the blood."[30]

The standard storyline of the modern Pentecostal narrative is that Parham was the doctrinal father, and Seymour was the herald of his teaching. A worthy debate continues to assess how much of Parham's teaching was actually dispensed by Seymour. Interpreters of Pentecostalism, like Walter Hollenweger, give higher valence to the influences from African religion distilled through Afro-Christian faith.[31] Parham hinted negatively in that direction with his excoriation of practices associated with "darky campmeetings."

Seymour's biographer, Douglas J. Nelson, keenly points out that the rupture between Parham and Seymour involved more than a disagreement over leadership; it also indicated a theological stake.[32] This rupture points to Seymour as theologian. It shows agency and reflection on the work of God that goes beyond direct experience and testimony. In Seymour there was the search for consistency between claims concerning God the Spirit found in the scriptures and the experiences of the present day. But more, his concerns reflected a passion for coherence between the move of God in revivals like the one at Azusa Street and the broader confessions of the church.

The quest for coherence became full blown and was acknowledged as such in the contest over Trinitarian confessions. This contest was comprehended clearly as theological. The same was so in the matter of works of grace and right experience of the Spirit. Some insisted on sanctification as a second work. Those who clung most tightly to the name "Pentecostal" insisted that speaking with tongues is necessary initial evidence of Spirit baptism. But the contest over matters of the Spirit's nature and work in liberation from political, social, and economic bondage, and in tearing down walls of partition within the body of Christ scarcely rose to the level of theological and confessional urgency.[33]

As had been the case nearly a century earlier, in the revivals out of which African churches emerged, issues of liberation and reconciliation were held as the core of the gospel. God's disposition in matters of bondage and liberty were essential to the divine nature and the calling of Christians. As Benjamin Mays points out, Bishop Richard Allen of the AME Church declared boldly that God is the first pleader of the slave's cause; Nathaniel Paul, a Baptist preacher, declared that if he believed for one minute that God approved slavery he would immediately denounce his faith; and Henry Highland Garnet, a Presbyterian minister, declared that because the first duty of the Christian is to fear and obey God, it was the duty of African Christians to free their brothers from their chains so they could bring them to the light of the gospel.[34]

Christianity as it is generally known in the twenty-first century bears many marks of what came to be known as Pentecostalism in the twentieth century. This has in part had to do with effectiveness of mission and the ecumenical movements, particularly where people were encouraged to preach and teach in their own language and idiom. Interestingly, Pentecostalism bore great cultural similarities with the lands into which it was taken. With translation of the Bible into the language of the people, influences began to drift into Western Christianity from other points on the globe. By the categorization of some, worldwide Christianity in the twenty-first century could indeed be called Pentecostal.

Among African Christians in the United States the pattern was well under way in the twentieth century. It was observed from as early as 1933 by Benjamin Mays and Joseph Nicholson in their classic study, *The Negro's Church,* that the second highest numbers in their study came from what they then called the Holiness churches.[35] Their categorization did not distinguish between Pentecostals and Apostolics or pay attention to other theological distinctions, much less address specific teaching on the Holy Spirit. Significantly, however, this work differed from other studies that used the taxonomy of sects and cults to classify Holiness and Pentecostal groups.[36] Mays and Nicholson's methods granted agency to those studied, giving consideration to what subjects had to say of their experience as children of God and attempting to comprehend how those who spoke and acted by prophetic unction shaped the church's vision. Their work expanded the grid to enable a glimpse of how those who named the Spirit as a prominent actor were members who influenced family dialogue rather than opting for a different discourse.

Hearing from Pentecostals is not merely a matter of "inclusiveness," or that all perspectives are heard. It has to do with the experience of God that is crucial for framing theological reflection and discourse in the twenty-first century. Without the voice of the "Holiness part of the family" being invested fully in the reflective life of the Black Church, specifically in matters of pneumatology, significant siblings are muffled, and the concern for power is uncoupled from rituals of sanctification.[37]

Since "pneumatology," as used here, critically reflects on the person and work of the Holy Spirit as third Trinitarian person, an account ought to be given for the existence of the Spirit in communion with the Father and the Son. The first moment is confessing the mystery of God (see 1 Tim. 3:16). As critical discourse, however, there must be keen awareness of the times. Statements of faith rooted in Scriptures and the tradition of the church are to be restated in such a manner as to anticipate and comprehend the objections raised against them. Belief in the Holy Spirit, the Lord and Giver of Life, is proclaimed with full knowledge that the destination is living communities at the beginning of the third millennium. The confession is made in such a manner as to expose the outer limits of the contemporary thought-world, and perhaps even to continue past them.

From the outer limits of modern thought, including objections to faith, pneumatology follows the path of the Spirit who searches the deep things of God and goes where creation touches its limits. The visible comes forth from the invisible, disclosing the limits of the reality to which we are accustomed. As with the wind, we do not know its origin or destiny. The Spirit carries the believing one into the nexus where there is the groaning in the creation that is caught in the tension between forces of estrangement and the work that completes and transfigures that creation. The task of pneumatology in its dogmatic phase is to state the truth to the best of its ability. Clarity is not to be neglected, or pneumatology, as with any other discourse, has no value. Yet, the first move necessarily risks being unpalatable to the enlightened mind, rather than speaking errors.

Similarly with experience; while the Holy Spirit bears witness to the human spirit, the tension remains in critical discourse. The Spirit of God can never be reduced to a projection of human experience—whether personal or corporate. Experience of the Spirit is more than "what God is to me" as if any person is the measure, or as if the meaning of experiencing God is self-evident. What cannot be overlooked are the historical and critical dimensions of knowledge of God, including claims that have been erroneous. Yet there also should be concern for knowledge mediated through experience of the Spirit. Put another way, pneumatology forces the issue of the reason (or logic) inherent in the life of God as the referee for any subsequent reason. Whatever is said concerning the Spirit anticipates what is said at every other point in the declaration of truth. Nothing can be claimed for the Spirit that denies the truth of the Father and the Son: the same is so of the church and the world. Conversely, nothing can be said as the truth of the latter that contradicts the truth of the Spirit, given by revelation.

If God is truth, we do not first arrive at some version of knowledge—even if the vendors are science and history—and subsequently fit in God. If God is Father, Son, and Spirit we cannot make the Father subject to laws, refashion the Son as the principle of philosophical reason, and consign the Spirit to a nonessential cipher that holds them together. No, the Spirit, with all the accompanying "nonrational data," is given in the life of God from whom proceeds plenary reality. This is the reality to which Pentecostalism insists consideration should be given as modern thought reaches its limit. This is the sense in which contemporary pneumatology can and should be critical postmodern discourse.

Pneumatology can neither slip into the ruts of tritheism nor blur the distinction between the Spirit and human experience. It is possible to speak of the Spirit in such a manner that one gets the sense of independent working (i.e., the Spirit told me this, the Spirit told me that) that fails to acknowledge the normative revelation of the Son. Without clarity that the Spirit carries humanity into the life of God through the Son, there is no limit to the credits the Spirit can receive. There is no direct identity between the Holy Spirit and the human spirit, or between the Holy Spirit and the ministry offices of the church. There is dependence on the Spirit, but not equation with the Spirit.

Pneumatology is disciplined speech concerning reality that falls on both sides of the boundary between the rational from the nonrational. It exposes how this boundary is set and offers a fuller version of reality. In other words, as critical Pentecostal discourse, pneumatology is radically theistic, confessing the presence of God in the entire world. It explores the fullest implications of the Spirit as the Lord and giver of life. However, the increasing number of Pentecostals pursuing theological studies does not guarantee more critical reflection. Theological study can be confused with Bible study that focuses primarily on language, adopting fundamentalist interpretation of the Scripture. Though such work may be theological, ironically, it disclaims the very theology being appropriated. Sometimes this antitheological bias appears under the banner of "giving nothing but the Word," subsuming the meaning of texts, the tradition of interpretation (or misinterpretation), and the construction all in one uncritical move.

The issue here is the coherence of knowledge with which theology is concerned. More than an answering discipline, it puts all claims of knowledge to the test. In some instances this means declaring the limits of knowledge. In other instances it means appropriating them and testifying of them, activities that Pentecostals might identify as following after the apostle in "bringing every thought into captivity to the obedience of Christ" (2 Cor. 10:4–5, NKJV).

The experience of God among African American Christians has ever placed strong emphasis on the Spirit, whose nature and marks are life, vitality, energy, power, and koinonia. Whereas copious references to the Spirit are far superior to benign neglect, this second-order speech is still no substitute for the critical and reflective discourse needed to guide the church. For at the same time speech concerning the Spirit is accented in the church, the spirits are put on trial. And this for the African Church has always been rooted in the confession concerning Christ—namely, whether the Son of God has come in the flesh. It is to be noted that this is no docetic love that shuns matter. Rather, it is an embrace of a world in the throes of decay. It is the insertion of the living Christ into the rot of humanity.

Pneumatology cannot profitably be pursued outside the matrix of ecclesial ministry. It is within the context of worship and ministry that the issues arose for the ancient church. Questions concerning the nature and person of the Spirit have everything to do with how believers confess their faith and the power by which the work of the ministry is affected. Our interest is in directly challenging the dictum that "the person with an experience has no need of an argument." The theologian dares to make the challenge for the sake of authentic experience. But the challenge can be made also for the sake of an authentic account, which often becomes the basis for teaching. The implicit pneumatology in the preaching and writing of Pentecostal pioneers ought to be made explicit. Often the pneumatology that is needed already exists in sermons, Bible lectures, and addresses that are extant in unpublished papers, tapes, and other texts.[38] The work of historians, biographers, and scholars from the widest range of fields is crucial.

No conversation in pneumatology can proceed without the wisdom of the church through the ages. To do so would fail to recognize the voluminous valuable work that is the gift of the church fathers and mothers. There should be recognition of the wealth of scholarship in this subfield of theology, which expanded exponentially in the latter half of the twentieth century in the wake of the interactions that carried Pentecostal distinctives back into the mainline churches.[39]

The flowering of pneumatology has gone hand in hand with the resurgence of Trinitarian theology, which is indispensable for avoiding ancient traps and heresies that are as real today as ever. Collapsing ancient meanings onto modern and pragmatic discourse is as problematic today as it was for Arius or Macedonius. Yet, mutual critiques among Trinitarian and Oneness theologians are essential and can be life-giving—as was the case with ancient debates between the East and the West.[40]

Openness to critiques of gendered language that limits the range of images and metaphors mediating revelation into the life of God is equally provocative and important. Exclusive use of the masculine pronoun for the Spirit should be reconsidered. Besides the suspect logic of such a move, we potentially forfeit the wealth of scholarship showing the historic use of feminine images and the difference that makes for knowledge of the Spirit, and thereby knowledge of God.[41]

Serious dangers are present in adopting a pneumatology that does not guard against imbibing the toxic nectars of racism, sexism, and classism. Coming of age requires rejecting false tokens of legitimacy. Baptizing heretical practices of imperialistic and materialistic culture invites embrace of the very idolatry Spirit-filled Christians are called to reject. Claims and practices are to be tested, rather than appropriated uncritically because of an appeal to the Spirit. Criteria for discernment are demanded of pneumatology as critical discourse since, for example, Pentecostalism and prosperity gospel are not identical; every tongue does not confess Jesus as Lord, and some forms of culture deny the power of godliness.[42] Just as no one can speak by the Spirit and curse Jesus, practices within the church and practices of the church in the world cannot be simultaneously "of the antichrist" and authored by the Spirit.

Conclusion

This essay attempted to accomplish two interrelated objectives: (1) to describe how African American Christian thought can contribute some critical perspective on pneumatology, and (2) to show how such contributions can enrich the Pentecostal theological task. Hence this is a prolegomenon to constructive Pentecostal theology, one that reflects on the changing discourses within Afro-Pentecostalism wherein the works of the liberating Spirit are gradually and more explicitly thematized, in this case, in dialogue with black liberation theology. The early mantra of black theology that "Jesus is the Liberator, and the gospel is freedom" begs for the pneumatological factor to be accented. As James Forbes, homiletician, theologian, and former pastor of Riverside Church in Manhattan, makes plain, the Christ of God is Jesus the anointed one.[43] As Forbes suggests, more needs to be made of the confession that he was sent by the Spirit and placed in the womb of a woman. As "pneumataphor" (bearer of the Spirit) Mary groaned as does the creation that awaits deliverance.

If the procession of the Spirit into history is marked by thoroughgoing works of liberty, what must be the nature of the Spirit from eternity? Without a doubt, Pentecostals have insisted that the interpenetration of the Son and the Spirit manifest in the economy of salvation sets at liberty those who are bruised, and heals those oppressed by the devil. Is the witness true who declared that "the Lord is that Spirit, and where the Spirit of the Lord is there is liberty" (2 Cor. 3:18, NKJV)? If God is faithful and cannot deny God's self, then the groaning of the creature subjected to the bondage of creation is utterly consistent with the nature of the Spirit. The Afro-Pentecostal experience thus has borne witness, in the sighs of afflicted bodies, to the liberating mission of the Spirit. The release in worship, visions, rapture, and manifestations of power are gestures away from the terror of history as a human tale of carnal rulers toward embrace the Spirit's mission. Black Pentecostals will insist that these sighs are more than complaints; rather, the cries of the faithful are shouts of the kingdom, which is righteousness, peace, and joy in the Holy Ghost. One might go even farther to say that these sighs, gestures, and shouts are also a summons for the reflective work that takes the shape of pneumatology.

NOTES TO CHAPTER 10

1. In the view of some, Pentecostalism and pneumatology are considered one and the same. Within certain Pentecostal circles, pneumatology begins and ends with "baptism in the Holy Spirit," and "operation of the gifts." From that viewpoint, pneumatology has or should have been conceded to Pentecostals by the rest of the church, who for neglect and "loss of first love" have quenched the fires of Pentecost.

2. I use the term "pneumatomonism" to name the absorption of theology under one rubric, as if the Spirit is all encompassing.

3. *The greatest growth* of Christianity is in the Southern Hemisphere, in those regions of the globe that have been referred to as the Third World. See Walbert Buhlman, *The Coming of the Third Church: An Analysis of the Present and Future of the Church* (Maryknoll, N.Y.: Orbis Books, 1977), and Amos Yong, *The Spirit Poured Out On All Flesh: Pentecostalism and the Possibility of Global Theology* (Grand Rapids, Mich.: Baker Academic, 2005). Issues of Western epistemology that were significant during and following the Enlightenment often are unimportant in this part of the world. The bias toward historical consciousness and rational proof as the verification for truth left little room for the Spirit, who comes and goes like the wind. However, this fascination with a limited domain of knowledge hastened the advance of skepticism and the erosion of faith, known as atheism.

4. See slave testimonies in Clifton Johnson, *God Struck Me Dead: Religious Conversion Experiences and Autobiographies of Ex-Slaves* (Philadelphia: Pilgrim Press, 1969).

5. Milton C. Sennett, *Afro-American Religious History: A Documentary Witness* (Durham, N.C.: Duke University Press, 1985), 166–67.

6. Joseph R. Washington, *Black Religion: The Negro and Christianity in the United States* (Boston: Beacon, 1966).

7. See early statements in Gayraud Wilmore and James Cone, eds., *Black Theology: A Documentary Witness, 1966–79* (Maryknoll, N.Y.: Orbis Books, 1980), and James Gardiner and J. Deotis Roberts, *Quest for a Black Theology* (Philadelphia: Pilgrim Press, 1971). Antecedents to this emerging field of scholarship are found in texts like Benjamin E. Mays, *The Negro's God, as Reflected in his Literature* (Boston: Chapman and Grimes, 1938), and the work of Howard Thurman, particularly his *Jesus and the Disinherited* (Boston: Beacon Press, 1949). See also Sue Bailey Thurman, *For the Inward Journey: The Writings of Howard Thurman* (Richmond, Ind.: Friends United Press, 1984). For the writings of

Martin Luther King Jr., see James Washington, *A Testament of Hope: The Essential Writing of Martin Luther King Jr.* (San Francisco: HarperCollins, 1991).

8. James H. Cone, *Black Theology and Black Power* (New York: Seabury Press, 1969).

9. Henry Mitchell, *Black Belief: Folk Beliefs of Blacks in American and West Africa* (New York: Harper and Row Publishers, 1975), 139.

10. E. Franklin Frazier, *The Negro Church in America* (New York: Schocken Books, 1974), 14–17.

11. Mitchell, *Black Belief*, 139.

12. Ibid., 143.

13. Albert Cleage, *Black Christian Nationalism: New Directions for the Black Church* (New York: William Morrow, 1972). Hereafter cited in text.

14. Reference here is to circulation of life among the Father, Son, and Spirit (see Jn. 14:10; 15:26).

15. James H. Cone, "Sanctification and Liberation in the Black Religious Tradition," in Theodore Runyon, ed., *Sanctification and Liberation: Liberation Theologies in Light of the Wesleyan Tradition* (Nashville, Tenn.: Abingdon, 1981), 174–92.

16. Ibid. 174.

17. Actually, the point is made with great force, and it is crucial for identifying pneumatological threads in black theology. Cecil Cone accents the encounter of the Almighty Sovereign God as the deepest node of Afro-Christian faith. See Cecil W. Cone, *The Identity Crisis in Black Theology* (Nashville, Tenn.: AMEC Publishing House, 1975). Leonard Lovett, "Black Holiness-Pentecostalism: Implications for Ethics and Social Transformation" (PhD diss., Emory University, 1979), is even more explicit in his exploration of how the ethical and ritual life within black Pentecostalism embodies motions toward social transformation.

18. Cone, "Sanctification and Liberation," 175.

19. Ibid., 188. In his article "Black Origins of the Pentecostal Movement," Lovett commented that "No man can genuinely experience the fullness of the Spirit and remain a bona fide racist" (in Vinson Synan, ed., *Aspects of Pentecostal-Charismatic Origins* [Plainfield, N.J.: Logos International, 1975], 140).

20. Cone, "Sanctification and Liberation," 190.

21. Ibid., 122.

22. Cone, *Black Theology of Liberation*, 122

23. Bishop R. L. Speaks, *The Prelude to Pentecost: A Theology of the Holy Spirit* (Pompano Beach, Fla.: Exposition Press, 1985).

24. Ibid., 67. In an almost cryptic manner Speaks telegraphed one of the most crucial problems that can arise without careful pneumatology. In attempting to illustrate his understanding of the Trinity, he spoke of a right triangle with three equal angles, indicating equality within the Godhead. But he called it an "isosceles" triangle. In the isosceles triangle only two sides are equal, the third side being unequal. This geometric error reflects a potential theological error. He wanted the angles to be equal with only two sides being equal. Similarly with the Trinity: he wanted to say that the Trinitarian persons are equal in substance, essence, will, and purpose but unequal in roles and functions. But that cannot be. Just as the sides of a triangle must be equal for the angles to be equal, so must the (work of the) divine persons be equal for their substance and essence to be equal.

25. Major Jones, *The Color of God: The Concept of God in Afro American Thought* (Macon, Ga.: Mercer University Press, 1987). Hereafter cited in text.

26. J. Deotis Roberts, *The Prophethood of Black Believers: An African American Political Theology for Ministry* (Louisville, Ky.: Westminster/John Knox Press, 1994).

27. Ibid., 38, 63.

28. Ibid., 38.

29. Parham's teaching included doctrines like the eighth-day creation to distinguish the "formed race" of Caucasians from the created race of blacks, browns, and "half-breeds." He saw the gift of tongues for evangelizing in the language of the nations and for sparing the righteous remnant from the great conflagration to come, and repudiated Seymour for his ventures in race mixing. See Charles Fox Parham, *The Everlasting Gospel* (Baxter Springs, Kans.: Apostolic Faith Church, 1911), 4, 100, 111ff; cf. Robert Mapes Anderson, *Vision of the Disinherited: The Making of American Pentecostalism* (New York: Oxford University Press, 1979), 81ff.

30. Frank Bartleman, *Azusa Street: The Roots of Modern-Day Pentecost* (1925; repr., Plainfield, N.J.: Logos International, 1980), 54.

31. Walter J. Hollenweger, *Pentecostalism: Origins and Developments Worldwide* (Peabody, Mass: Hendrickson, 1977), chap. 3.

32. Douglas J. Nelson, "For Such a Time as This: The Story of Bishop William J. Seymour and the Azusa Street Revival—A Search for Pentecostal/Charismatic Roots" (PhD diss., University of Birmingham [England], 1981).

33. The bottom line regarding the nature person and of the Spirit is no different from the critical question of William R. Jones to black theologians. He pressed it with great force in his book *Is God a White Racist? A Preamble to Black Theology* (Boston: Beacon Press, 1998).

34. Mays, *Negro's God*, 33ff.

35. Benjamin E. Mays and Joseph William Nicholson, *The Negro's Church* (New York: Institute of Social and Religious Research, 1933).

36. See, for example, Horace R. Cayton and St. Clair Drake, *Black Metropolis: A Study of Negro Life in a Northern City* (New York: Harcourt, Brace, 1945), and Arthur H. Fauset, *Black Gods of the Metropolis* (Philadelphia: University of Pennsylvania Press, 1944).

37. I am expanding Mays's category to include Holiness, Pentecostals, Apostolics, and other independents that identify with the theologies and worship practices that have been cultivated under these rubrics. See a fuller discussion of the perforated boundary among black evangelicals and Pentecostal groups in William C. Turner Jr., *The United Holy Church of America, Inc.: A Study in Black Holiness-Pentecostalism* (Piscataway, N.J.: Gorgias Press, 2006).

38. Cheryl Sanders's *Saints in Exile: The Holiness-Pentecostal Experience in African American Religion and Culture* (New York: Oxford University Press, 1996), and her archaeology into the treasures of Bishop Smallwood Williams are examples. There is also my work, *The United Holy Church*, as well as the published and unpublished works of Ithiel Clemmons, Leonard Lovett, Bishop A. W. Lawson, Bishop Ozro T. Jones, Robert C. Lawson, Garfield Haywood, and countless others known only within small circles and denominational churches—many of which are priceless in value.

39. The works of Augustine of Hippo and the Cappadocians are indispensable. Orthodox and Roman Catholics scholarship is exceedingly good for exposing these treasures. Guidance can be found in George Montague and Kilian McDonnell, *Christian Initiation and Baptism in the Holy Spirit: Evidence from the First Eight Centuries* (Collegeville, Minn.: Liturgical Press, 1991); Yves Congar, *I Believe in the Holy Spirit*, trans. David Smith, 3 vols. (New York: Seabury Press, 1986); and George Montague, *The Holy Spirit: The Growth of*

a Biblical Tradition (New York: Paulist, 1976; repr., Peabody, Mass.: Hendrickson, 1994). Classics among Protestants include the work of H. B. Swete, *The Holy Spirit in the Ancient Church: A Study of Christian Teaching in the Age of the Fathers* (London: Macmillan, 1912), and Abraham Kuyper, *The Work of the Holy Spirit*, trans. Henri De Vries (New York: Funk and Wagnalls, 1990). Recent work by Jürgen Moltmann, Michael Welker, Molly Marshall, Clark Pinnock, Jose Comblin, J. Rodman Williams, and Veli-Matti Karkkainen add to a growing body of work.

40. Amos Yong's insights on this matter in *Spirit Poured Out* possess great value.

41. See Donald Gelpi, *The Divine Mother: A Trinitarian Theology of the Holy Spirit* (Lanham, Md.: University Press of America, 1984), and Catherine LaCugna, *God for Us: The Trinity and Christian Life* (San Francisco: HarperSanFrancisco, 1992).

42. Leonard Lovett asserts that "Authentic liberation can never occur apart from genuine Pentecostal encounter, and likewise, authentic Pentecostal encounter does not occur without liberation" ("Black Origins of the Pentecostal Movement," 140).

43. James Forbes, *The Holy Spirit and Preaching* (Nashville, Tenn.: Abingdon Press, 1989), chap. 2. Theo Witvliet, in *The Way of the Black Messiah: The Hermeneutical Challenge of Black Theology as a Theology of Liberation*, trans. John Bowden (Oak Park, Ill.: Meyer Stone Books, 1987), put his finger on the same nerve, expanding the underdeveloped pneumatological hermeneutic that connects the liberating praxis of Jesus of Nazareth with black history and culture. His insights deserve attention. I would argue that good liberation theology is pneumatology, and good pneumatology is liberation theology.

11

On the Compatibility/ Incompatibility of Pentecostal Premillennialism with Black Liberation Theology

FREDERICK L. WARE

Introduction

One aspect of African American religion and culture is the tendency toward utopian and eschatological vision, what I call the mythic dimension of racial consciousness.[1] Here is where the turn to another reality takes place, and where belief and hope are born. Here is a nostalgic longing for recovery of a lost past or a dream of a promising future. Brought forcefully and violently into a new emerging global system, oppressed Africans and their descendents formed different ideas about American identity and the role of America and its future in the world.

This gaze forward into a time yet to come, but perceived as consequential for the present, is found in Pentecostalism and black theology. Both movements intersect in eschatology, the doctrine of the end times or of the last days (among other arenas). Black theology chooses eschatology as a central category for studying and interpreting the mythic dimension of racial consciousness. In Pentecostalism's aspiration to be colorblind or to transcend race, ethnicity, and other markers of human identity, eschatology centers on the nearness of Christ's return, the time at which Christ expects to be greeted by a unified church without regard to these identifiers.

The term "millennialism" refers to religious and political perspectives about the end of history. Often hoped for is a golden age of joy, peace, justice, and prosperity. In American civic life, influenced by the Christian hope of a glorious future, talk about the destiny of the United States is framed around optimism and the idea of progress. The American nation, whose best days always lie ahead, is believed to be God's instrument in ushering human civilization into a new stage of development. In Christian thought, this golden age is the millennium, the period when Christ will rule on earth. Based on convictions about when Christ will return (before, after, or not at all for the millennium), Christian millennialism divides into premillennialism, postmillennialism, and amillennialism. While political discourse about the future of the United States may be called simply "American millennialism," it shares in common with postmillennialism the view that the golden age is preceded by, possibly even hastened or caused by, improvement in human society.

African Americans altered American millennialism and thus created their own black millennialism to account for their past experience and secure their future participation in the United States and world history. Black millennialism grants African Americans meaningful inclusion in the coming golden age. Black millennialism is shaped by African American beliefs regarding the utility of American culture and social institutions in transforming the world, about the probability and aftermath of divine judgment of injustices in American society and Western civilization, and about the church's role in establishing a new era of earthly equality, justice, and prosperity. Black millennialism retains an American postmillennial orientation that emphasizes progress and a belief that the golden age is preceded by improvement in human society.

Pentecostal premillennialism (the pervasive conception of eschatology in Pentecostal churches) conflicts with black racial consciousness and is thus insufficiently compatible with a theology designed to empower black liberation. Unable to dislodge itself from its premillennialism or develop an alternative conception of eschatology, African American Pentecostals have developed instead their demonology and holiness codes in order to sanction their social activism. However, such a resort to demonology and holiness doctrine alone does not address the restrictions on social action imposed by premillennialist eschatology. In light of African American Pentecostals' move to name injustice as an "evil" that must be and can be overcome and their integration of social justice into their holiness teachings, an additional adjustment may make African American Pentecostalism a source of liberation theology: replacing premillennialism with a conception of eschatology derived from black folk sources and black Christian millennialism. I do not reject millennialism but instead propose for African American Pentecostals a reorientation toward a conception of eschatology derived from black religion, a covering term for black folk sources and black millennialism.

In spite of Pentecostal claims to interracial beginnings, imperatives to evangelize all peoples, and quest for an ecclesial and social unity that transcends race, African American Pentecostals are concentrated in "Black Churches," congregations and denominations that are membered predominately by persons of African descent. Since black theology focuses on matters impacting the humanity and quality of life of black people, within such situations African American Pentecostals cannot afford to neglect the black theological tradition.[2]

Although the term "black theology" has been in use since the 1960s; its meaning is hardly common. There is no uniform definition for black theology or, as it is sometimes called, black liberation theology. In this chapter, black liberation theology names a tendency in African American religion and culture as well as the academic writing that emerged as a result of African American clergy and scholars reflecting theologically on the civil rights and black power movements of the 1960s. In reflection on African Americans' experiences, primarily in their struggles to assert their humanity, black theology focuses on liberation as a major theme and ultimate goal.[3] While academic black theologians seek to portray accurately African American experience, their works do not represent it wholly or absolutely. Black theology is not one and the same with the academic literature produced by professional theologians. Alongside academic writings, there are other traditions with additional and possibly alternative meanings of liberation.[4] Further study needs to be done on these lived religious traditions embodied in the sayings, songs, stories, social organizations, and cultural beliefs of African Americans. In this chapter, I propose that cultural products such as black folk religion and black millennialism, which African American Pentecostals may claim as part of their ethnic and religious heritage, be mined for insight into eschatological thinking. Throughout, my focus is on urging a shift in Afro-Pentecostal theological discourse in general and eschatological thought in particular, away from what has remained fairly closely tethered to the classical Pentecostal theological tradition toward one that is more congruent with black theological sensibilities and commitments.

Eschatology in Black Religion

In the British colonies that would eventually become the United States, British Protestant Christians construed the settlement of the Americas as a divinely inspired and guided mission, favoring the expansion of a new people and nation entitled to opportunity, wealth, and power. These Christians believed that they were chosen to advance God's kingdom and glory on earth. By making a better world, they would hasten the millennium—a golden age in human civilization—after which Christ would return. This thinking on the role and future of the American nation has endured for centuries.[5] Excluded, in various ways, from this entitlement and grand mission were African slaves and their descendents, who were left out of this march toward progress and prosperity.

African slaves dreamed of another world, not based on racial caste and inequality. They imagined and strove for a place of destiny beyond and after America. They redefined and reshaped Christian eschatology in accordance with their experiences, values, and traditions.[6] Their beliefs in life beyond death, as well as possible existence beyond oppression, were expressed clearly in their narratives, tales, songs, sermons, aphorisms, prayers, and funeral and burial practices.[7]

A distinct conception of eschatology emerges from the spirituals and other folk sources. African slaves believed in the return of Christ and the establishment of God's kingdom on earth. Their hermeneutics is character-ized by literal and figurative interpretation of biblical texts, guided by val-ues of freedom and justice, and their eschatology is aimed at inspiring and assessing human effort. The kingdom of God is goal and norm; it is a symbol of destiny (on earth and/or in the afterlife) and standard by which to judge social practices and behaviors. Black eschatology is suspicious of the arro-gance and triumphalism of American millennialism. Blacks believe in the ultimacy of divine agency. The end, symbolized by catastrophe or the spec-tacular, is beyond what calculated human effort alone can achieve. While the end time is spoken of as "coming soon," there is little or no speculation or prediction about the precise moment of the end.[8] There is, however, certitude that justice will come.[9]

The kingdom of God is realized not only in the remote future but in the present.[10] In the present, God's reign is realized in the affirmation of black people's humanity, experiences of freedom and community, and fulfillment of needs and desires crucial for survival and quality of life.[11] Worse than death is the mode of existence marked by nonfulfillment. In the here and now, ecstatic experience is assurance of God's presence and promise. Through these and other encounters with God, black people's humanity is defined and dignified.[12] When certain spirituals were sung, slaves knew that these songs were coded messages about escape and flight to the North.[13] Heaven was not only above, in the sky, but also north of the Mason-Dixon Line or in Canada where slaveholding was not sanctioned by law. Heaven is a metaphor for community, where one is reunited with loved ones and is recognized and respected. In heaven, needs and desires are met adequately and fully.

Black Christian millennialism is much like the visions of eschatology in black folk sources.[14] African Americans expressed a number of views on the millennium, ranging from affirmation to disbelief. The types of black millennialism are (1) cultural (characterized by belief in transformation of the world through American principles and institutions), (2) racial (espousing belief in black leadership established for God's transformation of the world), and (3) progressive (marked by belief in the power of Christianity to transform the world through evangelism, missions, and social reform).[15]

Black Christian millennialism was developed and propagated in the latter part of the nineteenth century and early decades of the twentieth century, roughly from 1865 to 1925.[16] This is a period of African Americans' mass projections of self-identity and prolific institution building. They held public forums and utilized print media to clarify their racial identity and status as American citizens. Several African American institutions, including Christian denominations and colleges and universities, which are today recognized as "historic," may be traced to this period.

These widely varied black millennialist perspectives exhibit common beliefs including (1) belief in an imminent golden age that will start and spread from either the United States or the African continent, (2) belief that history is divinely ordained and controlled by God, (3) belief that the movement of history is progressive, (4) belief that the eradication of racism is of primary importance, (5) the belief that the kingdom of God is not identical to Western civilization or Christianity, in view of the injustices against African Americans and the distortion of Christianity to sanction these social injustices, and (6) belief that personal and social change involves human participation in God's plan of transforming the world. These core beliefs of black Christian millennialism are a refinement of themes found in folk sources. In the folk sources the terms "jubilee," "heaven," "kingdom of God," "millennium," and "golden age" are used, as in black millennialism, to describe possible and actual human experience here on earth. Black Christian millennialism offers further clarification on the location of the millennium (golden age), the distinction between the kingdom of God and Western civilization, which beliefs and practices of the American nation hasten the golden age, and which role African Americans fulfill in the coming of the millennium and establishment of the kingdom of God.

The theological roots of black Christian millennialism may lie in the Great Awakening and in the emergent perceptions of the contradiction of racism and oppression with the sacred mission of the American nation. "The revivalism of the Great Awakening, spread over time and space by evangelical preachers, created the conditions for large-scale conversion of [African American] slaves."[17] Jonathan Edwards and other revival preachers described the Awakening as the "dawning of a new day" and the conversion of African Americans as "showers of grace" preceding the "glorious times," that is, the millennium.[18] Edwards's postmillennialism appropriates the Puritans' sacred history of New England to describe the revivals. The Puritans believed that they were in the final stage of history. As they saw it, God's plan of history followed the principle of progress through struggle. They believed that the future would bring improvement. Better days, a millennium, would occur before the return of Christ. For Edwards, the revivals were a sign of the millennium that was starting in America and would spread to other parts of the world. Revival preaching, during and after the Revolutionary War, blended with the rhetoric of patriotism to produce an association of God's work in history with politics and government. American institutions were deemed essential for the propagation of the gospel. In the zeal of evangelical churches (Presbyterian, Baptist, and Methodist) to spread the gospel, strong positions were taken against slavery, and visions were cast for the reform of society. The evangelical churches challenge of the existing social order and African Americans' own adverse experience of racism and oppression provoked African Americans to propose alternative interpretations of the American nation and its mission.

Pentecostal Premillennialism

The emergence of Pentecostalism from the Holiness movement was accompanied by a parallel shift from postmillennialism to premillennialism.[19] With this shift, the postmillennial vision of the Holiness movement, marked by optimism and promise of social improvement, gave way to increasing disillusionment and doubt in the face of mounting decline and deterioration in the world. No longer convinced that the millennium could be achieved within history or by adoption of Christian ideals or human effort, radical Holiness leaders introduced premillennialism as an alternative interpretation of the condition of the world and how, and in what manner, the millennium would be possible.[20]

In premillennialism, it is believed that Christ will return visibly and bodily before his thousand-year reign on the earth, an important period at the end of the world. With premillennialism, the church has a limited role in society with respect to social change or social reform, and its mission is primarily to evangelize, so that individuals may be saved from a world that is doomed to destruction.

While premillennialism is a central feature and theological distinctive of Pentecostalism, not all early Pentecostal leaders had a well-developed theology of the end times. For example, in contrast to Charles Parham's eschatology that specified a chronology of events, William Seymour conceived eschatology very generally for practical and pastoral purposes.[21] For Seymour, it was a way of making real the sense of urgency of persons to come into the fullness of God (i.e., receive the baptism in the Holy Spirit) and become involved in the church's mission of spreading the gospel to those yet needing to hear about God's plan of salvation.

The Church of God in Christ (COGIC) has maintained this tradition of premillennialism growing out of the Azusa revival led by Seymour.[22] In the interest of maintaining unity and harmony, COGIC discourages speculation of the sort common to dispensational premillennialism, and its official statement is not explicit regarding which form of premillennialism it endorses. COGIC tolerates, rather than rejects, dispensational premillennialism. Nevertheless, it is squarely premillennialist in its orientation toward eschatology, believing that "Christ will return before the Millennium."[23] In the spirit of Seymour, COGIC makes a simple appeal to the doctrine of the imminent return of Christ in order to urge persons to live righteously in preparation for the coming of Christ. For COGIC, the fundamental truth that all believers can or should embrace is that "Christ will return to this earth for his church."[24] In light of this believed truth, individuals are urged to live in a state of preparation. COGIC affirms the imminent return of Christ as "a powerful factor in shaping conduct, quickening conscience, and enforcing the obligations of service for God and man."[25]

COGIC's belief in the imminent return of Christ is based on interpretation of passages from Paul's letters and the book of Revelation. In Paul's letters, it is evident that he and other early Christians believed that Christ would return in *their* lifetime, not centuries later. Paul goes to great lengths to console his fellow Christians, asserting that departed believers are not lost and will not miss out on Christ's return. In Revelation 20, the only passage where the notion of the thousand years is mentioned, Christ comes before the millennium and assumes rulership over the earth. Paul makes no reference, directly or indirectly, to the millennium. COGIC subscribes to classical premillennialism at the risk of minimizing (maybe even trivializing) the social, cultural, and historical setting of biblical literature. The expectation expressed in Paul's letters and the book of Revelation was unmet: the visible, bodily return of Christ during the lifetime of these early Christians did not occur. Their disappointment raises questions as to whether the imminent return of Christ is essential for the development of eschatology.

The Turn to Demonology and Holiness Teachings

It is through demonology and holiness teachings, and not eschatology, that African American Pentecostals justify their social and political engagement.[26] Pentecostals combat and seek to overcome various social problems by naming them as "evil," "demonic," or "Satanic." George McKinney's *The New Slave Masters* is illustrative of this tradition in COGIC.[27] McKinney, who is a bishop on the twelve-member governing board of the COGIC, names as evil and demonic the following realities: drugs, materialism, the mindless pursuit of pleasure and desire for instant gratification, racism, rage (misdirected frustration with racism), domestic violence, pornography, teenage pregnancy, and gangs—these are the forces of evil enslaving and destroying African American communities.[28] The advantage of McKinney's strategic turn to demonology is that these social matters may be taken seriously and addressed by Pentecostals. ·

McKinney argues that civil rights laws and other forms of legislation are limited tools for effecting change. He points out that after the removal of various legal barriers to black people's progress, they are hindered by their own lifestyle choices.[29] McKinney focuses attention on areas of private and personal life about which African Americans should be concerned and should be capable of addressing. According to McKinney, black people's realization of freedom comes about not only in the acquisition and exercise of civil rights but also the development of stable families as a key component for vibrant social and cultural life.

The shortcoming of McKinney's perspective is that the social problems he identifies are spiritualized to the point of disassociation from the actual processes and systems contributing to the formation of these problems.[30] Certainly, injustice and meaningless suffering is evil and demonic; there is something terribly wrong and harmful about these forms of experience. However, the attribution of causality chiefly to demons de-emphasizes human freedom and responsibility. Instead of human persons, demons are viewed as the culprits for almost all calamity and suffering. By successfully invading the human soul or mind, demons control persons, groups, and nations. The result is that humans are ultimately not held accountable for the condition and care of the world resulting from their choices. Demonology inhibits investigation of the complexity of human personal behavior and social interaction. It can aid us in labeling something as evil, but it does not supply us with tools for critical self-introspection and analysis of patterns of social behavior.

Rather than an analysis of processes and systems, McKinney proposes a form of morality grounded in middle-class values and centered on improving and normalizing family relationships. While family life should be valued and nurtured, McKinney's perspective is not informed by empirical study showing causal or correlative relations between family life and the problems that he identifies. The dualism that values soul over the body, or gifts of the Holy Spirit (ecstatic experience) over fruit of the Spirit (moral and ethical conduct), works against McKinney's integration of social activism into COGIC's holiness code.

Middle-class orientation is not radical or revolutionary; instead it often stands as an impediment to the achievement of social justice. The goal of the black middle class is to integrate, to "make it" in America. The middle class adopts mores that bring it into compliance with the norms of the ruling elite. By self-discipline, adherence to high moral standards, obedience to authority, hard work, education, and the exercise of financial responsibility, the black middle class believes that it will find and enjoy benefits in the American political and economic system.[31] Certainly, with the growth of the black middle class and the recent election of Barack Obama, the first person of African descent to the presidency of the United States, it would seem that the middle-class approach has worked for African Americans. Inequities still exists in America, however, with African Americans disproportionately cast among the poor. The lower classes struggle daily against poverty, violence, hunger, and lack of access to health care, quality education, affordable housing, and jobs that pay a living wage. Barred from the goods of society, the poor and oppressed are open to alternatives for attaining meaningful existence. True revolution, the break from the old and creation of a new order, comes from the poor.[32] Unfortunately, the protest arising from the poor and oppressed is skewed by the interests of the middle class, who are unlikely to support full-scale revolution, that is, the radical restructuring of society and redistribution of power and wealth.[33] Some African American leaders, holding middle- and upper-class status, depict poor blacks as backward and degenerate, and therefore needing to become civilized and moral, as if the problems in African American communities are primarily personal rather than the result of social injustice.[34] While the middle class seeks to increase its access to the goods of society, the poor are not only without the goods but also without any real means of access.

In spite of noble efforts at social reform, Pentecostals have invested the greater sum of their energy in combating perceived personal sins such as social dancing, styles of clothing (mostly women's fashions), lipstick and cosmetics, the use of tobacco products (cigars, cigarettes, snuff, chewing tobacco), alcoholic beverages, narcotics, gambling, premarital and extra-marital sex, divorce, homosexuality, and same-sex marriage.[35] The resort to demonology or emphasis on holiness teachings does not motivate social analysis and strategic planning on how to remedy societal and personal problems.[36] Pentecostals' experiments in social activism and reform thus have been sporadic and limited.[37] Social engagement is justified as a tool for evangelism rather than by its capacity to express the obligation of the church to serve the poor and combat injustices that cause their poverty.

Compatibility/Incompatibility of Pentecostal Premillennialism with Eschatology in Black Religion

The points at which Pentecostal premillennialism is compatible with eschatology in black folk sources and black Christian millennialism are (1) belief in the return of Christ and the establishment of the kingdom of God, (2) belief in the ultimacy of divine agency in the establishment of the king-dom of God, (3) suspicion of the optimism of American millennialism, and (4) belief in and desire for freedom.

McKinney uses the metaphor of slavery-emancipation to address prob-lems in African American communities about which he is concerned. That he seeks to set persons free from bondage is indicative of the place and value of freedom in his system of thought.[38] In this system, God does not act in the stead of human beings; rather God acts persuasively, inspiring and plac-ing before humans alternatives on which they must act in order to be deliv-ered from bondage and thereby enjoy life. God supplies the means, that is, a plan of salvation. Humans appropriate that means through their cooperation with God's plan. From McKinney's perspective, freedom is the absence of hindrance or restriction in the realization of one's potential. A person is free when he or she lives the life God intended for him or her.[39]

Where Pentecostal premillennialism is incompatible with eschatology in black folk sources and black Christian millennialism is in the areas of herme-neutics and realization of the kingdom of God. Unlike black folk eschatol-ogy, Pentecostal premillennialism entails a spiritual reading of the Bible that does not allow latitude in figurative interpretation. In black religion, because of the leeway given in biblical interpretation, heaven or the kingdom of God refers not only to the afterlife but corresponds to physical locations and situ-ations on this life, on the earth. The escape from bondage is not an exercise in spiritual disciplines only, but it is also a concerted effort to protest and resist systems of social oppression. Social justice and complete emancipation is the defining hope in black religion, which is very this-worldly.

Conclusion: Toward Liberation Theology and Constructive Theology

African American Pentecostalism falls short of restoring primitive Christianity and of renewing the Black Church by not articulating a sound eschatology. American millennialism distorts Christian eschatology by legitimating the imperialist aspirations of the American nation. Enslaved Africans constructed an alternative eschatological vision compatible with early Christians' resistance to the cult of the Roman Emperor. African American Pentecostalism's recovery of the eschatology of the "fathers and mothers" of black Christian faith will allow it to come closer to recapturing the spirituality and ethics of the early Christians' resistance.

The embrace of premillennialism raises identity problems for African American Pentecostals, hermeneutically, socially, and politically. Premillennialism entails a commitment to a certain reading of the Bible, which is especially problematic where the resolution of doctrinal issues could be achieved by openness to other interpretations of biblical texts. Also, premillennialism carries with it a pessimistic view of humanity's effort to do anything to substantially improve the condition and fate of society. The church is not perceived as a force for the restructuring of society. Its role is thus to simply evangelize (save as many individuals as possible from) a world doomed to destruction.[40] This world is viewed as a place to escape and, in Pentecostal churches influenced by the prosperity gospel, a place to exploit. This world is not seen as a place to love, engage, or build community.

Pentecostals' resort to demonology is fraught with complications. While naming social injustice as evil, these evils are spiritualized and removed from thorough social analysis. Although demonology has the potential to raise awareness about matters that are terribly wrong, the fixation on demons is more often excessive and unhealthy.[41] Without social analysis, black Pentecostalism lacks practical strategies for achieving substantive change in the world. The assertion of social justice as a mark of holiness is frustrated by the focus on personal moral failing and on uncritical adoption of prevalent cultural traditions, norms, and middle-class values.

One alternative that has been put forth by some Pentecostals to foster engagement with society and culture is dominion theology, which draws much of its symbolism from Christian eschatology.[42] Its aim is to place Christians in positions of power and influence in society. In spite of its rallying cry for Christians to reign until Christ returns, dominion theology is not an acceptable alternative. Rather, it is for the most part simply a negative response to religious and philosophical pluralism, and is not grounded in a commitment to social justice and solidarity with the poor but in a will to power.

Does black Pentecostal eschatology have to be premillennialist? My answer is no. African American Pentecostal churches may continue as an eschatological community awaiting the return of Christ, but if black Pentecostalism aspires to restore primitive Christianity or renew the Black Church, it cannot achieve this end through commitment to premillennialism. Traditional black Christian eschatology (i.e., eschatology in black religion) allows flexible (literal and figurative) interpretation and political engagement of the sort not found in Pentecostal premillennialism. Robert C. Lawson, an African American Pentecostal church leader, was able to develop a theological critique of racism in the Pentecostal movement because of his leanings toward black Christian millennialism.[43]

Among the various theological distinctives of Pentecostalism, eschatology (if radically altered) offers the greatest potential for addressing its apoliticalism and other excesses. While there is no universally accepted definition of Pentecostalism or consensus of what is Pentecostal belief, the movement may be defined in terms of a perspective that arises from a dialectic between certain valued experiences and the Bible. Persons claim to have a certain kind of encounter with God that influences the way that they read Scripture. Further, the manner in which they interpret Scripture influences their expectations and understandings of the nature of God and the parameters of the encounter with God. A major reorientation in eschatology—shifting from premillennialist, individualistic, and futuristic notions to more social and this-worldly conceptions of salvation—will change the way Pentecostals interpret Scripture, construct doctrine, and understand religious experience.

The shift suggested in this chapter may enable African American Pentecostalism to become a source for liberation theology and even fertile ground for constructive theology. As Afro-Pentecostal theology has never been static but always dynamic, the possibility for such a development should not be underestimated. Afro-Pentecostals are increasingly realizing the need to revise received theological doctrines and ideas and to recalibrate their beliefs so as to achieve a more coherent and consistent self-understanding of their cultural heritage and religious life. The result may even be a more liberative theological tradition conducive to achieving the realities that they hope for and aspire to.

1. See Charles H. Long, *Significations: Signs, Symbols, and Images in the Interpretation of Religion* (Aurora, Colo.: Davies Group Publishers, 1999), 184; "Passage and Prayer: The Origin of Religion in the Atlantic World," in Quinton Hosford Dixie and Cornel West, eds., *The Courage to Hope: From Black Suffering to Human Redemption* (Boston: Beacon Press, 1999), 17–18; and "African American Religion in the United States: A Bibliographic Essay," in Arvarh E. Strickland and Robert E. Weems, eds., *The African American Experience: An Historiographical and Bibliographical Guide* (Westport, Conn.: Greenwood Press, 2001), 371–72. Long defines religion as orientation in the ultimate sense, that is, how one comes to terms with the ultimate significance of one's place in the world. Religion is a way of relating and reconciling oneself to things and matters of ultimacy. Discernment of one's place in the world is fundamental to Long's interpretation of religion. By providing grounding and integration of one's consciousness (awareness) of and as a self, race is a medium for understanding one's place in and connections to the world and for gaining insight into the nature of the physical, social and cultural environment where one lives. Though race neither encompasses fully nor exhausts totally the meaning of human life, the religious significance of racial consciousness (i.e., awareness of the self as having a particular racial identity or belonging to a particular social group) is found in its contribution to the saga, the long and ongoing story of the human quest for a fulfilled existence. In the United States, the construction of black racial identity often encompasses visions of and aspirations for an improved future.

2. It may be that African American Pentecostalism has a unique calling not only as a movement in Christian spirituality but also as a contextual and liberation theology. According to William Turner, African American Pentecostalism is rooted in the tradition of black churches and stands as a call for the Black Church to be spiritual (intimately connected to God), prophetic (socially aware and active), and alive (a functional and authentic religious community). See William C. Turner, *The United Holy Church of America: A Study in Black Holiness-Pentecostalism* (Piscataway, N.J.: Gorgias Press, 2006), 113, 115, 118, 120.

3. In addition to liberation, other themes in African American religion and culture include: mystery, transcendence, survival, empowerment, uplift, fulfillment, and quest for self-understanding and community. See Frederick L. Ware, *Methodologies of Black Theology* (Cleveland, Ohio: Pilgrim Press, 2002), viii, 8; Charles H. Long, "African American Religion in the United States of America: An Interpretative Essay," *Nova Religio: The Journal of Alternative and Emergent Religions* 7.1 (July 2003): 23–24; and Gayraud S. Wilmore, *Pragmatic Spirituality: The Christian Faith through Africentric Lens* (New York: New York University Press, 2004), 44–59.

4. Ware, *Methodologies of Black Theology*, viii, 19–23. In addition to competing oral traditions of liberation thought in African American churches, there are different meanings of liberation in academic black theology. As I have argued and demonstrated in *Methodologies of Black Theology*, the fact of there being three schools of thought in academic black theology implies that liberation, if it is indeed the essential theme of African American religious thought, does not mean the same thing to all black theologians.

5. Dereck Daschke, "Millennial Destiny: A History of Millennialism in America," in Eugene V. Gallagher and W. Michael Ashcraft, eds., *Introduction to New and Alternative Religions in America*, vol. 1 (Westport, Conn.: Greenwood Press, 2006), 266–92.

6. Lewis V. Baldwin, "'A Home in Dat Rock': Afro-American Folk Sources and Slave Visions of Heaven and Hell," *Journal of Religious Thought* 41.1 (1984): 38–39.

7. Ibid., 38, 48. Baldwin's and Timothy E. Fulop's findings are confirmed in Benjamin Mays's prior study of African American folklore and literature. See Benjamin E. Mays, *The Negro's God as Reflected in His Literature* (Boston: Chapman and Grimes, 1938), 99–100, 126–27, 152–53, 246–50.

8. James H. Cone, *A Black Theology of Liberation* (Maryknoll, N.Y.: Orbis Books, 1990), 142.

9. James H. Cone, *The Spirituals and the Blues: An Interpretation* (New York: Seabury Press, 1972), 92–95.

10. Baldwin, "Home in Dat Rock," 44, 53, 55; Cone, *Spirituals and the Blues*, 83–87.

11. African American Womanists point out that the struggle for liberation and survival is not only in arenas external to black communities but also within these black communities. Accordingly, in contemporary African American Womanism, eschatological hope has come to be mean longings for autonomy and equality inside African American communities as well as in the larger society. See A. Elaine Brown Crawford, *Hope in the Holler: A Womanist Theology* (Louisville, Ky.: Westminster John Knox Press, 2002), 111.

12. Cone, *Spirituals and the Blues*, 87–92; James H. Cone, *Speaking the Truth: Ecumenism, Liberation, and Black Theology* (Grand Rapids, Mich.: Eerdmans, 1986), 18–22.

13. Baldwin, "Home in Dat Rock," 55; Cone, *Spirituals and the Blues*, 79–82.

14. Benjamin E. Mays's distinction between "mass" literature and "classical" literature is helpful for understanding the difference and similarities between eschatology in black folk sources, which Mays would say represents "mass" literature, and eschatology in versions of black Christian millennialism, which Mays would say represents "classical" literature. Mass literature includes Sunday School productions, prayers, sermons, and Spirituals. Classical literature includes slave narratives, biography, autobiography, public speeches, novels, poetry, and the writings of scholars of African American religion and culture. Eschatology from both sources is not a matter of difference but of degree.

15. These types are described in Timothy E. Fulop, "The Future Golden Day of the Race: Millennialism and Black Americans in the Nadir, 1877–1901," *Harvard Theological Review* 84.1 (1991): 75–99. In contrast to these views affirming some aspect of the millennium (golden age), there were some black Christians who were skeptical about the golden age. These skeptics argued that there is no golden age and that the kingdom of God is beyond/outside of human history. Progress is not inevitable. Any change, good or bad, in human society is the result of human action, not divine intervention. Here these skeptics seem to endorse a form of amillennialism that tends toward humanism and a view of history as open-ended. This black amillennialism, if construed as the idea that (1) there is no millennium or (2) the millennium is already taking place, is not an acceptable alternative for black liberation theology. That there is no millennium means that there is nothing to look forward to or no certainty that anything better will come. While there may be counter-evidence (moral evil, suffering, natural disaster, etc.) about the millennium as currently taking place, if the fate of humankind is solely only what we make it and the outcome of history is left totally to chance, humanity is without hope in this life. On earth, the dream of heaven is realizable, in part, by the rich and powerful. The poor and oppressed, if they look to heaven, are misled to believe that it is always aloof, realizable only after death or in another world.

16. Timothy E. Fulop, "The Future Golden Day of the Race"; Laurie Maffly-Kipp, "Mapping the World, Mapping the Race: the Negro Race History, 1874–1915," *Church History* 64 (1995): 610–26.

17. Albert J. Raboteau, *Slave Religion: The "Invisible Institution" in the Antebellum South* (New York: Oxford University Press, 2004), 148.

18. Ibid., 128.

19. Donald W. Dayton, *Theological Roots of Pentecostalism* (Grand Rapids, Mich.: Francis Asbury Press, 1987), 158–65.

20. D. William Faupel, *The Everlasting Gospel: The Significance of Eschatology in the Development of Pentecostal Thought* (Sheffield, England: Sheffield Academic Press, 1996), 72–75, 91–92. For an alternative interpretation of the decline of postmillennialism, based on crisis in theology and views on historical process, see James H. Moorhead, "The Erosion of Postmillennialism in American Religious Thought, 1865–1925," *Church History* 53.1 (1984): 61–77.

21. Douglas Jacobsen, *Thinking in the Spirit: Theologies of the Early Pentecostal Movement* (Bloomington: University of Indiana Press, 2003), 68–69, 81.

22. Frederick L. Ware, "The Church of God in Christ and the Azusa Street Revival," in Harold D. Hunter and Cecil M. Robeck Jr., eds., *The Azusa Street Revival and Its Legacy* (Cleveland, Tenn.: Pathway Press, 2006), 243–57.

23. *Church of God in Christ, Official Manual of the Church of God in Christ* (Memphis, Tenn.: Church of God in Christ Publishing Board, 1991), 63. Hereafter cited as *Official Manual*.

24. Ibid., 64.

25. Ibid., 61.

26. A seminal work in the study of spirituality and social ethics in COGIC and other African American Pentecostal churches is Leonard Lovett, "Black Holiness-Pentecostalism: Implications for Ethics and Social Transformation" (PhD diss., Emory University, 1979).

27. George D. McKinney, *The New Slave Masters* (Colorado Springs, Colo.: Cook Communications, 2005).

28. Ibid., 16–17. The book's chapters are broken down as follows: drugs (chap. 4), materialism (chap. 5); racism (chap. 6); desire for instant gratification and the mindless pursuit of pleasure such as pornography, unnecessary credit-card spending, and gambling (chap. 7); rage (misdirected anger resulting from repeated injustice and violation (chap. 8); gangs (chap. 9); and abortion, absent fathers, and lack of caring adults in children's lives (chap. 10).

29. Ibid., 9–10.

30. In Gilbert E. Patterson's *Here Comes the Judge: Finding Freedom in the Promised Land* (New Kensington, Pa.: Whitaker House, 2002), a more extreme but typical case of spiritualizing problems, he identifies despair, defeatism, helplessness, and depression as "satanic," of the "devil," but he does not address the social situations provoking these sorts of feelings. He claims that problems in life are ultimately spiritual or have a spiritual dimension and therefore have to be dealt with using spiritual means such as faith, prayer, and other religious disciplines. The devil is the archenemy of human souls. Patterson uses the situation of the Hebrews after the death of Joshua (a predicament where they arrived and settled but were periodically overcome by various invaders) as a metaphor for Christians today who profess faith in God but lack full enjoyment of God's promises in their lives.

31. James H. Cone, *Martin and Malcolm and America: A Dream or a Nightmare?* (Maryknoll, N.Y.: Orbis Books, 1991), 21, 71–79.

32. Frantz Fanon, *The Wretched of the Earth* (New York: Grove Press, 1966), 29, 48, 90, 123.

33. Cone, *Martin and Malcolm and America*, 116–18. In Malcolm X's "Message to the Grass Roots," using the analogy of the house Negro (black elite) and field Negro (black poor), he raises the specter of class in the civil rights movement. Malcolm claimed that the black liberation movement emerged among the black masses but was being thwarted by the black elite and their white liberal allies.

34. Wilson J. Moses, *The Golden Age of Black Nationalism, 1850–1925* (Hamden, Conn.: Archon Books, 1978), 10, 21, 23. Cone, *Martin and Malcolm and America*, 71–79, points out this black elitism even in Martin Luther King Jr.'s preaching and political rhetoric.

35. *Official Manual*, 93–94, 121–23, 125, 128–29; Vinson Synan, *The Holiness-Pentecostal Tradition: Charismatic Movements in the Twentieth Century*, 2nd ed. (Grand Rapids, Mich.: Eerdmans, 1997), 47, 81.

36. James H. Cone, *For My People: Black Theology and the Black Church* (Maryknoll, N.Y.: Orbis Books, 1984), 88–96, 120. The lack of social and economic analysis is a weakness that was present also in the early stages of contemporary black theology.

37. Grant Wacker, *Heaven Below: Early Pentecostals and American Culture* (Cambridge, Mass.: Harvard University Press, 2001), 223–26.

38. Even in Gilbert Patterson's *Here Comes the Judge*, he makes freedom conditional. Persons must act in order to be delivered from bondage and enjoy life. God supplies the means (plan of salvation). Humans contribute through their cooperation with God's plan.

39. McKinney, *New Slave Masters*, 116.

40. Wacker, *Heaven Below*, 257–63.

41. Harvey G. Cox, *Fire from Heaven: The Rise of Pentecostal Spirituality and the Reshaping of Religion in the Twenty-First Century* (Reading, Mass.: Addison-Wesley Publishing Company, 1995), 285–86.

42. Ibid., 289–95.

43. Jacobsen, *Thinking in the Spirit*, 268–69. Robert C. Lawson is founder of the Church of the Lord Jesus Christ of the Apostolic Faith. His millennialist perspective would be a form of black Christian millennialism that Fulop labels as millennial Ethiopianism.

V —

Afro-Pentecostalism in Global Context

The final two essays of this book highlight the historical intersection between African American Pentecostal and charismatic Christianity, and the phenomenal growth of Pentecostal spirituality throughout the Two-Thirds World. Indeed, at the beginning of the twenty-first century, the most explosive and exponential growth of Pentecostal spirituality is occurring not just among people of color among the global South, but in particular across the continent of Africa, as well as amid wide swaths of what is called the African diaspora (understood now to encompass South America, the Caribbean, and across Europe). This reality has implications for understanding the potential of Pentecostal spirituality, not only for revitalizing the Christian church but for forging social and political agendas that are more just throughout the world. The last two chapters of this book work within this context to shed light on two seemingly unrelated arenas—missions (Kalu) and liberation theology (Irvin)—as they have developed among people of the African diaspora and raise questions regarding the ongoing contribution of and the possible direction forward for the next generation of Afro-Pentecostal thought and practice. Simultaneously, both essays solidify the wider thesis regarding the African roots of modern Pentecostalism, especially as that has been popularized by the "Hollenweger School" of Pentecostalism (in the work of Walter Hollenweger and his students at the University of Birmingham—see the "Select Biography" at the end of the book) and close the loop in terms of explicating the Afro-morphic character of Pentecostal spirituality and religiosity as we head into the second century of the movement.

12

Black Joseph

*Early African American Charismatic
Missions and Pentecostal-Charismatic
Engagements with the African Motherland*

OGBU U. KALU

Introduction: God has a hand in it

The story of the African American charismatic–Pentecostal missionary enterprise to Africa beginning in the early twentieth century must be set within the larger framework of African American missionary engagement of Africa, which started in the nineteenth century. Ironically, black people who were brutally taken away from their ancestral homes have played enormous roles in the evangelization of their African homelands. The slave trade that had vitiated the missionary impulse between 1500 and 1800 yielded the resources for counteracting its effects on Africa. Yet because Europeans have dominated the storytelling about the expansion of Christianity into non-Western worlds, the roles of non-Western actors have remained cloaked in shadows.

Missionary re-engagement with the African motherland occurred in three phases: (1) nineteenth-century charismatic and Ethiopian missions, (2) twentieth-century Pentecostal missions, and (3) contemporary Pentecostal-charismatic engagements with Africa.[1] The latest phase of Pentecostal-charismatic missions has been inspired by the narrative of the biblical Joseph, who although sold into Egyptian slavery by his brothers, yet was in retrospect believed to be divinely ordained to serve and even save his family during the famine that later developed. This self-understanding of "initial exile for the sake of the homeland" not only characterizes contemporary Pentecostal-charismatic endeavors but is an appropriate lens to view the previous two centuries of African American missionary agency to Africa. From this perspective, the original African American evangelization of their African motherland that began in the nineteenth century can be seen as having generated along the way a charismatic spirituality, which laid the foundations for black Pentecostal spirituality and missionary praxis of later years. But the motivation for African American missions was not only evangelism. It was also a matter of racial pride and self-respect, precisely the qualities divinely bestowed on the biblical Joseph, in his subsequent elevation to authority. The result is that the African American engagement with Africa has differed from white missionary efforts so that "some careful distinctions need to be made before the black church is accused of engaging in the same cultural imperialism and racism that accompanied the white church's evangelical incursions into the third world."[2]

The Return of the Exiles: The Charismatic Spirituality of the Early African American Missions to Africa

Since the early 1980s a number of studies have documented various aspects of the history of African American evangelization of Africa. As the historian Sylvia Jacobs declared:

> Afro-Americans' historical identification with the continent of Africa is increasingly being seen as one aspect of their survival in the United States. Moreover, their responses to the events occurring on the continent demonstrate a continuing interest in the fate of the homeland. Recently, black Americans and Africans have come to accept the fact that their lives and histories have been intricately linked. Thus, we see a reaffirmation of this kinship bond by Afro-Americans and a concern for a rediscovery of their deep ties to Africa.[3]

African American presence was most conspicuous in Sierra-Leone, Gold Coast, Nigeria, Cameroon, Fernando Po, Congo, South Africa, Zimbabwe, Egypt, and Ethiopia.[4]

Although the ambivalence of Africa in the African American imagination has been the staple of many discourses,[5] the historian Lamin Sanneh's 1999 *Abolitionists Abroad* painted a less problematic canvas that privileged the achievements of the early African American missionaries.[6] Many years earlier, the anthropologist Jean Herskovitz Kopytoff dealt with their contributions in the making of modern Nigeria, and recently the historian Ade Ajayi's collection of essays on Adjai Crowther, the first African bishop within the Anglican Communion, has added to the recognition of the roles of blacks in evangelizing Africa. Such recognition inspired the battle cry of "Ethiopianism," the Black Nationalist ideology in the nineteenth century. This ideology is based on the promise in Psalm 68:31 that Ethiopia shall be significant in promoting the worship of God, and Ethiopia was seen as representing the entire black race.[7] As the missionary-scholar Edward Wilmot Blyden stated in *The Return of the Exiles* (1891), Africans across the diaspora, especially those in America, must return to evangelize Africa.[8] The following overview of nineteenth-century African American efforts to evangelize Africa focuses particularly on their motivations to return to the motherland, examines the racial factors involved, and identifies some reasons for the waning of this missionary enterprise toward the end of that period.

The roots of modern charismatic movements in Africa were nurtured within the heat of the return of African Americans to evangelize Africa. The beginnings of this story can be understood at least in part as involving the charismatic New Light spirituality that black Americans brought with them in their return to Africa.[9] As Sanneh recounts, "New Light converts received their anointing from the Spirit and consequently took their authority from God, not from earthly powers."[10] This charismatic courage was then imparted to others, especially to the indigenous bands of "recaptives" (slaves whose ships were intercepted in the Atlantic Ocean, taken to the Court of Admiralty in Freetown, and then freed) or Creoles (descendents of freed African Americans, Afro-Caribbeans, and Europeans) who were trained for the task of evangelizing other parts of Africa. Quite notably, before the first modern missionary society was founded in Britain by white Christians, African Americans from Nova Scotia and stouthearted Maroons (fugitive slaves from Jamaica or their descendents) had started the enterprise. They constituted one strand, while the "Ethiopians" who fostered the American Colonization Society, an organization founded to establish a colony in Liberia, constituted a second. Missionary activity by later Holiness and Pentecostal groups made up a third strand.

Building on the charismatic and assertive black consciousness of these early leaders, a golden age of black missionary enterprise opened in the 1870s.[11] It was suffused with an atmosphere of confident assertion of black leadership. The historian Adrian Hastings has commented that in nineteenth-century Africa, "Christian advance was black or it was nothing."[12] Thus, African American roots put a charismatic stamp on African Christianity and energized the drive to indigenize an African appropriation of the gospel. A typical example of African American influence was the Native Pastorate experiment in Sierra Leone in which blacks contested control over the churches by the white Anglican missionaries. Since funding of the clergy was the strong card, the blacks offered to constitute themselves into a Native Pastorate and to pay the salaries of their clergy. The tendency has been to interpret the Native Pastorate experiment in Sierra Leone as merely a brand of cultural nationalism, to say that the indigenes wanted to take control of the administration of churches without white supervision, and to insist that naturally, the white church leaders felt threatened because such nationalism could have led to the quest for political independence. But the missiologist Jehu Hanciles has delineated how the Native Pastorate controversy in Sierra Leone articulated the struggle of this generation to put an Africanist stamp on the face of Christianity and to achieve an African initiative in missions.[13] The Native Pastorate proposal was a radical challenge that contested the spirituality of Anglicanism against a more charismatic black spirituality. It was the quest for identity through charismatic spirituality, and it constituted the historical background to the rise of Pentecostalism in West Africa. The proponents of the Native Pastorate experiment propounded a different type of Christian expression and moved beyond loyalty to white structures to voice their dissent against white control of the church. They laid the groundwork for those who would later leave the Anglican Church to found "African Native Churches."

Both the early African American engagement of Africa in the eighteenth century and the following Ethiopian movement of the nineteenth century constitute the historical roots of the African Pentecostal movement in the twentieth century precisely because they contributed two important strands: charismatic spirituality, and a nationalism that sought to recover African identity through that spirituality. Later phases of African American Pentecostal missions in Africa used these to articulate part of their motivation.

Motivation in the black missionary enterprise is, however, quite complex. A sixfold typology is essential in conceptualizing what motivated black missionary activity because different types of black enterprises occurred and each generated its own nuance.

1. Some black missionaries stayed home but organized, raised funds, and supported missionary activities because they perceived the importance of missions from the imperative of the Great Commission in the New Testament.
2. Some supported programs to uplift the black people. They sponsored Africans who studied in the United States, then returned home to serve in their various countries and churches. These educated Africans helped to create the political ferment that produced political independence in their respective countries.
3. Some went to the mission field just like white people of their age because it was the fad of the period, as the northern globe intensified contacts with the southern globe after the slave trade era. Some of them were sponsored by the new burgeoning missionary societies while others journeyed out with personal funding.

4. Early on, some African Americans migrated to Africa with the hopes of practicing their charismatic Christianity freely and creating a new era for Africa. These emigrants believed in the "Blackman's Burden," a sacred duty to make Africa a garden of Eden again and to enable the black person to prove a sense of worth and ability. Others envisioned the leadership of Africans in Christianity. The anthropologist Walter L. Williams has used the sociological theory of metamotivation to explain this emigrant posture, arguing that while, after emancipation, the emigrants wanted land and opportunity, they also acted out of a great sense of racial duty. As Alfred Reidgel of the African Methodist Episcopal Church put the matter, "Often I think of leaving the field and returning to my friends and relatives where life would afford more base and comfort, but in the midst of these meditations, the voice of the man of sorrows comes down the ages: stand to your post. Hold the fort for I am coming."[14] The reverse theory of providential design argued that God brought Africans to North America so that they would be equipped as agents to bring the gospel home, and so that the status of the black person in the United States could change as a function of the success of the enterprise in Africa.[15]

5. Another type of black missionary motivation derived from the black churches themselves. As they matured, these churches sent missionaries to different parts of Africa as a symbol of their independence. Three black churches, the African Methodist Episcopal Church (AMEC), African Methodist Episcopal Zion (AMEZ), and the National Baptist Convention, sponsored seventy-six missionaries in Africa and educated thirty African students in the period between 1877 and 1900. Many of these students would later promote the spread of Pentecostalism, especially in South Africa. Meanwhile, the black churches in Sierra Leone sent missionaries to other parts of West Africa such as Nigeria, Gold Coast, Gambia, Liberia, and Cameroon. While the evangelical ardor among Holiness and Pentecostal groups at the turn of the twentieth century emerged from the interior of their spirituality, it was nevertheless deeply informed by the charismatic missionary vision of their African American forebears.

6. Some African Americans were recruited by various white organizations. Holiness churches, mainline churches, and Pentecostal churches recruited blacks because the climate in those regions made it difficult for whites.

The racial factor was important in the African American engagement of Africa. Some scholars, therefore, argue that the recruitment of blacks by white churches had less to do with climate and more to do with race. For instance, working with Episcopal data, the missionary and church leader Harold T. Lewis is convinced that nineteenth-century white Episcopalians recruited blacks as missionaries to solve the slavery issue, namely, to rid the country of surplus freed slaves, because they feared a possible insurrection by blacks and nursed other racist motives. After all, he argued, Episcopalians had been the least concerned with the abolitionist cause, playing no significant roles in abolitionist societies.[16] Yet, they appointed sixteen out of the twenty-five African Americans ordained between 1795 and the end of the Civil War as missionaries to Africa. The same church brought West Indians to supply the needs in local American parishes. The enterprise (the African Mission School Society) that set out to locate and train pious, intelligent Africans for cross-cultural missions failed partially because the early graduates preferred to work at home and to assist the cause of their enslaved kin. Indeed, opponents of the American Colonization Society (founded in 1816 to return blacks to freedom in Africa) argued that the organization was being hijacked for a different agenda by the racially motivated, and that those who could not argue against the enslavement of blacks in the United States were not honest in their show of concern for benighted Africans in the homeland.

Similarly, the missiologists Morrisine Mutshi and Stephen Bartlett determined that the Presbyterians sent fifty-nine African Americans to Liberia between 1833 and 1895, though this number dropped to twenty-six for the entire continent of Africa between the years 1956–1998.[17] While racial motives can be inferred, there were other reasons for whites to scout institutions such as Oberlin College, Lincoln and Fisk Universities, Hampton and Tuskegee Institutes, Gammon Theological Seminary in Atlanta, Stillman College in Alabama, and the Stewart Missionary Foundation, for able-bodied African Americans to be recruited for missions to Africa. Mosquitoes constrained the white presence as malaria decimated white missionary personnel in West Africa. Various missionary agencies arrived at the same conclusion: that black personnel must be the agency of sustainable cross-cultural mission. The Wesleyan Methodists in the Gold Coast attributed the longevity and success of one of their missionaries, Birch Freeman, to the fact that his mother was white but his father was black. The missionary Andreas Riis advised the Basel mission from Switzerland to recruit black missionaries from the West Indies. The missiologists Daniel Antwi and Paul Jenkins have reconstructed the efforts of the Basel mission to recruit black missionaries in this period.[18]

The quest for racial identity bred the Ethiopianist ideology that energized black missions, especially in white settler communities of southern and eastern Africa. For instance, Bishop Turner's tours of South Africa inspired Black

Nationalism and changed the religious landscape by establishing the African Methodist Episcopal churches. The campaign for African leadership in missions in the mid-nineteenth century crystallized around certain foci: developing a "Negro state" with a different type of education including a tertiary education facility; mobilizing Christian and Muslim resources in the larger African interest; voicing African protest against white control of decision-making processes in the church through black-owned newspaper and print media; preserving African culture, language, and racial distinction; and building an African church sans denominations so as to adequately counteract missionary cultural policy and racism. The church was the center of the enterprise and evangelism its primary instrument. Charismatic Christianity in Africa fed on this African American ideological heritage that promoted racial identity through a charismatic spirituality that rejected the inherited formalism of the Western missionary denominations.

With all this said, two questions must be asked: What were the results of the early African American missionary enterprise, and why did it run out of steam? Obviously different motives produced different types of missionary endeavors, and it would appear that while black settlers in Sierra Leone paid much attention to missions, those in Liberia did not (the chaotic governance in Liberia did not help in this regard). But in neither place was the vaunted ideal to carry the gospel into the hinterland fulfilled. The exigencies of the local contexts consumed the energy that black settlers could have invested in mission. Moreover, the intensity of black-sponsored missions slumped early because of poor funding.

It must be added that opposition to the concept of missions as "the return of the exiles" was robust because of the track records of various white churches in the abolitionist movement. In abolitionism, a distinction could be made between three aspects: a doctrinal stance against slavery; a proactive participation in an abolitionist society; and engagement in a repatriation program as a solution to the demographic bulge of freed slaves. Here the evidence is clearer with the Quakers on both sides of the Atlantic. The historian Christine Bolt has detailed the active roles of Quakers in the leadership of abolitionist societies and in funding local chapters from 1833 to 1877.[19] She argued that thirty-two out of the sixty-seven members of the central committee of the British and Foreign Anti-Slavery Society were Quakers spurred by a religious scruple about the sinfulness of the slavery system. Individuals such as John Sturge, a corn merchant from Birmingham, committed enormous amounts of funds to the cause. There is little evidence of the same level of engagement on the part of many American churches before the nightmare of living in equality with freed slaves.

A number of other factors also caused the waning of the African American missionary impulse. In southern Africa, for instance, whites felt that African indigenes' contacts with African Americans energized Black Nationalist movements and so attacked the black American efforts. As white settlers complained abroad, the home base could not support their black agents because of the shared racist ideologies. The historian Michael West provides a very good example with the fate of the African Orthodox Church in Zimbabwe, especially as that culminated during the first quarter of the twentieth century.[20]

Finally, some African Americans argued against emigration or felt less enthusiastic about cross-cultural missions. The missiologists Vaughn Walston and Robert Stevens contend that African Americans became insulated in nursing their wounds, engaged in enervating introspection, and lost the missionary zeal that was so fervent in the period between 1800 and 1920.[21] As Gayraud Wilmore puts it, "with the struggle against virtual genocide in an era of racial hatred and violence at home, together with the distractions of the First World War and Great Depression, black church support of missions gradually declined and much was left in disarray that had been so auspiciously begun during the last quarter of the nineteenth century."[22]

Some efforts did persist longer. For example, the impulse from the West Indies remained high for a longer period even though West Indians did not completely take over from the Americans, and many served the colonial government in West Africa.[23] Yet years later, in the heat of the church growth movement, Evangelical assessors such as G. W. Olson would characterize much of the missionary enterprise in Sierra Leone as a failure, and the author Joseph Wold titled his 1968 book *God's Impatience in Liberia* (1968).[24] Sanneh's optimism about the power of black republican ideals may have lost sight of the effect on African indigenous chiefs who were rejected by the African Americans.[25] Paul Gifford, a scholar of African Christianity, rightly argues that the dominance of the American Liberians and marginalization of the indigenous people weakened both state and church.[26] Master Sergeant Samuel K. Doe's coup in Liberia in 1982 reflected the revenge of the indigenous people who had been displaced from political and economic power through the centuries. Thus there were negative dimensions to the black missionary enterprise, especially as some black missionaries internalized the white image of indigenous Africans.

Yet despite these challenges, it is clear that the Ethiopianist and charismatic mission movements viewed their work as not only serving the uplift of the African motherland but also as an expression of their own divinely appointed vocation and calling. This already anticipates the later paradigmatic use of the Joseph story to highlight the theological conviction that whatever the horrors of the experience of slavery, there were divine purposes at work in the restoration of the African people, including those in the African American diaspora.

Called by the Spirit: Black Pentecostal Missions in the Twentieth Century

Interestingly, just when black missionary enterprise lost its force during the years between World War I and World War II, the Pentecostal missionary enterprise to Africa flowered. In various respects, the Spirit-empowered missionary motif that propelled black Pentecostalism was an extension of the charismatic spirituality of their ancestors, even as these early twentieth-century Afro-Pentecostal endeavors were driven by the racial pride and theological vision that were central elements of the self-understanding of their neo-Pentecostal and charismatic successors.

The image of Azusa Street as the New Jerusalem from which missionaries moved into fifty countries, including those of Africa, has been the staple diet of North American historiography.[27] The strongest agents of Azusa Street were missionaries from other Christian traditions who had been in the field. While serving in Africa, they were often targets of the early Azusa Street missionaries and evangelists. Later, while on furlough in the United States, many received the baptism of the Holy Spirit and the Azusa Street imprimatur. Samuel and Ardell Mead, for example, had been Methodist missionaries in Angola for twenty-one years, received the baptism during their furlough, and returned to Benguela, Angola. In the same year Julia Hutchins, the African American holiness pastor, left for Liberia with her husband, Willis, and niece, Leila McKinley. In this period, some were *sponsored missionaries* from Pentecostal groups such as William J. Seymour's Azusa Street ministry in California, or a Swedish group from Minnesota, who in 1904 sent Mary Johnson and Ida Andersson to Durban, South Africa.

Recent literature has reexamined the numbers, biographies, support systems, duration, character, and achievements of these missionaries. Initially, Azusa Street worked with many Holiness groups who were willing to cooperate. Many independent missionaries from small Holiness house cells who served with little organizational backing could be mistaken as Azusa Street missionaries. In this early period, there was little coordination, and the spiritual hyperbole in the house magazine *The Apostolic Faith* must be understood properly. Some of the missionaries may have had official blessings without financial support. For instance, in 1906 Lucy Farrow, who accompanied Seymour from Houston to California, went to Johnsonville, Liberia, with some black Pentecostal missionaries, as did George W and Daisy Batman, Mrs. Cook, and Mrs. Lee. The entire Batman family, Cook, and Lee died shortly thereafter from tropical fever. Farrow's service on the continent lasted only seven months. The group was self-supporting and had no financial backing from Azusa Street. Though Farrow claimed she was able to preach in the Kru language, the more successful mission among the Kru was led by Frank Cumming, Edward and Mollie McCauley (African Americans from Long Beach, California), and their associate Rosa Harmon, who went to Liberia in 1907, the same year as Henry M. Turney. During 1907–13 some reports emerged about the thriving Apostolic Faith church among the Kru. In that year, Isaac Neeley and his wife, Mattie, from Chicago's Stone Church joined the Assemblies of God mission in Liberia, which had been started by a Canadian, John Reid, a graduate of Lupton's school in Alliance, Ohio. By 1915 it was reported that the Neeleys opened a new mission among the Dorobo people. Another Chicago couple, James Hares and his wife, went to Sierra Leone in 1910 and worked among the Creoles. All these missionaries labored in the midst of unsettled political environments as the indigenous people fought the American Liberians who governed the country.

It is likely that some African Americans participated in the grand effort to coordinate Pentecostal groups to unite in missionary enterprises between the years 1909–10. Africa was one of the targeted mission fields.[28] Indeed, in 1909, an effort was made to found the Pentecostal Missionary Union. It failed in the United States, but motivated a missionary enterprise in Britain. The following year, the Bethel Pentecostal Assembly of Newark, New Jersey, organized the Pentecostal Mission in South and Central Africa and sent missionaries to Liberia, Swaziland, Mozambique, and South Africa. In 1910 they sent George Bowie, a Scot, who received the baptism of the Holy Spirit in America, to South Africa, where he founded the Pretoria Pentecostal Mission.

Others brands of Pentecostalism were established in various parts of Africa, especially the Assemblies of God (AOG), that had started with rural evangelism from the outset. Established in Sierra Leone in 1914, the AOG moved into French territories such as Burkina Faso in 1920. The pastors H. Wright, W. Taylor, their wives, and Misses M. Peoples and J. Fansworth initiated a successful rural mission among the poor Mossi of the central plateau, where they participated in the agricultural development of the semi-savannah ecosystem.[29] Later, the AOG moved into Côte d'Ivoire, Gold Coast (now Ghana), Republic of Benin (formerly Dahomey), and South Africa. Others groups that established African missions efforts included the Pentecostal Assemblies of Canada, Church of God in Christ, the Pentecostal Assemblies of the World, and International Pentecostal Holiness Church. The International Church of the Foursquare Gospel came in the late 1950s.[30] Thus, African American Pentecostals functioned in a competitive missionary field, jostling for prominence with many white Pentecostals. Within this context, it is often difficult to determine the racial character of some missionaries from the records.

Just when it appeared that African American evangelization of Africa was declining during the interwar years, the black Pentecostal missionary enterprise blossomed. Many African American Pentecostal missionaries in this period went to Liberia or to South Africa. They opted for Liberia, first, because it was founded by former American slaves in 1822; second, because the AMEC and AMEZ had opened the field; and third, because they could endure the climate in that region (and in southern African as well). A few missionary accounts will illustrate this.

The biographer Herman L. Greene has produced a fascinating story about an intrepid couple, Alexander and Margrete Howard, who landed in Cape Palmas in 1920.[31] In 1914 Alexander was employed as a porter at the Palmer House Hotel in Chicago. In the course of his duties, he heard a voice asking him to go to Africa. It seemed impossible but the urge persisted. He finally yielded, withdrew from his job, collected his little savings, and started the search for a sponsor. It was a forlorn hope because black churches could not afford the idea, and white churches told him explicitly that God could not call him.

Things changed four years later, when Alexander was directed to Rev. George Phillips, founder of Faith Holiness Church of the Apostolic Faith. Phillips's life story started with his youth in the Bahamas, where his father founded a group called "Christian Mission." But Phillips wanted to make money and as a teenager escaped to work in Guyana. At nineteen, he left for the United States. A near-death experience struck the fear of God in him, and he came in contact with the Nazarene Church, where Mary Vinton and her husband had started a charismatic ministry following the experience of the "fire" at Azusa Street. Phillips was baptized in the Spirit and responded to a call to the ministry. He was ordained in September 1916 in a colorful ceremony, and his ministry prospered. According to his biographer, "the normal capacity of the meeting house was overrun at every meeting, which inspired members to seek larger quarters."[32]

When Alexander met Phillips in 1919, some synergy occurred. Phillips mobilized two other Pentecostal churches founded by West Indian immigrants to facilitate Alexander's dream. The first was the Christian Mission

Holiness Church started by Rev. Alfred E. Cragwell from Barbados, British West Indies. He and his wife migrated to Cambridge, Massachusetts, where Cragwell rented a room on Harvard Street, bought a property on Main Street, and chartered his church in 1917. It blossomed as "a fire house and soul saving station for the people of God" until 1951 when he died.[33] The second was another West Indian church, the Apostolic Pentecostal Church (aka Abundant Life Church in Cambridge), pastored by Rev. Conrad Dottin. Later, on July 17, 1919, the three West Indian immigrants (Phillips, Cragwell, and Dottin) formed the United Pentecostal Council of the Assemblies of God (UPCAG)—with no connection to Assembly of God Springfield. Together, they sponsored Alexander and his wife to Cape Palmas.

Notably, Howard's biographers point to a key aspect of Pentecostal missionary engagement: "After having received the baptism of the Holy Ghost according to Acts 2:4, and having many other wonderful spiritual experiences, the Lord showed Mr. Alexander Howard that his field of labor was to be in Liberia, West Africa."[34] In the earlier phases of African American missionary enterprises, motivation was theologized from the perspectives of *theodicy* and *human liberation*. Among Pentecostals, the emphasis shifted to premillennial *eschatology*. This did not make them less sensitive to racial and social justice issues.

Alexander and Margrete showed their ideological commitment quite early. They refused to work on the coast and moved inland to the Fan ethnic communities. From here they moved north to Biabo and to Bonike in the southeast corner of Liberia, on the boundary with French Ivory Coast. Various missionary bands of the home-base church supported the effort through women and children's donation of cloths, sewing machines, and other materials for the welfare of the African communities. The mission would later spread into the Ivory Coast. In twenty-four years, the Howards built missions, compounds, village schools, and a boarding school named after Phillips. They engaged an indigenous pastor, Jaspeh Toeh, to aid the few missionary personnel and to develop palm oil and rubber farms to succor the finances. The Howards labored for years in spite of malaria attacks and other hardships, sustained by God through local chiefs and communities. In November 1943, the *Apostolic Messenger* mourned and honored the memories of Alexander Howard and his wife. Their work continued with Rosa Lee Wright, who sailed in 1937, and Maryne Hathaway of Chicago, who sailed in 1940. Among many failed enterprises in these early years, the legacy of the Howards survived, and in 1982 a team (Herman Greene and Marva Collins) went to appraise and shore up the legacy of the black Pentecostal missionaries.

Importantly, the Pentecostal missionary enterprise to West Africa involved the leadership of a number of black women who dared to serve in the interior. From the mid-1920s, both the Church of God in Christ (COGIC) and the Assemblies of God (AOG) started hinterland missions instead of perching on the developed coastal regions of Liberia. However, the significance of the COGIC women missionaries rested on the re-interpretation of what it meant to live a sanctified life. They extended it to engaging the public space and the plights of blacks in the African homeland.

COGIC organized the Home and Foreign Mission Board in 1925 and sent their first missionaries to Trinidad, Costa Rica, and Turks Island in 1927. Typical of the new Pentecostal enterprises, the motivation was expressed in very eschatological terms:

> The purpose of the organization shall be for the winning of lost souls to Christ and to establish the work of grace in the hearts of believers; to encourage a holy life and the Baptism of the Holy Ghost and Fire among all the nations of the earth, to make ready a people for the soon coming of the Lord Jesus Christ in love and unity of spirit and faith, by a clean, holy people who are walking in the light, with the fellowship of Saints, cleansed through the blood of Jesus by the washing of the water by the word.[35]

Two years later, the COGIC mission board recruited Elizabeth White to go to the island of Cape Palmas. She had served for three years under a certain Miss January, a self-sponsored female faith missionary in Liberia. Mother Elizabeth Robinson, National Supervisor of COGIC's Women's Department, invited White to a conference and mentored her. Returning under denominational sponsorship, she opened the COGIC mission at Bonike. In 1932 Mrs. Willis C. Ragland of Columbus, Georgia, joined White. During her furlough, Ragland recruited Beatrice Lott to go to Tubake while White moved to Wisseka. The Second World War disrupted COGIC missionary enterprises, but after the war COGIC recruited Martha Barber of Chicago who, with the help of an indigene, Valentine Brown, enabled the church to move into Monrovia in 1948. Five missionaries were deployed to the field between 1945 and 1956.

The historian Anthea Butler argues that one of the achievements of Elizabeth Robinson's leadership of the COGIC women was the inauguration of the Home and Foreign Mission Band in 1925. Against the opposition of some male ministers, Robinson defended this development as involving the active engagement of COGIC women in foreign missions, and saw it as a means of reinterpreting the theology of sanctified life to include a mandate to sanctify the society and the world. Butler writes:

> Slowly, mainstream life was beginning to encroach upon the women of COGIC. It was no longer enough to simply allow Holiness to change one's life: Holiness needed to change other lives as well. What was becoming increasingly clear was the civically based church education of Saints would redefine church mothers' teachings on sanctification. The new teachings would rely on civic engagement to sanctify the world.[36]

It could be conjectured that the appointment of Charles Pleas in 1945 as the COGIC bishop of Liberia and his visit with the president of the country consolidated the missionary work of COGIC women.[37] When William J. Taylor visited Monrovia and Cape Palmas in July 1956 as the secretary of COGIC's missionary agency, he found a receptive President Tubman, and a healthy missionary presence filled with new opportunities and land grants. He also found that the missionary field had become a competitive field sporting seven other African American agencies: Gibi Apostolic Church, United Pentecostal Mission, Carver Foreign Mission, Afro-American Missionary Crusade, Youth Mission of Life, United Church of America, and the Liberian branch of International Evangelistic Women's Workers Incorporated.[38] Significantly, Taylor's report shifted from the rhetoric of soul saving of heathens, concluding that, "The tremendous need on the field is for younger missionaries twenty-five to thirty-five years of age. It is not the Bible that is so acutely essential now, but machinists, scientists, in fact technical skills in every profession. Let us pray to the Lord of Harvests."[39]

A major aspect of the rise of Pentecostalism in southern and central Africa in this early period was the importance of South Africa in the charismatic evangelization of the rest of the region. It served as a nodal point from which black and white missionaries sallied forth into the region to Zimbabwe, Malawi, Zambia, Mozambique, and other countries. For the most part, migrant laborers and traders (*mutchona*) served as the core agents in the spread of Christianity of various hues.

The dynamics in the *azungu-atchona*, white-black relationship, became important for the story of early South African Pentecostalism. As racism divided the Apostolic Faith Mission in South Africa, Africans founded their own churches, and the Ethiopian churches grew. But David Maxwell, the African religious scholar, argues that the Ethiopian African churches constituted the means by which early Pentecostalism grew from 1908, and that

J. G. Lake, the leader of the Apostolic Faith Mission (South Africa), did not want to found a church and made enormous efforts to build into the existent religious landscape.[40] Maxwell noted that though charismatic experiences appealed to Boers and Africans alike, it appealed more to the latter because their economic disenfranchisement opened them to the possibility of using charismatism as a tool of resistance. Lake, therefore, participated in many AMEC conventions and received whole congregations into the AFM, though some later returned to their old denominations.

Perhaps the most significant aspect of African American influence on African Pentecostalism is that it catalyzed the nationalist strain that fused charismatism, identity, social justice, and Black Nationalism. This is best illustrated with the career of Nicholas Benghu (1909–86) in South Africa.[41] He was very much influenced by the nationalist ideology of the African Methodist Episcopal Church, and became a central actor in the development of Pentecostalism in southern Africa. Unlike the Apostolic Faith Mission, the AOG in South Africa was an umbrella association of many groups run by white, black, and colored leaders. Benghu became connected with the AOG in the 1930s and rose to prominence over the next decade through successful revival campaigns in Port Elizabeth and East London. By 1950, he founded the "Back-to-God Campaign" as an instrument for expansion into southern and central Africa. His ministry was distinguished by its capacity to address a combination of issues including personal renewal and racial and social justice themes. He imagined the continent of Africa as a sleeping giant that must awaken to its greatness, and proffered Christianity as an instrument for achieving this from the "Cape to Cairo."

Benghu's Pan-Africanism was grounded in the ideology of Ethiopianism and the nationalism of the era characterized by the Negritude movement that emerged among African and Caribbean students in Paris in the 1930s. Benghu's achievement was to provide the religious dimension of Pan-African nationalism, grounded in the interior of the gospel message. He inspired future Pentecostal leaders such as Ezekiel Guti of Zimbabwe and Mensah Otabil of Ghana. His theological quest for African identity through religious power underpins the ideology of the Intercessors for Africa, a movement that, in the tradition of nineteenth-century charismatic spirituality, turned prayer, land deliverance, and intercession into political praxis.

Ezekiel Guti, founder of the Zimbabwe Assembly of God Africa, urged Africans to build up their lives through hard work, hygiene, and discipline.[42] He constructed tight-knit communities in which members drew moral boundaries against popular cultural behavior such as drinking alcohol, gambling, dancing, and the use of traditional medicine. Members grew within the movement through discipleship or mentorship, continuous engagement in church activities, and energetic evangelism. Nicknamed the Black Billy Graham, Guti impressed commentators with his seriousness, commitment, confident demeanor, and the tensile strength of his simple faith. He became popular with African Americans, garnering support from many Western countries. From the mid-1950s, a number of American white Evangelical preachers toured eastern and southern Africa: William Branham, Oral Roberts, Frederick Bosworth, Lorne Fox, and Billy Graham. Benghu and Guti immediately adopted their style of holding revival campaigns with big tents.

Black Joseph: Contemporary African American Engagement of Africa

In various respects, Guti's life experience encapsulates the exile-and-return motif that has perennially characterized the self-understanding of the African American missionary enterprise to Africa. The difference now, however, is that the exilic sojourn and return that before occurred across generations were undertaken within a lifetime, even a decade or a few weeks. This aspect of the contemporary phenomenon of globalization and transnationalism has impacted the black Pentecostal missionary mentality. Several factors led to the African American Pentecostal rediscovery of Africa as a missionary field from the mid-1980s, in the process producing a variety of patterns of contemporary African American engagement with Africa as well as surfacing a number of new challenges.

To begin with, Guti himself became a link between African Pentecostal leadership and African American Pentecostal missionary endeavors. He is a prime example of the connection between a new crop of highly educated African Pentecostals and African Christianity with the global North, especially televangelists in the United States. In response to the crisis of legitimacy, economic collapse, and poverty, and amid the collapse of the Soviet Union at the end of 1980s (which heralded the second liberation of Africa from dictators), the media was liberalized, and the mass mediation of religion intensified. As the state retreated, private investors took over radio and television. Televangelism, Christian radio broadcasts, video recording, audio-cassettes, and advertisement through billboards and print combined to give charismatic spirituality a high profile. Pentecostals negotiated between sacred and profane music and dance, and incorporated popular culture in the competitive religious market. As a result, theology shifted from puritan ethics to an emphasis on prosperity motivated by mega institutions, high-profile leadership, and hermeneutical shifts in the doctrines of wealth and poverty. Some scholars connect the socioeconomic and political backdrop to the rapid expansion of the charismatic movement. Others argue that through crusades, conferences, training retreats, scholarships, pulpit sharing, and financial support, African Pentecostalism was locked into American Evangelicalism of various hues.[43]

In the midst of these developments, African American churches rediscovered Africa as a mission field. As Bishop Charles Blake of West Angeles COGIC put it:

From my teenage years, I have loved Africa, and I have sought to connect with my African heritage. I was blessed to begin visiting Africa in the 1980s and have done so annually since that time. In 1998, Rev Eugene Rivers and his congregation in Boston submitted to my Episcopal oversight. His activist aspirations to mitigate suffering in Africa were contagious. I joined him in founding the Pan African Charismatic Evangelical Congress in the year 2000 . . . addressing the HIV/AIDS pandemic. . . . We provide financial support, supplies and equipments, best practices consultation, and we employ a comprehensive approach to orphan care, incorporating principles developed by UNICEF and UNAIDS. . . . We cannot allow 40 million children in Africa to live, suffer and die without all the help we can give them. If not us, who? If not now, when? If not there, where?[44]

Significantly, the imagery underpinning the motivation changed. Blake argued that the motivation for promoting a broad-scale African American awareness of the plight of Africa and the need for the mobilization of a movement as intense and comprehensive as the civil rights movement was because

Blacks were also sold into slavery, many times by our brothers in Africa. Like Joseph, our forefathers endured many trials, much humiliations and suffering. But Joseph held to his dreams. . . . Through a series of supernatural and providential events Joseph was blessed by God to become the vice-president of Egypt. We through a series of phenomenal and supernatural events have by God's grace come to success and power in this land of our captivity . . . Joseph realized that this blessed promotion had taken place so that he could fulfill his God-given destiny of reaching back to those same brothers who sold him into slavery and save them from starvation and death.[45]

The new missionaries represented themselves as Black Josephs. In a similar vein, Rev. LaVerne Hanes Stevens formed the *Joseph Project* in Tyrone, Georgia, after an emotional visit to Ghana in 2001.[46] The project promotes group visits by churches to different parts of Africa, especially West Africa. The visits are like therapeutic corporate ministries of sustaining, healing, and reconciling. Many hope to reconcile with the progenies of those who sold slaves and thereby restore dignity of both parties. In this pattern of reconnection the emphasis is on projects that combat poverty and disease, not on direct evangelism. Thus, the prominent areas of noticeable impact include black racial ideology, theological education and ministerial formation, social welfare projects, responses to poverty and HIV/AIDS, capacity building and empowerment, and cultural and ministerial exchanges.

From a broader perspective, these developments fit the general pattern of Protestant missions from the global North to the global South. The volume of the missionary impulse from the South is increasing at the same time that the northern missionary impulse is declining in its intensity, but showing a measure of resilience and diversification of its strategy. When the North American Protestant data is read closely, by removing the large number of short-term missionaries, there is a measure of decline among those missionary bodies. But a new trend is emerging among Evangelicals: thousands are connecting as visiting and short-term missionaries with the new Christian centers in the global South as Evangelicals, at least in some circles, are turning away from singly focused attention on domestic issues (abortion and sexual orientation) to global social concerns over ecology, poverty, and HIV/AIDS.

There are eight identifiable patterns of contemporary African American engagement with missions in Africa:

1. Historic denominations such as COGIC, AMEC, and AMEZ have retained their missionary presence. Some (e.g., COGIC) claim a measure of growth mostly in southern and central Africa. But the charismatic landscape has changed significantly in Africa.
2. Some African American mega ministries have opened branches in Africa, such as T. D. Jakes's Potter's House.
3. Others invite African pastors to international retreats and pulpit exchanges.
4. Many super-evangelists such as Juanita Bynum undertake evangelistic crusades in Africa.
5. Others, such as Bishop W. R. Portee of Southside Christian Palace Church in Los Angeles, combine huge evangelistic crusades with poverty alleviation projects. His wife uses the Wailing Wall organization as a mode of

access to womenfolk. He testifies that God told him about the importance of Africa, especially Nigeria, in the end times. This resonates with the type of prophecies given by Intercessors for Africa and Nigeria Prayer House. Portee has invested millions of dollars in evangelistic electronic equipment and buses for large crusades and rural evangelism. He has teamed up with some Nigerian bishops whom he ordained to do "apostolic visitations" and crusades in southwestern Nigeria. He appears regularly on TV One (Chicago), preaching and canvassing for contributions.

6. A number of the Black Joseph projects function as NGOs, sourcing from government and public funds. This is exemplified by Bishop Blake's *Save Africa's Children Fund/Pan African Children's Fund*. Such alliances may hinder the capacity of the church to speak prophetically about the government's foreign policy in Africa. African compatriots learn to coddle politicians for patronage. Internally, such projects compete virulently. Bishop Blake said that he was saddened by the negative effects of rivalry. In his address to the Interfaith Summit, he admonished: "I believe that it was John Maxwell who said, *it takes teamwork to make a dream work.* We must respect the actualities and potentials of every participant. We must work together to maximize our collective impact. We are much better working together with respect, than we are apart."[47]

7. Many African American churches organize visits to Africa. They come bearing gifts, sponsoring small projects, or with a team of medical professionals. Short-term and safari missionary excursions run the risk of functioning without adequate knowledge of the mission field, resulting in wrong strategies and failed endeavors.[48] They also run the risk of the functioning like the nineteenth-century missionaries who failed to be dialogical, that is, to learn from the people and give something to the people without the rescuer mentality. Philanthropy has hidden paternalistic traps. Yet quite often rural communities have benefited from these interactions.

8. Many African American churches engage in leadership development whereby they network with African pastors, grant them academic degrees, and ordain them as bishops under the American jurisdiction. Some create Houses of Bishops empowered to ordain bishops in various African nations.

There is little doubt that African Americans have influenced the religious culture of African Pentecostalism in a number of broad ways. First, the beliefs of many Africans resonate with the spirituality of some leading African American ministers such as Bishop T. D. Jakes. Second, African American pop culture has powerfully permeated Pentecostal culture. Examples go beyond the gospel music of Ron Kenoly, who holds a chieftaincy title in Ghana and has popularized Yoruba songs in America. This new culture does not depend solely on external sources, but has emerged in the responses to both indigenous and urban cultures, dance, and music. Pentecostalism has utilized various aspects of hip-hop culture to popularize a genre of music and dance known as "praiseco."[49] The relationship of a Christian form to popular culture, materialism, and issues of social justice could be quite crucial to its survival.

The problem for African Pentecostalism lies in how it borrows and absorbs ingredients of African American culture and style. On the positive side, many of the international initiatives and contacts provide confidence-building, visibility, and a high public profile for individual pastors and their ministries, and networking creates a global Pentecostal culture. On the negative side, it creates the "big man of the big God" syndrome, promoting a pastor who has international connections, jets around the world, and is not accountable to any local assembly of believers. International conferences and the sharing of pulpits have been useful when properly utilized.

Ethical and moral criticisms of African Pentecostalism have arisen because of the movement's capitulation to the materialism and individualism of American cultural values. It is important to analyze the ways that the movement has gestated and utilized the negative side effects because the quality of African Christianity and stewardship depend on the moral accountability of its leadership. Malpractice threatens charismatic ministries. Two examples will suffice: manpower development, and polity. The rapid growth has intensified the manpower problem. Many African Pentecostals use their connections with America to acquire unaccredited degrees, especially doctorates. Africans and African Americans share the same propensity of hankering after titles, fancy cars, clothes, and the like. This tendency has also produced the rash of episcopal ordinations and the legitimization of houses of bishops in Africa by well-meaning Americans. Thus, the Pentecostalism that started with egalitarian congregational polities in the 1970s established episcopal polity within two decades.

Conclusion

We have seen that the African American quest to reconnect with Africa has used competing imageries over the centuries to express the motivation. These imageries changed as African American engagement with Africa flowed through various phases. In the immediate aftermath of abolition and emancipation, the predominant imagery was derived from the exodus-from-

Egypt motif (as articulated most forcefully by Edward Wilmot Blyden) and the potential return of the exiles. Then, a period of intense adjustment and withdrawal followed during and between the decades of the world wars. After that, the Negro became black and, finally, African American in a process of revamped racial identification in the face of American culture wars.

The quest to reconnect with Africa blossomed thereafter with the dominant imagery emerging from stories of Joseph's fate in the Bible: as understood by many contemporary Pentecostals, charismatics, and even others in the Black Church community, Joseph was sold into slavery by his brothers but prospered in Egypt sufficiently to rescue his entire family from famine. In the same manner, African Americans have prospered in the land of slavery under their white "pharaohs" and returned to rescue their guilty brothers from the scourge of poverty. African American charismatics and Pentecostals have played central roles in this unfolding story, laying the foundation in the beginning, and continuing to have an essential roles in black American engagement with Africa.

For these and other reasons, the recent surge of African American engagement of African Christianity is an important field of research. The motivation and rhetoric continue to change. Yet, its impact speaks to the heart of the fortunes of African Pentecostalism precisely because the quality of Christian witness is often challenged by the contest between gospel and culture. Popular culture can compromise the holiness ethic that is essential to stewardship. Happily, public disenchantment has not slowed the growth curve, but the negotiation with popular culture and the morality issues arising from materialism and absorption of American culture may cause problems in the future if left unattended.

NOTES TO CHAPTER 12

1. Editors' note: For a typology of Pentecostalism and its contemporary charismatic types, see the editors' introduction to this volume. Kalu's distinction maps onto that typology as follows: "Pentecostalism" includes classical Wesleyan-Holiness Trinitarian Pentecostals and classical Apostolic (Jesus' name or "oneness") churches, while "contemporary Pentecostal-charismatic" refers to charismatic independent congregations or networks, and recent neo-Pentecostal currents within the wider Black Church tradition.

2. Gayraud S. Wilmore, "Black Americans in Mission: Setting the Records Straight," *International Bulletin of Missionary Research* 10.3 (July 1986): 98.

3. Sylvia Jacobs, ed., *Black Americans and the Missionary Movement in Africa* (Westport, Conn.: Greenwood Press, 1982), xi; see especially the bibliographical essay on 229-37.

4. Morrisine Flennaugh Mutshi and Stephen Bartlett, eds., *African Americans in Mission: Serving the Presbyterian Church from 1833 to the Present* (Louisville, Ky.: Office of Global Awareness and Involvement, 2000).

5. This is the point in R. G. Weisbord, *Ebony Kinship: Africa, Africans, and the Afro-American* (Westport, Conn.: Greenwood Press, 1974).

6. Lamin Sanneh, *Abolitionists Abroad: American Blacks and the Making of Modern West Africa* (Cambridge, Mass.: Harvard University Press, 1999).

7. J. H. Kopytoff, *A Preface to Modern Nigeria: The Sierra-Leonians in Yorubaland, 1830–1890* (Madison: University of Wisconsin Press, 1965), and J. Ade Ajayi, *A Patriot to the Core: Bishop Adjai Crowther* (Ibadan, Nigeria: Spectrum Press, 2001).

8. Edward Wilmot Blyden, *The Return of the Exiles and the West African Church* (London: W. B. Whittingham and Co., 1891).

9. For more on the New Light religious ideas and the impact among freed slaves, see Sanneh, *Abolitionists Abroad*, 59–65.

10. Ibid., 59.

11. Ibid., 74–101.

12. Adrian Hastings, *The Church in Africa* (Oxford: Clarendon Press, 1994), 437.

13. Jehu Hanciles, *Euthanasia of Mission: African Church Autonomy in a Colonial Context* (Westport, Conn.: Praeger, 2002); see also Hollis Lynch, *Edward Blyden* (London: Oxford University Press, 1964), and Ogbu U. Kalu, *The History of Christianity in West Africa* (London: Longmans,1980), 270–92.

14. Cited in Walter L. Williams, *Black Americans and the Evangelization of Africa, 1877–1900* (Madison: University of Wisconsin Press, 1982), 90.

15. Articulated by Bishop Henry Turner's "God is a Negro"; see Gayraud S. Wilmore, *Black Religion and Black Radicalism: An Interpretation of the Religious History of African Americans* (Maryknoll, N.Y.: Orbis, 1973), 152.

16. Harold Lewis, "Black Episcopalians as Missionaries to Africa in the Nineteenth Century," in Lynne Price, Juan Sepulveda, and Graeme Smith, eds., *Mission Matters* (New York: Peter Lang, 1999), 21–34.

17. See Mutshi and Bartlett, eds., *African Americans in Mission*; the nineteenth-century figure is mentioned in Mutshi's introduction, xvii.

18. Daniel Antwi and Paul Jenkins, "The Moravians, the Basel Mission and the Akuapem State in the Early Nineteenth Century," in Holger Bernt Hansen and Michael Twaddle, eds., *Christian Missionaries and the State in the Third World* (Oxford: James Currey, 2002), 39–51.

19. Christine Bolt, *The Anti-Slavery Movement and Reconstruction: A Study of Anglo-American Cooperation, 1833–1877* (Oxford: Oxford University Press, 1969).

20. Michael O. West, "Ethiopianism and Colonialism: The African Orthodox Church in Zimbabwe, 1924–1934," in Hansen and Twaddle, *Christian Missionaries*, 237–54.

21. Vaughn J. Walston and Robert J. Stevens, eds., *African-American Experience in World Mission: A Call Beyond Community* (Pasadena, Calif.: William Carey Library, 2000).

22. Wilmore, "Black Americans in Mission," 100.

23. Nemata A. Blyden, *West Indians in West Africa, 1808–1880: The African Diaspora in Reverse* (Woodbridge, UK: Boydell and Brewer, 2000).

24. G. W. Olson, *Church Growth in Sierra Leone* (Grand Rapids, Mich.: Eerdmans, 1969), and J. C. Wold, *God's Impatience in Liberia* (Grand Rapids, Mich.: Eerdmans, 1968).

25. See Sanneh, *Abolitionists Abroad*.

26. Paul Gifford, *Christianity in Doe's Liberia* (Cambridge: Cambridge University Press, 1993).

27. See Allan Anderson, "The New Jerusalem: The Role of the Azusa Street Revival in the Global Expansion of Pentecostalism," paper delivered at the Thirty-fifth Annual Meeting of the Society for Pentecostal Studies, Pasadena, California, March 23–25, 2006; and Anderson, *Spreading Fires: The Missionary Nature of Early Pentecostalism* (Maryknoll, N.Y.: Orbis, 2007), 149–90, for further discussion and detailed documentation of what is summarized in the this and the next paragraph.

28. See Andre Corten and Ruth Marshall-Fratani, eds., *Between Babel and Pentecost: Transnational Pentecostalism in Africa and Latin America* (Bloomington: Indiana University Press, 2001), esp. pt. 3 on Africa.

29. See the work of Pierre-Joseph Laurent: "Les conversions aux Assemblees de Dieu du Burkina Faso," *Journal des Africanistes* 47 (1998): 67–97; *Les Pentecostistes du Burkina Faso: Mariage, Pouvoir et Guerison* (Paris: Karthala, 2003); and "Transnationalism and Local Transformation: The Example of the Church of Assemblies of God of Burkina Faso," in Corten and Marshall-Fratani, *Between Babel and Pentecost*, 256–73.

30. See Ebenezer O. Adeogun, *A Transplant of the Vine: Forty Years of Foursquare History in Nigeria* (Lagos: Foursquare Gospel Church in Nigeria, 1999).

31. Herman L. Greene, *UPCAG—The First 90 Years*, vol. 1: *1919 to1945* (Sussex, N.J.: Geda Publications, 2005).

32. Ibid., 4.

33. See Rev. Alfred E. Cragwell, as cited on the "Christian Mission Holiness Church: Church History" webpage; see http://www.christianmissionholiness.org/history.html (last accessed December 31, 2007).

34. Greene, *UPCAG*, 11.

35. Charles H. Pleas, *Fifty Years of Achievement, from 1906–1956: A Period in History of the Church of God in Christ* (1956; repr., Memphis, Tenn.: COGIC, 1991), 24.

36. Anthea D. Butler, *Women in the Church of God in Christ: Making A Sanctified World* (Chapel Hill: University of North Carolina Press, 2007), 115.

37. As discernible in Pleas, *Fifty Years of Achievement*.

38. Elder J. W. Denny, *A Nostalgic Look at Yesterday* (Memphis, Tenn.: COGIC, ca. 1995).

39. *World Mission's Digest*, October 13, 1956.

40. David Maxwell, *African Gifts of the Spirit: Pentecostalism and the Rise of a Zimbabwean Transnational Religious Movement* (Oxford: James Currey, 2006), 41–45.

41. Further details about Benghu can be found in Maxwell, *African Gifts of the Spirit*, 69–73, and Ogbu Kalu, *African Pentecostalism: An Introduction* (New York: Oxford University Press, 2008), 55–60.

42. Maxwell's *African Gifts of the Spirit* covers the life and ministry of Ezekiel Guti.

43. Paul Gifford, "Some Recent Developments in African Christianity," *African Affairs* 93.373 (1994): 513–34.

44. Bishop Charles E. Blake Sr., address to "Faith-Based Solutions to Social Issues: Interfaith Summit on Africa," July 19, 2006; see enclosure in *From Faith to Action: A Resource for Faith-Based Groups* (Santa Cruz, Calif.: Firelight Foundation, 2006).

45. Blake, address to "Faith-Based Solutions to Social Issues."

46. Stevens's story is told in *Charisma* (July 2007): 23.

47. Blake, address to "Faith-Based Solutions to Social Issues."

48. This came out strongly during my interview in Accra in June 2007 with Bishop Victor L. Powell and a team from Rhema Word International Ministries, Albany, Georgia.

49. I have collected photocopies of advertisements in *Charisma* magazine tracing which ministries invited and advertised African Pentecostal pastors. See Ogbu U. Kalu, "Holy Praiseco: Negotiating Sacred and Popular Music and Dance in African Pentecostalism," *Pneuma: Journal of the Society for Pentecostal Studies* 32.1 (2010): 16–40.

13

Meeting Beyond These Shores

*Black Pentecostalism, Black Theology,
and the Global Context*

DALE T. IRVIN

More than thirty years have passed since Leonard Lovett's dissertation, "Black Holiness-Pentecostalism: Implications for Ethics and Social
Transformation," first appeared.[1] In that work, Lovett sought to lay the
groundwork for a fuller dialogue between black theology and the black Pentecostal movement. Three decades later that dialogue has still hardly begun.
Over the intervening years, Pentecostalism has grown exponentially as a
global movement. In the process, the significance of the African American
contributions to the formation of Pentecostalism globally has been somewhat obscured, ignored, or even erased. I will not re-argue here the thesis
regarding the African American origins of Pentecostalism in the United
States. Suffice it to say that I am convinced of this particular historical thesis,
and in this chapter will more or less assume it.[2] I will also not try here to
sort out the complex question of the precise relationship between American
Pentecostalism and global Pentecostalism, which is a much larger question.[3]

Analysis of the historical relationship between the two modes of Pentecostalism has often come down to a discussion of the role of the Azusa Street
Revival of 1906–09 in Los Angeles in the history of the global Pentecostal
movement. One must acknowledge that Azusa Street played an important
role in the emergence of Pentecostalism globally, without necessarily trying
to determine the precise nature or significance of that role.[4] It is important,
on the other hand, to note explicitly the African American context out of
which the Azusa Street experience emerged. Thanks to the historical work
of Cecil M. Robeck, there can no longer be any doubt that not only William
J. Seymour but the entire Azusa Street Mission and Revival that he led were
fully within the Black Church tradition. Azusa Street was many things, but
it was first of all a Black Church.[5] We cannot truly understand or appreciate
Pentecostalism as a global Christian phenomenon without understanding its

deep (although not exclusive) roots in the African American religious world and in the Black Church tradition, specifically the black Holiness church tradition, of the late nineteenth and early twentieth centuries. Without such an understanding, global Pentecostalism has found itself in an identity crisis.

Black theology has also undergone its own fuller global engagement over the last several decades, primarily through its sustained dialogue with other liberation theologies around the world. Black theology has had, from its inception as a discursive and self-reflective practice in the 1960s, a significant, if sometimes somewhat obscured, global identity. Black theology as a movement has also since the 1970s struggled with questions of its "identity." The theologian Cecil Wayne Cone's important book that responded to the work of his brother and preeminent proponent of black theology, James Hall Cone, was titled *The Identity Crisis in Black Theology*.[6] Cecil Cone's critique of black theology was that it had not rooted itself deeply enough in the language and practice of the Black Church. Black theology appeared to him, at least, to have depended too much on white European-American sources and thus faced a fundamental crisis regarding the blackness of its identity. The movement's engagement with the wider global community of liberation theologies from the so-called Third World was in no small part a response to this critique.

Over the three decades since Cecil Cone published his critique and Leonard Lovett sought to open a discussion, the conversation between black Pentecostalism and black theology has not been entirely silent. On the contrary in fact, in the academic world there has been a very lively engagement resulting in a rich body of work drawing these two streams together. One need only consult the works of Cheryl J. Sanders, Clarence E. Hardy, and others in this regard to see the results of the conversation.[7] Nevertheless, these academic efforts have not had a great deal of impact on the life of black churches.

This is especially true for black Pentecostals. While a number of black Pentecostal scholars have been engaged directly with black theology, taking the latter movement forward in significant directions, black Pentecostal churches as a whole have not always embraced these efforts. Of course, this has not been universally true. One can point to a number of churches or church leaders whose identities were forged in a black Pentecostal context and who have embraced explicitly and enthusiastically even the most radical commitments of black theology to justice and inclusion.[8] In other cases, black Pentecostals have become more socially active without fully embracing the liberation agenda.[9] For the most part, however, these churches have remained relatively silent on the themes that have animated black theology, not necessarily denouncing the liberation agenda but, nevertheless, keeping it somewhat at arms length. This has especially been the case among the black Charismatic or neo-Pentecostal churches, for whom the so-called prosperity gospel has offered of an alternative route to liberation.[10]

There are a number of signs that this situation is changing, and that the distancing of black Pentecostal churches from black theology and the wider commitments of liberation theology are breaking down. In part this may be due to the fact that a number of younger black Pentecostal leaders have come through programs in theological education where black theology was regarded as a staple. In part it may also result from the growing impact of women whose leadership in black Pentecostal churches has always been strong, and for whom Womanist theological themes resonate in particularly powerful ways.[11] Given the current state of flux in global intellectual, political, economic, social, and religious life, and the crisis that people of African descent especially face globally on these fronts, continuing that dialogue is crucial. The crisis of people of African descent globally needs now more than ever a merger of the energy and dynamism of black Pentecostalism and the liberationist commitments of black theology.

Black Pentecostalism and black theology are never going to get an adequate conversation underway, however, if their dialogue takes place predominantly on European or North American intellectual and social terrain. Black theology, as was noted above, came to that conclusion decades ago, in part as a response to the crisis in its identity that Cecil Cone wrote about. The global dimensions of black theology during its formative years have not always been appreciated. Many still recall the encounter between Latin American liberation theologians and black theologians from the United States at the 1975 "Theology in the Americas" conference in Detroit as being confrontational in nature. It was at times. But it was also this meeting that launched black theology into its first decade of global theological engagement. The more serious confrontation for James Cone and other black theologians at the Detroit conference was not with Latin Americans but with other North Americans. Cone was blunt; most of the North American delegates at Detroit, he told the conference, were not people whom he "regarded as in the struggle for oppression" or people who "came out of actual concrete struggles, people that I wouldn't have to be as suspicious about. . . . But most of the North American participants here are people I suspect."[12] Two years later, at the Atlanta meeting of the project, Cone said, "Our active involvement in the 'Theology in the Americas,' under whose aegis this conference is held, is an attempt to enlarge our perspective in relation to Africa, Asia, and Latin America as well as to express our solidarity with other oppressed minorities in the U.S."[13]

Clearly Cone's perspective was not drawn from and did not depend on sources extraneous or alien to the black religious experience. It was drawn from his experience and the long, collective experience of people of African descent in North America. That experience of "Otherness" and oppression, of being marginalized, excluded, and rendered an "outsider," not only engendered suspicion; it was the source for the desire for and experience of solidarity with those who had been "minoritized" and oppressed in North America and those who had been "minoritized" and oppressed globally through the modern era. The global dimensions of black theology's perspectives were not grounded in the theological sources that it borrowed from the dominant European and European-American experience or context.[14] Black theology was grounded in its own global memory and experience, and in the solidarity with others throughout the world who have been on the oppressed end of the modern global colonial experience.

These global dimensions were already at work in and on the civil rights and black power movements from which black theology sprang in the 1960s. These movements, in their own ways, manifested global or transnational dimensions. This is a point James Cone makes in *Martin and Malcolm and America: A Dream or a Nightmare.*[15] The direction that both Martin and Malcolm were taking, Cone points out, was to move the Civil Rights struggle, which was discursively if not historically located within a U.S. social and intellectual context, in a more global direction. Martin Luther King linked civil rights to the global anticolonial movement in his famous April 1967 speech at Riverside Church when he came out against the Vietnam War.[16] Malcolm had already made a similar connection in speeches dating more than a decade before, but then brought it into a more public arena when he sought to get the United Nations to debate the oppression of African Americans as a matter of human rights and genocide.[17]

Malcolm's effort is often portrayed against the backdrop of a longer and deeper Pan-African intellectual current that runs through his life and work. This Pan-African tradition is in fact critical for understanding both black Pentecostalism and black theology, and must continue to inform the ongoing effort to reopen the dialogue between them. The work of scholars such as Josiah U. Young is important in this area, as are the efforts of David D. Daniels, Ogbu Kalu, and others studying Pentecostalism in the African diaspora.[18]

A recent article by Clarence E. Hardy has pointed to the importance of the transnational impulse for both black Pentecostalism and black theology. Hardy's work stands in a steam of scholarship that runs from Benjamin E.

Mays's *The Negro's God as Reflected in His Literature* (1938) [19] through Arna W. Bontemps and Jack Conroy's *They Seek a City* (1945).[20] That latter text was republished two decades later in a revised and expanded edition, which was fittingly retitled *Anywhere But Here*.[21] Hardy listens in on the turn-of-the-nineteenth- and early-twentieth-century conversations that later animated the work of Mays, Bontemps, and others to hear in a fresh way the transnational impulses that were coming to expression in and through the African American experience. He points to the importance of the work of Charles Price Jones, a leading black Holiness teacher from Jackson, Mississippi, who was a close colleague of Charles H. Mason prior to their split over the issue of the doctrine of speaking in tongues in 1907.[22] Jones had undergone a conversion experience in 1884 and originally felt called to Africa to serve as a missionary. After graduating from Arkansas Baptist College, he elected to minister instead among his fellow sons and daughters of Africa in the United States. In 1902 Jones published a collection titled *An Appeal to the Sons of Africa: A Number of Poems, Readings, Orations and Lectures, Designed Especially to Inspire Youth of African Blood with Sentiments of Hope and True Nobility as well as to Entertain All Classes of Readers and Lovers of Redeemed Humanity*.[23] The wider circle of intended readership he termed "redeemed humanity" was significant in his work. Jones was not just a Pan-Africanist; he was a proponent of what many today would call "cosmopolitanism"[24]

Jones, Mason, Seymour, and others had their roots in the African American experience in the South, with its memories of slave religion and the revitalizing power of the Spirit in the midst of oppression. But they were also part of a generation on the move. Both Jones and Seymour ended their ministries in Los Angeles and were part of the African American migration to the West. While Mason continued to make Memphis the organizational center of the Church of God in Christ, he traveled widely throughout the country, planting churches and overseeing a burgeoning national body with strong congregations in major cities in both the North and the West.

Hardy notes that during this period the African American migrants from the South to the North and West did not find the Promised Land as they had hoped.

What they found instead was a broader space to further interrogate old conceptions of racial identity they had already begun to question as Reconstruction's promise faded. Whether they found themselves in the ranks of emerging black Holiness groups hoping finally to escape sin and stultifying conformity or among emigrationists seeking to remake Africa for Christ and civilization, the children of slaves began to embrace the global stage as the principal context for constructing notions of (black) communal identity and the divine.[25]

That global stage was especially prominent at Azusa Street. Indeed, it is the key to unlocking both the self-understanding of the leadership there, especially Seymour, and the importance of Azusa Street for world Pentecostalism. Albert J. Raboteau and David W. Wills, in their preliminary editorial description of *African-American Religion: A Documentary History Project*, argue that 1906 marks the beginning of what they call "the global phase of African-American religious history."[26] For them, the defining event for that history is the Azusa Street Revival under the leadership of Seymour, whom they describe as "a southern black preacher."

Their description of Seymour has been fleshed out in greater detail in Robeck's study of the Azusa Street Mission and revival.[27] The Azusa Street Mission was a black church to which persons of various ethnic backgrounds came to worship, and from which they went out in ministry and mission. At the height of the revival from 1906 through 1909, the ethnic makeup of the congregation at the daily meetings on Azusa Street was by all accounts quite diverse. Some merely passed through Azusa Street as visitors and thus spread reports of its distinctive Pentecostal experience abroad. Others were considered members or regular participants in the mission and were commissioned by the leadership, under Seymour, to go out as missionaries. In either case, a black church was at the center of an emerging global nexus. People of diverse ethnicities came to a black church to worship and receive their Pentecostal experience. Many left Azusa Street with their former theological understandings relatively intact, in effect adding a Pentecostal dimension to previously formed constructs.[28] But this does not negate the fact that Seymour and the mission as a whole were both grounded in and belonged fully to the Black Church tradition.[29]

Under Seymour's leadership emerged a vision of mission to reach across the entire globe. The experience of hearing and speaking what were considered to be foreign tongues or languages was a critical factor in shaping this global missionary vision. The Azusa Street Mission commissioned African American missionaries to go mostly to Africa, but it also commissioned European Americans to go to other continents. In this regard Azusa Street may well have been the first black church to commission missionaries to go to places outside the United States other than to Africa, or to children of the African diaspora. Raboteau and Wills argue that Seymour's ministry on

Azusa Street "foreshadows" the increased involvement of African Americans "with the entire globe." They summarize the implications well:

> Writing about the Azusa Street meetings, Seymour placed them on a worldwide landscape. "People of all nations came and got their cup full," he said. "Some came from Africa, some came from India, China, Japan, and England." Rhetoric such as this, which reaches both eastward back to Africa and Europe and westward to Asia, and connects the whole world to a spiritual event occurring in a largely black context in California, signals the beginning of a new era in African-American religious history. In this global era to put it abstractly, African-American religion develops in the context of a set of sustained and interrelated human interactions that are increasingly worldwide in their extent.[30]

Seymour's vision of ministry, shaped as it was in the context of the Azusa Street Revival, was global in scope. The global dimension was manifested in a concrete manner primarily through the experience of speaking in tongues. Participants in the revival believed they were hearing and miraculously empowered by the Spirit to speak various other languages that represented the peoples and cultures of the earth.[31] This in turn led concretely to the global missionary efforts that the revival spawned. Missions were the predominant means by which churches of the world expressed their global ecumenical consciousness during the first decades of the twentieth century.[32] While other concrete forms of solidarity would emerge through the course of the century, including international conferences, fellowships, councils and programs for partnership and exchange, missions would continue to be an important means of expressing global awareness and identity for churches throughout the world.

The global vision of the Azusa Street Revival, and the mission efforts that it launched to realize that vision, gave it an important, if not central role in the emergence and formation of the Pentecostal movement worldwide in the twentieth century.[33] The full implications of this vision were slow to take root beyond the immediate experience of the mission itself on the other hand. Azusa Street was an interracial and intercultural experience, yet within a decade the Pentecostal churches, fellowships, and denominations that emerged from it and looked back on as part of their origins were mostly racially and ethnically segregated.

The late Bishop Ithiel C. Clemmons argued that the legacy of Seymour and the Azusa Street Mission were carried on most directly in the life and practice of black Pentecostal churches. The most direct line of descent,

Clemmons argued, was in the Church of God in Christ under the leadership of Bishop C. H. Mason.[34] Yet the black Pentecostal churches and denominations that formed in the wake of the Azusa Street Revival in the first part of the twentieth century, including the Church of God in Christ under Bishop Mason, did not continue at first to pursue Seymour's global vision so intentionally or explicitly. The missiological impulses among the first generation of black Pentecostal churches following Azusa Street continued to purse the reconstruction of African American life in the United States and to a lesser degree the Pan-Africanism of Jones and others.[35]

The Church of God in Christ organized a mission board in 1926 under the leadership of Elder Searcy, who had previously headed the independent House of Prayer International Home and Foreign Mission Board in Portland, Oregon. The new department in the Church of God in Christ was located under the Women's Department for the first decade.[36] Until 1945 the mission work it carried on outside the United States was in the Caribbean and West Africa. Similar patterns of global engagement characterized the mission work of other black Pentecostal churches and denominations from the period of 1909 through 1945. Most efforts were directed to the islands of the Caribbean and to the entire African continent. The fuller contours of Seymour's global vision were, for at least a generation, institutionally eclipsed for the most part in black Pentecostalism, even as they continued, as Hardy argued, to live on in the imaginations of African American peoples.

There are signs that things are changing. Black Pentecostal churches and leaders are demonstrating a more robust engagement with churches and movements in Asia, Africa, and Latin America where Pentecostalism is flourishing, and not just through the one-way traffic of sending missionaries but through mutual engagement and partnerships on a global scale. Such engagement was demonstrated vividly in the highly visible role played by numerous black Pentecostal leaders in the centennial celebration of the Azusa Street Revival in April 2006, which more than fifty thousand people from around the world gathered in Los Angeles to commemorate.

Drawing on its roots in Azusa Street, black Pentecostals should see such engagement with the wider currents of the global Pentecostal movement not as something extraneous to their identity, but as an intrinsic component of it, even if it was partially eclipsed for a time. A wider global arena of engagement will, in turn, prove essential for a more robust conversation between black Pentecostalism and black theology. Global dimensions of black Pentecostalism and black theology are not extraneous to either movement but are intrinsic to and critical for the identities of both. Pan-African consciousness remains an important element in this regard, but is by no means the limit of their global awareness and engagement. Seeking consciously to carry on their dialogue in a more global theological arena or context does not negate their Pan-African heritage, but in fact enhances it.

Both black Pentecostalism and black theology are exilic and diasporic movements that were forged in the crucible of oppression of children of African descent. But both also have sought to expand beyond the African context from their inception, to engage global theological discourses more fully. Black Pentecostalism has done so primarily through the mechanisms of foreign missions, while black theology has done so by identifying with so-called Third World liberation theologies and seeking to engage in solidarity with the oppressed in every place. On both counts, the result has been a conscious engagement with those whose experiences of faith lie outside the historical boundaries of Western Christendom, linking them with movements of resistance that have been forged within the territorial domains of the West.

Pentecostalism and black theology have engaged in sustained critique of the dominant paradigms of modern Western theology, albeit on differing methodological grounds. Black Pentecostalism has largely followed a post-secular, post-Enlightenment paradigm of embracing signs and wonders, and resisting the reduction of Christian faith and practice to rational categories forged in the modern West, often doing so from a location on the "underside."[37] Its critiques of modernity and of the dominant theologies of the West have been more generally religious and cultural in character. Black theology has also emerged from the underside. It has tended to follow a more explicitly political line of criticism, however, although it has followed this with a sustained religious and cultural critique.[38] Despite their convergence around the role of traditional religious practices and the resistance such can engender against oppression, one still detects lingering ambiguities on the part of the black theology concerning the canons of modernity and the standards of rationality that tend to shape (Pentecostals are often tempted to say "distort") theological discourses that follow in the wake of the European Enlightenment. Lovett was getting to this in the last chapter of his dissertation in part by noting that black theology has not been able yet to fully engage dimensions of the Spirit. It has been a bit deficient, one might say, in its pneumatology. It also appears, to some at least, to still be too committed to modernist canons of respectability, in that it seems to want to avoid dealing with signs and wonders, or with the workings of the Spirit in a way that might be participatory or signal their embrace. On this point black Pentecostalism has an important contribution to make to black theology.

For its part, black Pentecostalism has at times been criticized for not being committed enough to transformational praxis. Black Pentecostalism does indeed present itself fully as a praxis theology, but the praxis it embraces has been predominantly that of spiritual praise. Given the privatization of spirituality in much recent theology, such a practice can tend toward individualizing the blessings that are promised in ways that lead to the distortions of prosperity doctrine and its consumerist ethos. In the deliberations of black Pentecostalism, especially in its theology of signs and wonders, liberation has often seemingly given way to an emphasis on attaining those material goods that are the signifiers of a global ideology of consumption.

Black theology has an important critique to make regarding the effectiveness of liberation when it takes place on a personal level, be it spiritual or material, without a corresponding collective or political dimension.[39] Black theology as a movement over the past two decades has not been able to register the sustained growth and public awareness that characterized black Pentecostalism over this same period. It has, for the most part, remained confined to the upper echelons of graduate theological educational discourse and practice. Its impact has been felt in the black churches, without question. However, it has generally been a muted influence, often mediated through the memory of the U.S. civil rights movement and providing supplemental support for the project of resistance against white oppression.

Black theology needs an infusion of vitality characterized by the Spirit that black Pentecostalism can provide.[40] Black Pentecostalism, on the other hand, needs the critical reminder that material signifiers do not constitute liberation, that prosperity demands a clearer and more explicit social and political critique, and that numerical growth does not on its own constitute sufficient evidence of faithfulness to the gospel of Jesus Christ—all of which black theology can provide.

These movements need each other. They can best meet one another, and through mutual engagement discover resources that each needs to move forward, in contexts that are clearly demarcated as being "beyond the shores" of Western theology, infused as it is with its colonial memories, still dominated by the canons of authority that derive exclusively from modern Western experience, and exercising such oppression. Such a dialogue, however, need not be physically located in spaces outside North America. The experience of the Ecumenical Association of Third-World Theologians has demonstrated that critical postcolonial discourse can be carried out in geographical terrains within the West. The West itself is undergoing significant transformation under the impact of global transnational migrations.[41] One can find the alternative contexts of world Christian experience close at hand. Such a meeting "beyond the shores" and in the context of world Christianity is consistent with the identity of both black Pentecostalism and black theology.[42] The contributions of a fuller dialogue between the two —not only to each other but to world Christianity in general—would, without question, be enormous.

NOTES TO CHAPTER 13

1. Leonard Lovett, "Black Holiness-Pentecostalism: Implications for Ethics and Social Transformation" (PhD diss., Emory University, 1978).

2. See Dale T. Irvin, "Pentecostal Historiography and Global Christianity: Rethinking the Question of Origins," *Pneuma: Journal for the Society of Pentecostal Studies* 27.1 (2005): 35–50. For the main contours of the argument for the African American origins of Pentecostalism see, among others, James S. Tinney, "William J. Seymour: Father of Modern-Day Pentecostalism," *Journal of the Interdenominational Theological Center* 4.1 (1976): 34–44; Tinney, "Exclusivist Tendencies in Pentecostal Self-Definition: A Critique from Black Theology," *Journal of Religious Thought* 86.1 (1979): 32–45; Leonard Lovett, "Perspective on the Black Origins of the Contemporary Pentecostal Movement," *Journal of the Interdenominational Theological Center* 1.1 (1973): 36–49; Walter J. Hollenweger, *Pentecostalism: Origins and Developments Worldwide* (Peabody, Mass.: Hendrickson, 1997); Hollenweger, "The Black Roots of Pentecostalism," in Allan Anderson and Walter J. Hollenweger, eds., *Pentecostals after a Century: Global Perspectives on a Movement in Transition* (Sheffield, UK: Sheffield Academic Press, 1999), 33–44; Iain MacRobert, *The Black Roots and White Racism of Early Pentecostalism in the USA* (London: Macmillan, 1988); Douglas J. Nelson, "For Such a Time as This: The Story of William J. Seymour and the Azusa Street Revival" (PhD diss., University of Birmingham, 1981); David Douglas Daniels, "The Cultural Renewal of Slave Religion: Charles Price Jones and the Emergence of the Holiness Movement in Mississippi" (PhD diss., Union Theological Seminary, New York, 1992). Challenges to this historical argument include, among others, James R. Goff, Jr., *Fields White unto Harvest: Charles F. Parham and the Missionary Origins of Pentecostalism* (Fayetteville: University of Arkansas Press, 1988), and Edith L. Blumhofer, *Restoring the Faith: The Assemblies of God, Pentecostalism, and American Culture* (Urbana: University of Illinois Press, 1993). For a concise summary of the historiography of early U.S. Pentecostalism, see August Cerillo Jr. and Grant Wacker, "Bibliography and Historiography of Pentecostalism in the United States," in Stanley M. Burgess and Eduard M. Van der Maas, eds., *The New International Dictionary of Pentecostal and Charismatic Movements* (Grand Rapids, Mich.: Zondervan, 2002), 383–405, s.v. "Pentecostalism."

3. See Allan Anderson *An Introduction to Pentecostalism: Global Charismatic Christianity* (Cambridge: Cambridge University Press, 2004); Amos Yong, *The Spirit Poured Out on All Flesh: Pentecostalism and the Possibility of Global Theology* (Grand Rapids, Mich.: Baker Academic, 2005); and David D. Bundy, "Bibliography and Historiography of Pentecostalism outside North America," in *New International Dictionary of Pentecostal and Charismatic Movements*, 405–17, s.v. "Pentecostalism."

4. See Allan Anderson, *Spreading Fires: The Missionary Nature of Early Pentecostalism* (London: SCM Press, 2007); and Cecil M. Robeck Jr., "Pentecostal Origins from a Global

Perspective," in Harold D. Hunter and Peter D. Hocken, eds., *All Together in One Place: Theological Paper from the Brighton Conference on World Evangelization* (Sheffield: Sheffield Academic Press, 1993), 166–80.

5. See Cecil M. Robeck Jr. *The Azusa Street Mission and Revival: The Birth of the Global Pentecostal Movement* (Nashville, Tenn.: Thomas Nelson, 2006).

6. Cecil Wayne Cone, *The Identity Crisis in Black Theology* (Nashville, Tenn.: African Methodist Episcopal Church, 1975).

7. See for instance Cheryl J. Sanders, *Saints in Exile: The Holiness-Pentecostal Experience in African American Religion and Culture* (New York: Oxford University Press, 1999); Sanders, *Empowerment Ethics for a Liberated People* (Minneapolis, Minn.: Augsburg Fortress Press, 1995); and Clarence E. Hardy III, *James Baldwin's God: Sex, Hope, and Crisis in Black Holiness Culture* (Nashville: University of Tennessee Press, 2003).

8. The example of Bishop Yvette Funder of City of Refuge Community Church in San Francisco comes to mind in this context, along with that of Bishop Carlton Pearson, pastor of New Dimensions Church in Tulsa, Oklahoma. Bishop Flunder is also author of *Where The Edge Gathers: Building A Community of Radical Inclusion* (Cleveland: Pilgrim Press, 2005).

9. The sociologist Omar M. McRoberts, in his article "Understanding the New Black Pentecostal Activism: Lessons from Ecumenical Urban Ministries in Boston," *Sociology of Religion* 60.1 (1999): 47–70, regards the social activism of the black Pentecostal churches he studied in the Boston area as the result of the effort of a new generation of black Pentecostal leadership to recover the legacy of the civil rights movement, and not necessarily as the result of the impact of black theology upon their ministries. Even though black theology is heavily indebted to the civil rights movement, the relationship of black theology to black Pentecostalism even in these instances seems to be more of a shared legacy than direct influence.

10. For a critical analysis of the rise of the prosperity gospel among black churches, see Shayne Lee, *T. D. Jakes: America's New Preacher* (New York: New York University Press, 2005); Stephanie Mitchem, *Name It and Claim It? Prosperity Preaching in the Black Church* (Cleveland: Pilgrim Press, 2007); and Robert M. Franklin *Crisis in the Village: Restoring Hope in African American Communities* (Minneapolis, Minn.: Fortress Press, 2007).

11. See Cheryl Townsend Gilkes, "The Role of Women in the Sanctified Church," *Journal of Religious Thought* 43.1 (1986): 18–24; Gilkes, *If It Wasn't for the Women . . . : Black Women's Experience and Womanist Culture in Church and Community* (Maryknoll, N.Y.: Orbis Books, 2000); and Estrelda Alexander, *The Women of Azusa Street* (Cleveland, Ohio: Pilgrim Press, 2005).

12. James Cone, in "Black Theology Panel: Excerpts from the Discussion," in John Eagleson and Sergio Torres, eds., *Theology in the Americas* (Maryknoll, N.Y.: Orbis Books, 1976), 354.

13. James H. Cone, "Black Theology and the Black Church: Where Do We Go from Here?" *Risks of Faith: The Emergence of A Black Theology of Liberation, 1968–1998* (Boston: Beacon Press, 2000), 49.

14. In this regard the participation of black theologians from the United States in the Ecumenical Association of Third World Theologians (EATWOT), especially in the 1980s, proved to be not only a critical means but an expression of black theology's global identity. See especially James H. Cone, "Black Theology: Its Origin, Methodology, and Relationship to Third World Theologies," in Virginia Fabella and Sergio Torres, eds.,

Doing Theology in a Divided World: Papers from the Sixth International Conference of the Ecumenical Association of Third World Theologians, January 5–13, 1983, Geneva, Switzerland (Maryknoll, N.Y.: Orbis Books, 1985), 93–105.

15. James Hall Cone, *Martin and Malcolm and America: A Dream or a Nightmare* (Maryknoll, N.Y.: Orbis Books, 1992).

16. Martin Luther King Jr., "Beyond Vietnam: A Time to Break Silence," in James M. Washington, ed., *A Testament of Hope: The Essential Writings and Speeches of Martin Luther King Jr.* (San Francisco: HarperSanFrancisco, 1990).

17. In his April 1964 speech "The Ballot or the Bullet," Malcolm X said: "When you expand the civil-rights struggle to the level of human rights, you can then take the case of the black man in this country before the nations in the UN." Quotation taken from Joy James, *Imprisoned Intellectuals: America's Political Prisoners Write on Life, Liberation, and Rebellion* (Lanham, Md.: Rowman and Littlefield, 2003), 58.

18. Josiah U. Young, *Pan African Theology: Providence and the Legacies of the Ancestors* (Trenton: Africa World Press, 1992); David D. Daniels, "'Everybody Bids You Welcome': A Multicultural Approach to North American Pentecostalism," in Murray W. Dempster, Byron D. Klaus, and Douglas Petersen, eds., *The Globalization of Pentecostalism: A Religion Made to Travel* (Oxford: Regnum Books, 1999), 222–52; Daniels, "Teaching Afresh the History of Global Christianity," in David V. Esterline and Ogbu U. Kalu, eds., *Shaping Beloved Community: Multicultural Theological Education* (Louisville, Ky.: Westminster John Knox Press, 2006), 211–25; and Ogbu U. Kalu, *African Pentecostalism: An Introduction* (New York: Oxford University Press, 2008).

19. Benjamin E. Mays, *The Negro's God as Reflected in His Literature* (Boston: Chapman and Grimes, 1938).

20. Arna W. Bontemps and Jack Conroy, *They Seek a City* (Garden City, N.Y.: Doubleday, Doran and Co., 1945).

21. Arna W. Bontemps and Jack Conroy, *Anywhere But Here* (New York: Hill and Wang, 1966).

22. See Dale T. Irvin, "Charles Price Jones: Image of Holiness," in James R. Goff and Grant Wacker, eds., *Portraits of a Generation: Early Pentecostal Leaders* (Fayetteville: University of Arkansas Press, 2002), 37–51.

23. Charles Price Jones, *An Appeal to the Sons of Africa: A Number of Poems, Readings, Orations and Lectures, Designed Especially to Inspire Youth of African Blood with Sentiments of Hope and True Nobility as well as to Entertain All Classes of Readers and Lovers of Redeemed Humanity* (Jackson, Miss.: Truth Publishing, 1902).

24. For a fresh look at "cosmopolitanism" in a voice that Jones would have appreciated, see Kwame Anthony Appiah, *Cosmopolitanism: Ethics in a World of Strangers* (New York and London: W.W. Norton Co., 2006).

25. Clarence E. Hardy III, "From Exodus to Exile: Black Pentecostals, Migrating Pilgrims, and Imagined Internationalism," *American Quarterly* 59.3 (2007): 750.

26. On-line at http://www3.amherst.edu/~aardoc/Global_Phase.html, accessed 08/21/2008.

27. Robeck, *Azusa Street Mission and Revival.*

28. This is the point made by Joe Creech, "Visions of Glory: The Place of the Azusa Street Revival in Pentecostal History," *Church History* 65.3 (September 1996): 405–24, in his critical assessment of the place of Azusa Street in Pentecostal history.

29. It should be noted here that prior to the Azusa Street Revival, although Seymour had worked in interracial contexts, notably with Charles Fox Parham in Texas, his pastoral leadership had been shaped in churches that were fully immersed in the African American religious tradition. Following the 1906–09 revival, the Azusa Street Mission under Seymour incorporated as a church. Both the published work from this period and descriptions of the congregation make it clear that Azusa Street church under Seymour after 1910 belonged to the Black Church tradition.

30. Online at http://www3.amherst.edu/~aardoc/Global_Phase.html, accessed August 21, 2008.

31. See Dale T. Irvin, "'Drawing All Together in One Bond of Love': The Ecumenical Vision of William J Seymour and the Azusa Street Revival," *Journal of Pentecostal Theology* 6.1 (1995): 25–53.

32. See Dale T. Irvin, *Hearing Many Voices: Dialogue and Diversity in the Ecumenical Movement* (Lanham, Md.: University Press of America, 1994), 123–55.

33. See Harold D. Hunter and Cecil M. Robeck Jr., eds. *The Azusa Street Revival and Its Legacy* (Cleveland, Tenn.: Pathway Press, 2006); Grant McClung, ed. *Azusa Street and Beyond: 100 Years of Commentary on the Global Pentecostal, Charismatic Movement*, rev. ed. (Gainesville, Fla.: Bridge-Logos, 2006); and Dempster, Klaus, and Petersen, *Globalization of Pentecostalism.*

34. Ithiel C. Clemmons, *Bishop C. H. Mason and the Roots of the Church of God in Christ* (Bakersfield, Calif.: Pneuma Life Publishing 1996).

35. Black churches through the end of the nineteenth and first half of the twentieth centuries generally understood the work of reconstruction of African American life, especially in the South, to be fully missiological in nature, as can be seen in John Wesley Edward Bowen, ed., *Africa and the American Negro: Addresses and Proceedings of the Congress on Africa: Held under the Auspices of the Stewart Missionary Foundation for Africa of Gammon Theological Seminary in Connection with the Cotton States and International Exposition December 13–15, 1895* (Atlanta, Ga.: Franklin Printing and Publishing Co., 1896).

36. See Anthea Butler, "A Peculiar Synergy: Matriarchy and the Church of God in Christ" (PhD diss., Vanderbilt University 2001), 50–51.

37. The experience has been described by Frank D. Macchia, "The Struggle for Global Witness: Shifting Paradigms in Pentecostal Theology," in Dempster, Klaus, and Petersen, *Globalization of Pentecostalism*, 12, as "sub-modern."

38. This is seen most clearly in one of the foundational texts of black theology, James H. Cone, *Black Theology and Black Power* (New York: Seabury Press, 1969; repr. Maryknoll, N.Y.: Orbis Books, 1997). The subsequent fuller cultural analysis was provided not only by Cone himself, in works such as *The Spirituals and the Blues: An Interpretation* (New York: Seabury Press, 1972), but by others such as Dwight N. Hopkins, *Shoes That Fit Our Feet: Sources for a Constructive Black Theology* (Maryknoll, N.Y.: Orbis Books, 1993); Theophus H. Smith, *Conjuring Culture: Biblical Formations of Black America* (New York: Oxford University Press, 1995); Victor Anderson, *Beyond Ontological Blackness: An Essay on African American Religious and Cultural Criticism* (New York: Continuum, 1995); and Anderson, "Secularization and the Worldliness of Theology," in Delwin Brown, Sheila Greeve Davaney, and Kathryn Tanner, eds. *Converging on Culture: Theologians in Dialogue with Cultural Analysis and Criticism* (New York: Oxford University Press, 2001), 71–85.

39. See Linda E. Thomas, *Under the Canopy: Ritual Process and Spiritual Resilience in South Africa*, (Columbia: University of South Carolina Press, 1999).

40. See Marlon Millner, "Can a Dead Black Theology Be Resurrected as a Pentecostal Theology? A Review Essay of *The Rise and Demise of Black Theology* by Alistair Kee," in *Pneuma: Journal of the Society for Pentecostal Studies* 30.2 (2008): 291–98.

41. See Manuel A. Vásquez and Marie Friedmann Marquardt, *Globalizing the Sacred: Religion Across the Americas* (New Brunswick, N.J.: Rutgers University Press, 1993); and Jehu J. Hanciles, *Beyond Christendom: Globalization, African Migration, and the Transformation of the West* (Maryknoll, N.Y.: Orbis Books, 2008).

42. One finds precedence for this in the work of black Pentecostal leaders such as Frank Chikane of South Africa. An ordained minister in the Apostolic Faith Mission of South Africa, Chikane has a long and distinguished history of providing leadership for liberation and justice in both church and society. For a concise and compelling account of Chikane's role in the ending of Apartheid in South Africa, see David Goodman, *Fault Lines: Journeys into the New South Africa*, rev. ed. (Berkeley: University of California Press, 2002), 23–65. Chikane was a member of the Institute for Contextual Theology and is generally credited with being one of the primary authors of the "Kairos Document" that was published in 1985. For the text of the document, see *The Kairos Document: Challenge to the Church: A Theological Comment on the Political Crisis in South Africa,* 2nd ed. (Grand Rapids, Mich.: Eerdmans, 1986).

Selected Bibliography

Alexander, Estrelda, and Amos Yong, eds. *Philip's Daughters: Women in Pentecostal-Charismatic Leadership.* Eugene, Ore.: Pickwick Publications, 2009.

Andrews, William L., ed. *Sisters of the Spirit: Three Black Women's Autobiographies of the Nineteenth Century.* Bloomington: Indiana University Press, 1986.

Best, Wallace D. *Passionately Human, No Less Divine: Religion and Culture in Black Chicago, 1915–1952.* Princeton, N.J.: Princeton University Press, 2005.

Billingsley, Scott. *It's a New Day: Race and Gender in the Modern Charismatic Movement.* Tuscaloosa: University of Alabama Press, 2008.

Butler, Anthea D. *Women in the Church of God in Christ: Making a Sanctified World.* Chapel Hill: University of North Carolina Press, 2007.

Clemmons, Ithiel. *Bishop C. H. Mason and the Roots of the Church of God in Christ.* Bakersfield, Calif.: Pneuma Life, 1996.

Corten, Andre, and Ruth Marshall-Fratani, eds. *Between Babel and Pentecost: Transnational Pentecostalism in Africa and Latin America.* Bloomington: Indiana University Press, 2001.

Creech, Joe. "Visions of Glory: The Place of the Azusa Street Revival in Pentecostal History," *Church History* 65.3 (September 1996): 405–24.

Cruz, Samuel. *Masked Africanisms: Puerto Rican Pentecostalism.* Dubuque, Iowa: Kendall/Hunt Publishing Company, 2005.

Daniels, David D., III. "Doing All The Good We Can: The Political Witness of African American Holiness and Pentecostal Churches During the Post-Civil Rights Era," in Maryann N. Weidt and R. Drew Smith, eds., *New Day Begun: African American Churches and Civic Culture in the Post-Civil Rights America.* Durham, N.C.: Duke University Press, 2003, 164–82.

———. "'Gotta Moan Sometime': A Sonic Exploration of Earwitnesses to Early Pentecostal Sound in North America," *Pneuma: Journal of the Society for Pentecostal Studies* 30.1 (Spring 2008): 5–32.

———. "'Live So Can Use Me Anytime, Lord, Anywhere': Theological Education in the Church of God in Christ, 1970 to 1997," *Asian Journal of Pentecostal Studies* 3.2 (July 2000): 295–310.

DuPree, Sherry Sherrod. 1996. *African-American Holiness Pentecostal Movement: An Annotated Bibliography.* New York: Garland, 1996.

Franklin, Robert M. *Crisis in the Village: Restoring Hope in African American Communities* (Minneapolis: Fortress Press, 2007).

Frederick, Marla F. *Between Sundays: Black Women and Everyday Struggles of Faith.* Berkeley: University of California Press, 2003.

Gilkes, Cheryl Townsend. "The Role of Women in the Sanctified Church," *Journal of Religious Thought* 43.1 (Spring/Summer 1986): 18–24.

Hardy, Clarence E., III, "From Exodus to Exile: Black Pentecostals, Migrating Pilgrims, and Imagined Internationalism," *American Quarterly* 59.3 (2007): 737–57.

———. *James Baldwin's God: Sex, Hope, and Crisis in Black Holiness Culture*. Nashville: University of Tennessee Press, 2003.

Harrison, Milmon. *Righteous Riches: The Word of Faith Movement in Contemporary African American Religion*. New York: Oxford University Press, 2005.

Hollenweger, Walter. *Pentecostalism: Origins and Developments Worldwide*. Peabody, Mass.: Hendrickson, 1997.

Hunter, Harold D., and Cecil M. Robeck Jr., eds. *The Azusa Street Revival and Its Legacy*. Cleveland, Tenn.: Pathway Press, 2006.

Hurston, Zora Neale. *The Sanctified Church*. Berkeley, Calif.: Turtle Island, 1983.

Jones, Charles Edwin. *Black Holiness: A Guide to the Study of Black Participation in Wesleyan Perfectionist and Glossalalic Pentecostal Movements*. Metuchen, N.J.: The American Theological Library Association and Scarecrow, 1987.

Lee, Shayne. *T. D. Jakes: America's New Preacher*. New York: New York University Press, 2005.

Lovett, Leonard. "Black Origins of the Pentecostal Movement," in Vinson Synan, ed., *Aspects of Pentecostal-Charismatic Origins*. Plainfield, N.J.: Logos International, 1975, 123–41.

———. "The Spiritual Legacy and Role of Black Holiness-Pentecostalism in the Development of American Culture," *One in Christ* 23.1/2 (1987): 144–56.

MacRobert, Iain. *The Black Roots and White Racism of Early Pentecostalism in the USA*. New York: St. Martin's Press, 1988.

McKinney, George D. *The New Slave Masters*. Colorado Springs, Colo.: Cook Communications, 2005.

McRoberts, Omar. *Streets of Glory: Church and Community in a Black Urban Neighborhood*. Chicago: University of Chicago Press, 2003.

———. "Understanding the 'New' Black Pentecostal Activism," *Sociology of Religion* 60.1 (1999): 47–70.

Michel, David. *Telling the Story: Black Pentecostals in the Church of God* (Cleveland, Tenn.: Pathway Press, 2000).

Mills, Robert A. "Musical Prayers: Reflections on the African Roots of Pentecostal Music," *Journal of Pentecostal Theology* 12 (April 1998): 109–26.

Mitchem, Stephanie. *Name It and Claim It? Prosperity Preaching in the Black Church*. Cleveland. Ohio: Pilgrim Press, 2007.

Paris, Arthur E. *Black Pentecostalism: Southern Religion in an Urban World*. Amherst: University of Massachusetts Press, 1982.

Richardson, James C., Jr. *With Water and Spirit: A History of Black Apostolic Denominations in the U.S.* Washington, D.C.: Spirit Press, 1980.

Sanders, Cheryl J. *Saints in Exile: The Holiness-Pentecostal Experience in African American Religion and Culture*. New York: Oxford University Press, 1999.

Taylor, Clarence. *Black Religious Intellectuals: The Fight for Equality from Jim Crow to the Twenty-first Century*. New York: Routledge, 2002.

Tinney, James S. "Exclusivist Tendencies in Pentecostal Self-Definition: A Critique from Black Theology," *Journal of Religious Thought* 36.1 (Spring/Summer 1979): 32–49.

Turner, William C., Jr., *The United Holy Church of America: A Study in Black Holiness-Pentecostalism*. Piscataway, N.J.: Gorgias Press, 2006.

Walton, Jonathan. *Watch This! The Ethics and Aesthetics of Black Televangelism*. New York: New York University Press, 2009.

Yong, Amos. "Justice Deprived, Justice Demanded: Afropentecostalisms and the Task of World Pentecostal Theology Today," *Journal of Pentecostal Theology* 15.1 (October 2006): 127–47.

Contributors

ESTRELDA Y. ALEXANDER is Professor of Theology, Regent University School of Divinity, Virginia Beach, Virginia.

VALERIE C. COOPER is Assistant Professor of Religion, The University of Virginia, Charlottesville, Virginia.

DAVID D. DANIELS III is Professor of Church History, McCormick Theological Seminary, Chicago, Illinois.

LOUIS B. GALLIEN JR. is Dean and Professor of Education, Oakland University School, Rochester, Michigan.

CLARENCE E. HARDY III is Assistant Professor of the History of American Christianity, Yale Divinity School, New Haven, Connecticut.

DALE T. IRVIN is Professor of World Christianity and the eleventh President of New York Theological Seminary, New York City, New York.

OGBU U. KALU was the Henry Winters Luce Professor of World Christianity and Mission, McCormick Theological Seminary, Chicago, Illinois.

LEONARD LOVETT is Executive Director of the Office of Ecumenical Relations and Urban Affairs, Church of God in Christ, Alexandria, Virginia.

CECIL M. ROBECK JR. is Professor of Church History and Ecumenics, Fuller Theological Seminary, Pasadena, California.

CHERYL J. SANDERS is Professor of Christian Ethics, Howard University School of Divinity, Washington, D.C.

CRAIG SCANDRETT-LEATHERMAN is Adjunct Instructor in Anthropology and Religious Studies, Washington University, St. Louis, Missouri.

WILLIAM C. TURNER JR. is Associate Professor of the Practice of Homiletics, Duke Divinity School, Durham, North Carolina.

FREDERICK L. WARE is Associate Professor of Theology, Howard University School of Divinity, Washington, D.C.

AMOS YONG is J. Rodman Williams Professor of Theology, Regent University School of Divinity, Virginia Beach, Virginia.

Index

cross, 103, 112–13nn25, 26; theology of, 103, 115n61
Crowther, Adjai, 210

Dabney, Robert Lewis, 99–100
dance, 107–8
Daniels, David D., 143–44, 236
Darwinism, 75
Daughtry, Herbert, 143
Dayton, Donald W., 79n27, 143
demonology, 198, 201
diaspora, African, 8, 114n48
Doe, Samuel K., 216
Dollar, Creflo, 4, 146
dominion theology, 201
Dorsey, Thomas, 49
dreams, 85
Driver, E. R., 53
DuBois, W. E. B., 55, 156–57
Dubose, James, 103
Dyson, Michael Eric, 117, 124, 131, 135

Ecumenical Association of the Third-World Theologians, 242, 244n14
Edwards, Jonathan, 195–96
egalitarianism, 81n44
Elaw, Zilpha, 68
electoral politics, 52–52, 55
emancipation, 73, 86, 213
Emancipation Proclamation, 108
eroticism, 135n3
eschatology, 191, 193
Ethiopianism, 210, 214, 223
Eurocentrism, 155, 160
Evangelicalism, 67–68, 72, 141
Evans, May, 29
Evans, W. G., 29
Evening Light Saints, 75–76, 81n44. See also Church of God (Anderson, Indiana)

Faith Holiness Church of the Apostolic Faith, 219
Farrow, Lucy, 218
Father Divine, 90–91
Fauset, Arthur, 83–84, 89–90
Federal Bureau of Investigation, 91, 104

Federal Council of Churches, 58
feminism, proto-, 76–77
Fillmore, Charles, 90
Fire Baptized Holiness Church of America, 2–3, 48
First African Methodist Episcopal Church, 26
Flack, Roberta, 118, 126–27
folk church, 31, 33–34, 40n72
Foote, Julia, 68, 71–72, 77
Forbes, James A., Jr., 8, 143, 185
Ford, Louis Henry, 143
Franklin, Aretha, 120–23, 136nn12, 19
Franklin, C. L., 122–23
Franklin, John Hope, 156
Franklin, Kirk, 120
Franklin, Robert, 144
fraternal orders, 40n71, 50–51, 55
Frazier, E. Franklin, 157–58, 173
Frederick, Marla F., 144, 146–47
From the Heart Ministries, 6
Full Gospel Baptist Church Fellowship International, 3
Fuller Theological Seminary, 161
Fulop, Timothy E., 74–75, 204n15, 206n43
Flunder, Yvette, 244n8

Gardner, Clinton, 160
Garfunkel, Art, 121
Garnet, Henry Highland, 180
Garvey, Marcus, 59
Gaye, Marvin, 117–18, 127–34
Geertz, Clifford, 99
Gerloff, Roswith, 159
Gettysburg Address, 74
Gifford, Paul, 216
Gilkes, Cheryl Townsend, 67
Girard, Rene, 111n18
glossolalia. See speaking in tongues
Goodwin, Bennie, 8
Goff, James R. Jr., 17n1, 36n9
gospel music, 49, 135n1
Goss, Howard, 57
Graham, Billy, 224
Great Awakenings, 68, 195
Great Migration, 2, 36, 44, 47